LIVING LANGUAGE®

ESSENTIAL SPANISH FOR HEALTHCARE

THE LIVING LANGUAGE® SERIES

Living Language Basic Courses, Revised & Updated

*Spanish** *Japanese** *Portuguese (Brazilian)*
*French** *Russian* *Portuguese (Continental)*
*German** *Italian** *Inglés/English for Spanish Speakers*

Living Language Intermediate Courses

Spanish 2 *French 2*
German 2 *Italian 2*

Living Language Advanced Courses, Revised & Updated

Spanish 3 *French 3*

Living Language All the Way™ (Ultimate™)

*Spanish** *Japanese** *Russian 2* (1998)*
*French** *Spanish 2** *Japanese 2* (1998)*
*German** *French 2** *Inglés/English for Spanish Speakers**
*Italian** *German 2** *Inglés/English for Spanish Speakers 2**
Russian (1998)* *Italian 2** *Chinese (1999)*

Living Language Children's Courses

Spanish *French*

Living Language Conversational English

for Chinese Speakers *for Korean Speakers*
for Japanese Speakers *for Spanish Speakers*
for Russian Speakers

Living Language Essential Language Guides

Essential Spanish for Healthcare
Essential Spanish for Law Enforcement

Living Language Fast & Easy™

Spanish *Italian* *Portuguese*
French *Russian* *Czech*
German *Polish* *Hungarian*
Japanese *Korean* *Mandarin (Chinese)*
Arabic *Hebrew* *Inglés/English for Spanish Speakers*

Living Language All-Audio

Spanish *Italian*
French *German*

Living Language Speak Up!® Accent Elimination Courses

Spanish *American Regional*
Asian, Indian and Middle Eastern

Fodor's Languages For Travelers

Spanish *Italian*
French *German*

LIVING LANGUAGE MULTIMEDIA™ TriplePlay *Plus!*

Spanish *English* *Japanese*
French *Italian* *Hebrew*
German

LIVING LANGUAGE MULTIMEDIA™ Your Way 2.0

Spanish *French* *Inglés/English for Spanish Speakers*

LIVING LANGUAGE MULTIMEDIA™ Let's Talk

Spanish *French* *English*
Italian *German*

*Available on Cassette and Compact Disc

LIVING LANGUAGE®

ESSENTIAL SPANISH FOR HEALTHCARE

Written by

Dr. Miguel Bedolla

Hispanic Center for Excellence

University of Texas, San Antonio, Texas

Edited by

Helga Schier, Ph.D.

Living Language, A Random House Company

New York

Published by Living Language, a division of Crown Publishers, Inc., 201 East 50th Street, New York, New York, 10022. Member of the Crown Publishing Group.

Random House, Inc., New York, Toronto, London, Sydney, Auckland
http://www.livinglanguage.com/

Living Language is a registered trademark of Crown Publishers, Inc.

Printed in the United States of America

Designed by Cynthia Dunne

Library of Congress Cataloging in Publication Data is available upon request.

ISBN 0-609-80138-4

10 9 8 7 6 5 4 3 2 1

First Edition

ACKNOWLEDGMENTS

My sincere thanks to my wife, Roble Bedolla, whose help and support made this book possible, and to my brother, Raphael Bedolla, whose input was very valuable. Many thanks also to Crown's Living Language® staff: Helga Schier, Kathryn Mintz, Ana Suffredini, Lisa Alpert, Christopher Warnasch, Liana Parry, Lenny Henderson, Cynthia Dunne, and Erin Bekowies. Special thanks to Carole Horky at Cedars Sinai Medical Center in Los Angeles, California, and Dr. Martin Kantrowitz at the Medical School of the University of New Mexico in Albuquerque, New Mexico.

OMNIA AD MAIOREM DEI GLORIAM

CONTENTS

INTRODUCTION

Living Language® Essential Spanish for Healthcare offers a fast, efficient, and cost-effective way to learn the Spanish skills you'll need on the job. The program gives you *only* the vocabulary and phrases relevant to medical procedures. The phrasebook format lets you speak and understand Spanish immediately, without hours of serious study. The notes on vocabulary, grammar, and culture that you'll find throughout the book will help you use the language and interact with Spanish speakers more effectively.

Essential Spanish for Healthcare takes you through the most typical situations in which successful communication is a potentially life-saving skill. You'll learn how to take medical history, discuss symptoms, conduct general examinations, deliver diagnoses, and communicate with the family and friends of your patients, all in Spanish. Unlike any other program, *Living Language® Essential Spanish for Healthcare* not only teaches the questions you'll ask and the instructions you'll give but also includes possible responses you'll get to make sure that you are properly equipped to deal effectively with any situation.

The complete program consists of this text and three hours of recordings. However, if you are already comfortable with your Spanish pronunciation, this manual may also be used on its own.

Course Materials

• THE MANUAL •

Living Language® Essential Spanish for Healthcare consists of nine sections, seven of which deal with different aspects of healthcare: *Administration and Preliminary Examination, The Patient Interview, Medical Procedures, The Prognosis,*

Discussing the Follow-Up, Emergency Procedures, and *Patients with Special Conditions.* Each section includes several dialogues about specific on-the-job situations related to the general topic. For example, *The Patient Interview* provides dialogues on issues such as *Medical History of the Patient* and *Life and Lifestyle History; The Prognosis* highlights issues such as *Delivering and Discussing the Prognosis* and *Discussing the Treatment;* and *Patients with Special Conditions* features *The Alcohol-Abusing Patient* and *Home Healthcare for the Elderly and/or Physically Challenged.* The dialogues branch out in several directions to account for the most likely outcomes of each situation.

Communication is not a one-way street. Therefore, speaking skills *and* comprehension skills are taught to guarantee that you can ask the questions *and* understand the answers. Therefore, culture notes address different customs in the Spanish-speaking community that will help you do your job better. And vocabulary and grammar notes will improve your ability to speak Spanish.

The other two sections in the manual include our introductory section, *The Bare Essentials,* which provides an overview of the Spanish language and culture, and our *Reference* section in the back includes a concise grammar summary, a two-way glossary, and an easy-to-use index.

• THE REFERENCE GUIDE •

The pocket reference guide is designed to be used on the job. It features the most important words, phrases, and sentences from the manual, including helpful phrases for emergency situations. In addition, the reference guide serves as a transcript for the recordings. All of the material in **boldface** and ***boldface italics*** can be found on the two ninety-minute cassettes included in this package.

• THE RECORDINGS (two ninety-minute cassettes) •

The cassettes feature the most important words and phrases in the manual. You'll hear the Spanish phrases with their English translations, and pauses are provided for you to repeat after the native Spanish speakers. The recordings can be used without the manual or the reference guide—perfect for learning and practicing on the go.

And one last note...

Living Language® Essential Spanish for Healthcare is an indispensable tool for anyone working in the medical field. However, the skills that are required to deal with life-and-death situations safely and effectively go well beyond the linguistic realm. This program is not meant to override the medical training you received or the strategies you developed in your experience with your patients. *Living Language® Essential Spanish for Healthcare* is a valuable source for the Spanish language skills you'll need in your profession—no more and no less—and is, thus, not a replacement but a crucial supplement to your training as a healthcare professional.

SECTION A

THE BARE ESSENTIALS

1. The Spanish Alphabet

a	ah	*n*	EH-neh
b	beh	*ñ*	EH-nyeh
c	seh	*o*	oh
ch	cheh	*p*	peh
d	deh	*q*	koo
e	eh	*r*	EH-reh
f	EH-feh	*rr*	EH-rreh
g	heh	*s*	EH-seh
h	AH-cheh	*t*	teh
i	ee	*u*	oo
j	HOH-tah	*v*	veh
k	kah	*w*	doh-bleh-OO
l	EH-leh	*x*	EH-kees
ll	EH-yeh	*y*	ee-gree-EH-gah
m	EH-meh	*z*	SEH-tah

2. Pronunciation Chart

• VOWELS •

SPANISH SOUND	APPROXIMATE SOUND IN ENGLISH	EXAMPLE
a	(father)	*trabajar* (to work)
e	(ace, but cut off sharply)	*señor* (mister)
i	(fee)	*día* (day)
o	(note)	*pistola* (pistol)
u	(rule)	*mucho* (much)
y	(feet)	*y* (and) [only a vowel when standing alone]

• DIPHTHONGS •

SPANISH SOUND	APPROXIMATE SOUND IN ENGLISH	EXAMPLE
ai/ay	(aisle)	*bailar* (to dance) *hay* (there is, there are)
au	(now)	*auto* (car)
ei	(may)	*peine* (comb)
ia	(yarn)	*gracias* (thanks)
ie	(yet)	*siempre* (always)
io	(yodel)	*adiós* (bye)
iu	(you)	*ciudad* (city)
oi/oy	(oy)	*oigo* (I hear) *estoy* (I am)
ua	(wand)	*cuando* (when)
ue	(wet)	*bueno* (good)
ui/uy	(sweet)	*cuidado* (care) *muy* (very)

• CONSONANTS •

The letters *k* and *w* appear in Spanish in foreign words like *kilowatt, kilometer*. In some countries, the *k* is spelled with the Spanish equivalent, *qu: quilómetro*. The *w* in Spanish sounds like an English *v: kilowatt.*

SPANISH SOUND	APPROXIMATE SOUND IN ENGLISH	EXAMPLE
l/m/n/p/s/t	similar to English	
b	at the beginning of a word or after *m,* similar to English	*bueno* (good)
	elsewhere similar to English, but softer, allowing air to pass between lips, like *v*	*cabeza* (head)
c (before e/i)*	s (<u>c</u>ertain)	*cena* (dinner)
d	similar to English, but softer, allowing air to pass between lips, like th (<u>th</u>e)	*verdad* (truth)
	after *n,* as in English: d (<u>d</u>o)	*corriendo* (running)
c (before a/o/u)	k (<u>c</u>atch)	*como* (how)
cc	cks (a<u>cc</u>ent)	*acción* (action)
ch	ch (<u>ch</u>urch)	*mucho* (much)
g (before a/o/u)	hard go (<u>g</u>o)	*gasolina* (gas)
g (before e/i)	hard h (<u>h</u>e)	*gente* (people)
h	always silent	*alcohol* (alcohol)
j	hard h (<u>h</u>e)	*jefe* (boss)
ll	In Latin America: y (<u>y</u>et) In Spain: lli (mi<u>ll</u>ion)	*llamar* (to call)
ñ	ny (ca<u>ny</u>on)	*niño* (child)
qu	k (<u>k</u>ite)	*que* (that)
r	in the middle of a word, single trill (th<u>r</u>ow)	*pero* (but)
r	at the beginning of a word, double trill	*ropa* (clothes)
rr	double trill	*carro* (car)
v	v (<u>v</u>ote, but softer, allowing air to pass between lips)	*viernes* (Friday)

*In some regions of Latin America: *s* (vision).

x	cks (ro<u>cks</u>)	*taxi* (cab)
y	y (<u>y</u>et)	*yo* (I)
*z**	s	*zona* (zone)

3. The Spanish Language

Although Spanish is a language different from English, there are many rules which are identical between the two. Just like in English, the basic word order of Spanish is subject-verb-object.

This patient has an appointment. *Este paciente tiene una cita.*

The subject is the word referring to the agent (*este paciente*), the one who performs the action. The verb describes the action (*tiene*), and the object is the word referring to the thing or person receiving the action (*una cita*).

Just like the English verb, the Spanish verb can have different tenses and thus specify whether the action is performed in the present, past, or future. The "moods" of the verb express whether an action is really happening (indicative), may happen (conditional), or is hypothetical (subjunctive and potential).

Spanish verbs have different endings depending on whether the subject is singular or plural, you, me, he, we, or they.

You have an appointment. *Usted tiene una cita.*
They have an appointment. *Ellas tienen una cita.*

Since the verb ending can indicate what or who the subject is, you don't always have to make explicit reference to the subject of the verb.

(I) am a doctor. *Soy doctor.*
(We) are doctors. *Somos doctores.*

* In parts of Spain, z—and also *c* before *e* or *i*—is pronounced like English *th*. Examples: *zona, cera, cinco.*

All Spanish nouns have a gender, i.e. they are either masculine or feminine. In some cases, the gender is obvious: a man is masculine, and a woman is feminine.

the man	*el hombre*	the woman	*la mujer*
a man	*un hombre*	a woman	*una mujer*

In most cases, however, gender and meaning are unrelated, and it is the ending of the noun that determines the gender. The adjective, a word that describes the noun, always has to agree with the gender and number of the noun it describes. That means that the adjective endings have to be either masculine or feminine, singular or plural, just like the noun it describes.

the black man	*el hombre negro*	the black woman	*la mujer negra*
the black men	*los hombres negros*	the black women	*las mujeres negras*

So, it makes quite a difference whether you're speaking about or to a woman or a man.

Are you hurt?	(addressing a male)	*¿Está usted herido?*
	(addressing a female)	*¿Está usted herida?*

In this book we will list both whenever necessary:

Are you hurt?	*¿Está usted herido(a)?*

It is important to remember that, unlike English, Spanish has two different forms of address depending on how well you know a person. *Tú* is the familiar form of address used with family members, friends, children, and pets. *Usted* is the polite form of address used towards everyone else. Using *tú* with someone you are not on familiar terms with is considered inappropriate and disrespectful. Therefore it is best to always use *usted* on the job, unless you are dealing with children. Similarly, it is uncommon to use a person's first name in Spanish unless you are very well acquainted. For this reason, it is best to address everyone by his/her last name and with the polite form of address, again unless you are dealing with children.

Spanish uses accent marks on written words. Sometimes, words that look alike have different meanings depending on whether they have an accent mark or not.

you	*tú*	your	*tu*
is	*está*	this	*ésta*
I know	*sé*	yourself, himself, herself, itself, to him, to her, to you, to them	*se*
you, give!	*¡dé!*	of, from	*de*
yes	*sí*	if	*si*

If you remember these few rules, there's no need to worry about grammatical details. The phrases and sentences in this book are written for you to use them as printed. All you have to do is familiarize yourself with them, and you're ready to go. Should you be curious, however, please refer to the individual grammar notes throughout the book, and to the grammar summary in the appendix.

4. The Latino Culture

A. A QUICK OVERVIEW OF THE HISTORY OF IMMIGRATION

By the year 2000, Americans of Hispanic and/or Latino descent will comprise the largest minority living in the U.S., and they are expected to make up between 10 and 22 percent of the entire U.S. population by the year 2050. Their contributions span all areas of public life: from agricultural fields to the political arena; from science, education, literature, and art to the world of business. Terms such as "Latino" and "Hispanic" have emerged only recently to describe the ethnic background of a group of Americans with various cultural and national backgrounds. Because the word "Hispanic" often carries an association with Spain and the negative implications of the conquest and colonization of America, the term "Latino" is often preferred by the Spanish-speaking people of this continent. However, many Latinos and Hispanics don't think about themselves as such, but refer to themselves as Mexican-American, Tejano, Puerto Rican, Colombian, or other cultural and national designators describing any of the Spanish speaking countries from which they or their ancestors may have come. In fact, the terms "Hispanic" and "Latino" at times seem to be nothing but an attempt to simplify a very complex cultural phenomenon, similar to classifying Englishmen and New Zealanders within the same ethnic category just because both speak English. Therefore, the most respectful and neutral approach is to allow people to classify and name themselves.

The Hispanics and Latinos living in the U.S. are comprised of the following main groups: Cubans and Cuban-Americans, Puerto Ricans, Mexican and Mexican-Americans, Central Americans, Spaniards, and South Americans.

Cubans have been living in the U.S. since the eighteenth century. Today, there are three generations of Cuban-Americans living in the U.S. Most of them—more than half a million—live in Florida. Cuban immigration was mainly motivated by politics and began around 1959 with the communist revolution in Cuba. Immediately after Fidel Castro came to power, a huge number of Cubans fled to the U.S. A second major wave of immigration took place in 1976, when Castro opened his jails and put 125,000 political prisoners in boats and sent them to the U.S., where they were accepted by the Carter Administration.

Puerto Rico is an American protectorate, and Puerto Ricans are U.S. citizens. Exposure to mainland prosperity after serving in the U.S. military in World War II, coupled with the population explosion on the island, caused many Puerto Ricans to move to the mainland, seeking better economic opportunities. One third of all Puerto Ricans—2.3 million—live in one of the fifty U.S. states. In New York City alone, there are 900,000. Drugs, crime, and an alarming lack of educational opportunities in New York City's *El Barrio* are some of the reasons why the population of this area has become one of the most socially disadvantaged Latino groups.

Mexicans and Mexican-Americans represent the largest and most culturally complex group—20 million people. Their cultural heritage dates back centuries. Originally, the American Southwest was a Spanish colony which was incorporated into Mexico and was settled by Spaniards and "mestizos," who had a mixture of Spanish or Mexican and Indian ethnicity. In 1848, this territory was lost to the U.S. Although the resulting treaty of Guadalupe Hidalgo assigned land rights to Mexicans who homesteaded in Texas, many Americans ignored these rights and subjected Mexicans to abuse and cultural or racial discrimination. The Spanish language was banned from schools, the Mexican culture looked down upon, and the American English language and culture became dominant. Today, many Americans of Latino background are mistaken for Mexicans, no matter what their national origin.

As a result of past discrimination and abuse, some Mexican-Americans may be sensitive to identity issues. Many were raised with the belief that abandoning their Mexican roots would lead to a brighter future in Anglo-American society. Therefore, many may have grown up hearing the Spanish language at home but do not speak it themselves. They may consider themselves Mexican when talking to Anglo-Americans, but American when talking to Mexican nationals.

Americans with Mexican-Indian roots refer to themselves as Chicanos. Inspired by the Civil Rights movement in the 1960's, the Chicano movement—which is political, social, cultural, and intellectual by nature—emerged to protest the discrimination against Mexican-Americans and to restore their cultural identity.

Central Americans and South Americans started entering the United States in greater numbers in the late 1970's and continued in the 1980's and 1990's. Economic hardship in the Dominican Republic, Colombia, and Peru, as well as political persecution in countries such as Nicaragua, El Salvador, and

Guatemala brought many new citizens to this country. New York has the world's second largest Dominican population—about 800,000—and about 500,000 Salvadorans live in Los Angeles. There are also thousands of Argentinians, Panamanians, and Ecuadorians who come to this country today to work and make a better life for themselves and their families, as millions of people from Europe did many years ago.

Spaniards have immigrated into the U.S. for centuries, ever since Cristopher Columbus "discovered" America in 1492. Spaniards came as explorers, *conquistadores,* missionaries, refugees, and as individuals attracted by the riches of the "land of opportunity."

B. DEALING WITH CULTURAL STEREOTYPES

The U.S. is a multicultural society. As a healthcare professional, you meet and communicate with people from a variety of cultural and national backgrounds on a daily basis. An awareness of the stereotypes many non-Hispanic Americans may have about the Latino culture, and vice versa, will increase your cultural sensitivity, and will make your encounters with the Latino community easier, more cordial, and successful.

Stereotypes are strategies to help us make sense of actions, customs, and beliefs that seem foreign and strange to us. Some stereotypes may be partially true, in a general sense, but are usually not true at all when dealing with a particular individual face to face. For example, some widespread stereotypes are that Americans drink beer only out of cans, chew gum at all times, and often carry a gun. Without a doubt, everyone would agree that this is a rather simplistic view of American culture, recognize these as stereotypes that need explanation, or even dismiss them as nonsense. Nonetheless, similarly simplistic views of Latino culture are taken rather seriously.

Latinos don't like to work, take siestas all the time, and are in this country illegally. Sound familiar? Without a proper explanation, nothing could be further from the truth. While it is true that the work day is divided by a siesta time in southern regions of the globe to escape the midday heat, it is not true that Latinos don't like to work. Instead, a typical work day in Latin American countries and Spain is extended far into the evening hours. The long break at midday is used to share the biggest meal of the day with family, friends, or associates the way Americans do at dinner time. And while it is true that there are illegal immigrants in the U.S., it is also true that most Latinos are either legal aliens or American citizens, contributing to the gross national product and paying taxes as much as American citizens of other backgrounds do. Only a very small percentage of both legal and undocumented Latinos take advantage of the welfare programs this country offers—5 percent uses free medical care and 1 percent lives on food stamps.

Stereotypes are a fact of life. They will probably always exist, but that doesn't mean that they have a place in healthcare. On the contrary, stereotypes contribute to misunderstandings and inappropriate behavior in situations which call for objectivity and cultural sensitivity. Cultural differences don't make one group better or worse than another, just different. Armed with this open-minded attitude, your work among Latinos in your community may become easier, more enjoyable, and rewarding.

5. Essential Phrases

Good...	*Buenos(as)...*	BWEH-nohs(nahs)...
• morning.	• *días.*	• DEE-ahs.
• afternoon.	• *tardes.*	• TAHR-dehs.
• night.	• *noches.*	• NOH-chehs.
Hello.	*Hola.*	OH-lah.
Good-bye.	*Adios.*	Ah-DYOHS.
How are you?	*¿Cómo está?*	¿KOH-moh ehs-TAH?
Good.	*Bien.*	Byehn.
Bad.	*Mal.*	Mahl.

Fine.	*Bien.*	Byehn.
Better.	*Mejor.*	Meh-HOHR.
Worse.	*Peor.*	Peh-OHR.
The same.	*Igual.*	Ee-GWAHL.
How may I help you?	*¿Cómo puedo ayudarle?*	¿KOH-moh PWEH-doh ah-yoo-DAHR-leh?
Do you speak English?	*¿Habla inglés?*	¿AH-blah een-GLEHS?
Do you understand me?	*¿Me comprende?*	¿Meh kom-PREHN-deh?
I don't understand.	*No comprendo.*	Noh kom-PREHN-doh.
Sorry.	*Lo siento.*	Loh SYEHN-toh.
Excuse me.	*Discúlpeme.*	Dees-KOOL-peh-meh.
Please repeat that.	*Por favor, repita.*	Pohr fah-VOHR, reh-PEE-tah.
Please speak slowly.	*Por favor, hable más lento.*	Pohr fah-VOHR, AH-bleh MAHS LEHN-toh.
Would you feel more comfortable speaking to an interpreter?	*¿Se sentiría mejor hablando con un intérprete?*	¿Seh sehn-tee-REE-ah meh-HOHR ah-BLAHN-doh kohn oon een-TER-preh-teh?
Would you like to speak to a Spanish speaker?	*¿Quisiera hablar con alguien que hable español?*	¿Kee-SYEH-rah ah-BLAR kohn AHL-gyehn keh AH-bleh ehs-pah-NYOHL?
I'll call an interpeter.	*Llamaré a un intérprete.*	Yah-mah-REH ah oon een-TER-preh-teh.
Are you in pain?	*Está adolorido(a).*	Ehs-TAH ah-doh-loh-REE-doh(dah).
Yes.	*Sí.*	SEE.
No.	*No.*	Noh.
Show me where it hurts.	*Dígame donde le duele.*	DEE-gah-meh DOHN-deh leh DWEH-leh.
Here.	*Aquí.*	Ah-KEE.
There.	*Ahí.*	Ah-EE.

Are you allergic to any medication?	*¿Es usted alérgico(a) a alguna medicación?*	¿Ehs oos-TEHD ah-LEHR-hee-koh(kah) ah ahl-GOO-nah meh-dee-kah-SYOHN?
I don't know.	*No sé.*	Noh seh.
Are you pregnant?	*¿Está embarazada?*	¿Ehs-TAH em-bah-rah-SAH-dah?
I'm here to help you.	*Estoy aquí para ayudarla.*	Ehs-TOO-ee ah-KEE PAH-rah ah-yoo-DAHR-lah.
Calm down.	*Cálmese.*	KAHL-meh-seh.
You'll be okay.	*Usted estará bien.*	Oos-TEHD ehs-tah-RAH byehn.
No reason to cry.	*No hay porque llorar.*	Noh ay pohr-KEH yoh-RAHR.
It's okay to cry.	*Está bien llorar.*	Ehs-TAH byehn yoh-RAHR.
Would you like… to be present?	*¿Quiere que… esté presente?*	¿KYEH-reh keh…ehs-TEH preh-SEHN-teh?
• your spouse	• *su esposo(a)*	• soo ehs-POH-soh(sah)
• your family	• *su familia*	• soo fah-MEE-lyah
• your father/mother	• *su padre/madre*	• soo PAH-dreh/MAH-dreh
• your son/daughter	• *su hijo/hija*	• soo EE-hoh/EE-hah
• your friend	• *su amigo*	• soo ah-MEE-goh
• your priest/rabbi/minister	• *su sacerdote/rabino/ministro*	• soo sah-sehr-DOH-teh/rah-BEE-noh/meeh-NEEHS-troh
Does he/she/do they speak English?	*¿Habla/hablan inglés?*	¿AH-blah/AH-blahn een-GLEHS?
Please.	*Por favor.*	Pohr fah-VOHR.
Thank you.	*Gracias.*	GRAH-syahs.
You're welcome.	*De nada.*	Deh NAH-dah.
May I?	*¿Puedo?*	¿PWEH-doh?

May I ask you a few questions?	*¿Puedo hacerle unas preguntas?*	¿PWEH-doh ah-SEHR-leh OOH-nahs preh-GOON-tahs?
May I touch you?	*¿Puedo tocarla(o)?*	¿PWEH-doh toh-KAHR-lah(loh)?
Who?	*¿Quién?*	¿KYEHN?
What?	*¿Qué?*	¿KEH?
When?	*¿Cuándo?*	¿KWAHN-doh?
Today.	*Hoy.*	Oy.
Tomorrow.	*Mañana.*	Mah-NYAH-nah.
Yesterday.	*Ayer.*	Ah-YEHR.
Last ____.	*El (la) pasado(a) ____.*	Ehl (lah) pah-SAH-doh(dah) ____.
____ ago.	*Hace ____.*	AH-seh ____.
Since ____.	*Desde ____.*	DEHS-deh ____.
Where?	*¿Dónde?*	¿DOHN-deh?
Why?	*¿Por qué?*	¿Pohr KEH?
How?	*¿Cómo?*	¿KOH-moh?
How often?	*¿Con qué frecuencia?*	¿Kohn KEH freh-KWEN-syah?
How much?	*¿Cuánto?*	¿KWAHN-toh?
What's your…	*¿Cuál es…*	¿KWAHL ehs…
• name?	• *su nombre?*	• sooh NOHM-breh?
• address?	• *su dirección?*	• sooh dee-rek-SYOHN?
• telephone number?	• *su número de teléfono?*	• sooh NOO-meh-roh deh teh-LEH-foh-noh?
• social security number?	• *su numero de seguro social?*	• sooh NOO-meh-roh deh seh-GOO-roh soh-SYAHL?
• date of birth?	• *su fecha de nacimiento?*	• sooh FEH-chah deh nah-see-MYEHN-toh?

6. Numbers

A. CARDINAL NUMBERS

zero	*cero*	SEH-roh
one	*uno*	OO-noh
two	*dos*	dohs
three	*tres*	trehs
four	*cuatro*	KWAH-troh
five	*cinco*	SEEN-koh
six	*seis*	sehs
seven	*siete*	SYEH-teh
eight	*ocho*	OH-choh
nine	*nueve*	NWEH-veh
ten	*diez*	dee-EHS
eleven	*once*	OHN-seh
twelve	*doce*	DOH-seh
thirteen	*trece*	TREH-seh
fourteen	*cartorce*	kah-TOHR-seh
fifteen	*quince*	KEEN-seh
sixteen	*dieciséis*	dyeh-see-sehs
seventeen	*diecisiete*	dyeh-see-SYEH-teh
eighteen	*dieciocho*	dyeh-see-OH-choh
nineteen	*diecinueve*	dyeh-see-NWEH-veh
twenty	*veinte*	VEHN-teh
twenty-one	*veintiuno*	VEHN-tee-OO-noh
twenty-two	*veintidós*	VEHN-tee-DOHS
twenty-three	*veintitrés*	VEHN-tee-TREHS
thirty	*treinta*	TREHN-tah
forty	*cuarenta*	kwah-REHN-tah
fifty	*cincuenta*	seen-KWEHN-tah
sixty	*sesenta*	seh-SEHN-tah

seventy	*setenta*	seh-TEHN-tah
eighty	*ochenta*	oh-CHEHN-tah
ninety	*noventa*	noh-VEHN-tah
one hundred	*cien*	SYEHN
one hundred one	*ciento uno*	SYEHN-toh OO-noh
one hundred two	*ciento dos*	SYEHN-toh dohs
one hundred twenty	*ciento veinte*	SYEHN-toh VAYN-teh
one hundred thirty	*ciento treinta*	SYEHN-toh TREHN-tah
two hundred	*doscientos(as)*	dohs-SYEHN-tohs(tahs)
three hundred	*trescientos(as)*	trehs-SYEHN-tohs(tahs)
four hundred	*cuatrocientos(as)*	kwah-troh-SYEHN-tohs(tahs)
five hundred	*quinientos(as)*	kee-NYEHN-tohs(tahs)
six hundred	*seiscientos(as)*	says-SYEHN-tohs(tahs)
seven hundred	*setecientos(as)*	seh-teh-SYEHN-tohs (tahs)
eight hundred	*ochocientos(as)*	oh-choh-SYEHN-tohs (tahs)
nine hundred	*novecientos(as)*	noh-veh-SYEHN-tohs (tahs)
one thousand	*mil*	meel
two thousand	*dos mil*	dohs meel
three thousand	*tres mil*	trehs meel
one million	*un millón*	oon mee-YOHN
two million	*dos millones*	dohs mee-YOH-nehs

B. ORDINAL NUMBERS

first	*primero* *primer(a)*	pree-MEH-roh pree-MEHR (MEH-rah)

second	*segundo(a)*	seh-GOON-doh(dah)
third	*tercero* *tercer(a)*	tehr-SEH-roh tehr-SEHR(SEH-rah)
fourth	*cuarto(a)*	KWAHR-toh(tah)
fifth	*quinto(a)*	KEEN-toh(tah)
sixth	*sexto(a)*	SEHKS-toh(tah)
seventh	*séptimo(a)*	SEHP-tee-moh(mah)
eighth	*octavo(a)*	ohk-TAH-voh(vah)
ninth	*noveno(a)*	noh-VEH-noh(nah)
tenth	*décimo(a)*	DEH-see-moh(mah)

SECTION B

ADMINISTRATION AND PRELIMINARY EXAMINATION (BY A NURSE)

1. Reception: Welcome and Sign-in

RECEPTIONIST	*RECEPCIONISTA*	
Good…	*Buenos(as)…*	BWEH-nohs(nahs)…
• morning.	• *días.*	• DEE-ahs.
• afternoon.	• *tardes.*	• TAHR-dehs.
• evening.	• *noches.*	• NOH-chehs.
Do you have an appointment?	*¿Tiene una cita?*	¿TYEH-neh OO-nah SEE-tah?
PATIENT	*PACIENTE*	
Yes, I have an appointment.	*Sí, tengo cita.*	See, TEHN-goh SEE-tah.
No, I don't have an appointment.	*No, no tengo cita.*	Noh, noh TEHN-goh SEE-tah.
But I would like to see the doctor.	*Pero me gustaría ver al doctor.*	PEH-roh meh goos-tah-REE-ah vehr ahl dohk-TOHR.

CULTURE NOTE ••••

GREETINGS Greetings are very important to Hispanics. They acknowledge each other's presence and greet each other every time they meet, even if they meet several times in one day. And, every time they will probably ask each other *Hola, ¿cómo estás?* (Hi, how are you? [informal]) or *¿Cómo está usted?* (How are you? [formal]). Please be aware that using the familiar *tú* with Latinos you don't know well is considered disrespectful or condescending. Use the formal *usted,* unless you are dealing with children or teenagers. When greeting someone, a handshake may be expected. Most likely the patient will wait for you to extend your hand first.

If there is more than one physician in the office, you may ask:

RECEPTIONIST	*RECEPTIONISTA*	
Which doctor do you have the appointment with?	*¿Con cuál doctor tiene la cita?*	¿Kohn KWAHL dohk-TOHR TYEH-neh lah SEE-tah?
PATIENT	***PACIENTE***	
I have an appointment with Doctor ____.	*Tengo cita con el(la) Doctor(a) ____.*	TEHN-goh SEE-tah kohn ehl(lah) Dohk-TOHR (TOH-rah)____.
RECEPTIONIST	***RECEPTIONISTA***	
Is it urgent?	*¿Es urgente?*	¿Ehs oor-HEHN-teh?
PATIENT	***PACIENTE***	
No, it is not urgent.	*No, no es urgente.*	Noh, noh ehs oor-HEHN-teh.
Yes, it is urgent.	*Sí, es urgente.*	See, ehs oor-HEHN-teh.

RECEPTIONIST	***RECEPTIONISTA***	
Why?	*¿Por qué?*	¿Pohr KEH?
PATIENT	***PACIENTE***	
Because…	*Porque…*	POHR-keh…
• I am very sick.	• *estoy muy enfermo(a).*	• ehs-TOY moo-ee ehn-FEHR-moh (mah).
• I cannot stand the pain anymore.	• *ya no aguanto el dolor.*	• yah noh ah-GWAHN-toh ehl doh-LOHR.
RECEPTIONIST	***RECEPTIONISTA***	
I will ask you a few questions.	*Le haré unas preguntas.*	Leh ah-REH OO-nahs preh-GOON-tahs.
Then, I will inform the doctor that it is urgent.	*Luego informaré al (a la) doctor(a) que es urgente.*	LWEH-goh een-fohr-mah-REH ahl (ah lah) dohk-TOHR(TOH-rah) keh ehs oor-HEHN-teh.
PATIENT	***PACIENTE***	
Thanks.	*Gracias.*	GRAH-syahs.
Yes.	*Sí.*	See.
Fine.	*Está bien.*	Ehs-TAH byehn.
Good.	*Bueno.*	BWEH-noh.
Go ahead.	*Adelante.*	Ah-deh-LAHN-teh.

CULTURE NOTE ••••

NAMES AND LAST NAMES Latinos use two surnames called *apellidos:* the father's and the mother's last name. If only one single last name is reported, it is most likely in order to adapt to American customs. In these cases usually the father's last name is used.

Juan Antonio Pérez García	*Pérez* is the father's name. *García* is the mother's name. *Antonio* is not abbreviated as it is often done with middle names in English.
María Elena Ríos Fuentes de Pérez	*de Pérez* is María Elena's married name. *Ríos* is her father's name. *Fuentes* is her mother's name.

If Juan Antonio and María Elena have a son named José María, his full name would be:

José María Pérez Ríos

There are two ways to ask for somebody's name:

What's your name?
- *¿Cómo se llama?* (form.)
- *¿Cómo te llamas?* (inf.)
- *¿Cuál es su nombre?* (form.)
- *¿Cuál es tu nombre?* (inf.)

And two ways to answer.

My name is _____.
- *Mi nombre es* _____.
- *Me llamo* _____.

When you need somebody's name for a document, ask for:

Name and last names, please.	*Nombre y apellidos, por favor.*

Don't abbreviate any of the two last names when filling out forms, as they are both legal and identifying names.

RECEPTIONIST	*RECEPTIONISTA*	
What is your name?	*¿Cómo se llama?*	¿KOH-moh seh YAH-mah?
Please tell me slowly how you spell your name.	*Por favor, dígame despacio como se deletrea su nombre.*	Pohr fah-VOHR, DEE-gah-meh dehs-PAH-syoh KOH-moh seh deh-leh-TREH-ah soo NOHM-breh.
Is this the first time you are coming to see this doctor?	*¿Es la primera vez que viene a ver a este(a) doctor(a)?*	¿Ehs lah pree-MEH-rah vehs keh VYEH-neh ah vehr ah EHS-teh(tah) dohk-TOHR(TOH-rah)?
PATIENT	***PACIENTE***	
Yes, this is the first time.	*Sí, es la primera vez.*	See, ehs lah pree-MEH-rah vehs.
No, I've been here before.	*No, había venido antes.*	Noh, ah-BEE-ah veh-NEE-doh AHN-tehs.
RECEPTIONIST	***RECEPTIONISTA***	
When was the last time you came to see the doctor?	*¿Cuándo fue la última vez que vino a ver al (a la) doctor(a)?*	¿KWAHN-doh fweh lah OOL-tee-mah vehs keh VEE-noh ah vehr ahl (ah lah) dohk-TOHR(TOH-rah)?
Thank you.	*Muchas gracias.*	MOO-chahs GRAH-syahs.
I am going to get your chart.	*Voy a traer su expediente.*	Voy ah trah-EHR soo ehks-peh-DYEHN-teh.

GRAMMAR NOTE ••••

ADDRESSES AND PHONE NUMBERS When giving an address in Spanish, begin with the name of the street, followed by north, south, east, west, and the number.

What's your address?	*¿Cuál es su dirección?*
My address is 99 East Pine Street.	*Mi dirección es Calle Pine Este, número noventa y nueve.*

Phone numbers are grouped in pairs:

What's your phone number?	*¿Cuál es su número de teléfono?*
My number is 733-2285.	*Mi número de teléfono es el 7-33-22-85. (siete-treinta y tres-veintidós, ochenta y cinco)*

If this is the first time the patient is coming to see the physician, you may ask:

RECEPTIONIST	*RECEPTIONISTA*	
Who recommended that you come?	*¿Quién le recomendó que viniera?*	¿KYEHN leh reh-koh-mehn-DOH keh vee-NYEH-rah?
PATIENT	***PACIENTE***	
My spouse.	*Mi esposa(o).*	Mee ehs-POH-sah(soh).
A friend.	*Un(a) amigo(a).*	Oon(OO-nah) ah-MEE-goh(gah).
Dr. ____.	*El (la) Doctor(a) ____.*	Ehl (lah) Dohk-TOHR-(TOH-rah) ____.
RECEPTIONIST	***RECEPTIONISTA***	
What is your…	*¿Cuál es su…*	¿KWAHL ehs soo…
• Social Security number?	• *número de seguro social?*	• NOO-meh-roh de seh-GOO-roh soh-SYAHL?

• address and ZIP code?	• *dirección y zona postal?*	• dee-rehk-SYOHN ee SOH-nah pohs-TAHL?
• phone number?	• *número de teléfono?*	• NOO-meh-roh deh teh-LEH-foh-noh?
How old are you?	*¿Qué edad tiene?*	¿KEH eh-DAHD TYEH-neh?
What is your date of birth?	*¿Cuál es su fecha de nacimiento?*	¿KWAHL ehs soo FEH-chah deh nah-see-MYEHN-toh?
Where were you born?	*¿Dónde nació?*	¿DOHN-deh nah-SYOH?
In which…	*¿En qué…*	¿Ehn KEH…
• city?	• *ciudad?*	• syoo-DAHD?
• state?	• *estado?*	• ehs-TAH-doh?
• country?	• *país?*	• pah-EES?
Are you single or married?	*¿Es usted soltera(o) o casada(o)?*	¿Ehs oos-TEHD sohl-TEH-rah(roh) oh kah-SAH-dah(doh)?
What is your spouse's name?	*¿Cómo se llama su esposo(a)?*	¿KOH-moh seh YAH-mah soo ehs-POH-soh(sah)?
Are you…	*¿Es usted…*	¿Ehs oos-TEHD…
• divorced?	• *divorciada(o)?*	• dee-vohr-SYAH-dah(doh)?
• separated?	• *separada(o)?*	• seh-pah-RAH-dah (doh)?
• a widow(er)?	• *viuda(o)?*	• VYOH-dah (doh)?
Where do you work?	*¿Dónde trabaja?*	¿DOHN-deh trah-BAH-hah?
PATIENT	*PACIENTE*	
I do not work.	*No trabajo.*	Noh trah-BAH-hoh.
I am unemployed.	*Estoy sin empleo.*	Ehs-TOY seen ehm-PLEH-oh.
I work…	*Trabajo…*	Trah-BAH-hoh…
• at home.	• *en mi casa.*	• ehn mee KAH-sah.
• in the fields.	• *en el campo.*	• ehn ehl KAHM-poh.

• in a factory.	• *en una fábrica.*	• ehn OO-nah FAH-bree-kah.
• in an office.	• *en una oficina.*	• ehn OO-nah oh-fee-SEE-nah.
• in a store.	• *en una tienda.*	• ehn OO-nah TYEHN-dah.
• at ____.	• *en ____.*	• ehn ____.
I am…	*Soy…*	Soy…
• an agricultural worker.	• *trabajador(a) agrícola.*	• trah-bah-hah-DOHR (DOH-rah) ah-GREE-koh-lah.
• a factory worker.	• *obrero(a).*	• oh-BREH-roh(rah).
• an office worker.	• *oficinista.*	• oh-fee-see-NEES-tah.
• a sales person.	• *vendedor(a).*	• vehn-deh-DOHR (DOH-rah).
RECEPTIONIST	***RECEPTIONISTA***	
What is the…of your employer?	*¿Cuál es…de la empresa/compañía donde trabaja?*	¿KWAHL ehs…deh lah ehm-PREH-sah/kohm-pah-NEE-AH DOHN-deh trah-BAH-hah?
• name	• *el nombre*	• ehl NOHM-breh
• address	• *la dirección*	• lah dee-rehk-SYOHN
• phone number	• *el teléfono*	• ehl teh-LEH-foh-noh
In case of emergency, whom should we talk to?	*En caso de emergencia, ¿con quién quiere que hablemos?*	Ehn KAH-soh deh eh-mehr-HEHN-syah, ¿kohn kyehn KYEH-reh keh ah-BLEH-mohs?
Give me the…	*Déme el (la)…*	DEH-meh ehl (lah)…
• name.	• *nombre.*	• NOHM-breh.
• address.	• *dirección.*	• dee-rehk-SYOHN.
• phone number.	• *teléfono.*	• teh-LEH-foh-noh.
What is your relationship to this person?	*¿Cuál es su relación con esta persona?*	¿KWAHL-ehs soo reh-lah-SYOHN kohn EHS-tah pehr-SOH-nah?

PATIENT	***PACIENTE***	
He/she is my...	*Es mi...*	Ehs mee...
• father/mother.	• *papá/mamá.*	• pah-PAH/mah-MAH.
• brother/sister.	• *hermano/hermana.*	• ehr-MAH-noh/ehr-MAH-nah.
• son/daughter.	• *hijo/hija.*	• EE-hoh/EE-hah.
• friend.	• *amigo(a).*	• ah-MEE-goh(gah).
• colleague.	• *colega.*	• Koh-LEH-gah.
• boss.	• *patrón.*	• pah-TROHN.
RECEPTIONIST	***RECEPTIONISTA***	
Do you know how much the doctor charges per visit?	*¿Sabe usted cuánto cobra el doctor por una visita?*	¿SAH-beh oos-TEHD KWAHN-toh KOH-brah ehl dohk-TOHR pohr OO-nah vee-SEE-tah?
Where should we send the bill?	*¿Dónde vamos a enviar la cuenta?*	¿DOHN-deh VAH-mohs ah ehn-VYAHR lah KWEHN-tah?
PATIENT	***PACIENTE***	
I will pay now.	*Pagaré ahora.*	Pah-gah-REH ah-OH-rah.
Send it to me.	*Me la envía a mí.*	Meh lah ehn-VEE-ah ah mee.
Send it to...	*La envía a...*	Lah ehn-VEE-ah ah...
• my insurance.	• *mi seguro.*	• mee seh-GOO-roh.
• my employer.	• *mi patrón.*	• mee pah-TROHN.
RECEPTIONIST	***RECEPTIONISTA***	
Are you going to pay...	*¿Va a pagar...*	¿Vah ah pah-GAHR...
• in cash?	• *al contado?*	• ahl kohn-TAH-doh?
• with a check?	• *con un cheque?*	• kohn oon CHEH-keh?
• with a credit card?	• *con tarjeta de crédito?*	• kohn tahr-HEH-tah deh KREH-dee-toh?
What is...	*¿Cuál es el...*	¿KWAHL ehs ehl...
• the name of your insurance?	• *nombre de su seguro?*	• NOHM-breh deh soo seh-GOO-roh?

• your policy number?	• *número de su póliza?*	• NOO-meh-roh deh soo POH-lee-sah?
What is the name on the insurance policy?	*¿A nombre de quién está el seguro?*	¿Ah NOHM-breh deh KYEHN ehs-TAH ehl seh-GOO-roh?

If the patient urgently needs to see the physician:

I will tell the doctor that you need to see him/her urgently.	*Le diré al (a la) doctor(a) que necesita verlo(la) urgentemente.*	Leh dee-REH ahl (ah lah) dohk-TOHR (TOH-rah) keh neh-seh-SEE-tah vehr-loh(lah) uhr-hehn-teh-MEHN-teh.
The doctor will see you as soon as he/she can.	*El (la) doctor(a) la (lo) verá tan pronto como pueda.*	Ehl (lah) dohk-TOHR (TOH-rah) lah (loh) veh-RAH tahn PROHN-toh KOH-moh PWEH-dah.
Please take a seat.	*Por favor, tome asiento.*	Pohr fah-VOHR, TOH-meh ah-SYEHN-toh.
We will call you when it is your turn.	*Le llamaremos cuando llegue su turno.*	Leh yah-mah-REH-mohs KWAHN-doh YEH-geh soo TOOR-noh.
The doctor…	*El (la) doctor(a)…*	Ehl (lah) dohk-TOHR (TOH-rah)…
• is not in at the moment.	• *no está en este momento.*	• noh ehs-TAH ehn EHS-teh moh-MEHN-toh.
• is on his/her way.	• *está en camino.*	• ehs-TAH ehn kah-MEEN-noh.
• is making rounds.	• *está haciendo visitas.*	• ehs-TAH ah-SYEHN-doh vee-SEE-tahs.
• is in surgery.	• *está operando.*	• ehs-TAH oh-peh-RAHN-doh.
• is delivering a baby.	• *está atendiendo un parto.*	• ehs-TAH ah-tehn-DYEHN-doh oon PAHR-toh.

If we can help you in any way until the doctor arrives, please let us know.	*Si le podemos ayudar en algo hasta que llegue el doctor, por favor díganos.*	See leh poh-DEH-mohs ah-yoo-DAHR ehn AHL-goh AHS-tah keh YEH-geh ehl dohk-TOHR, pohr fah-VOHR DEE-gah-nohs.
Please fill out... while you wait.	*Por favor, llene... mientras espera.*	Pohr fah-VOHR, YEH-neh... MYEHN-trahs ehs-PEH-rah.
• these forms	• *estos formularios*	• EHS-tohs fohr-moo-LAH-ryohs
• this questionnaire	• *este cuestionario*	• EHS-teh kwehs-tyoh-NAH-ryoh
Do you need help with these forms?	*¿Necesita ayuda con los formularios?*	¿Neh-seh-SEE-tah ah-YOO-dah kohn lohs fohr-moo-LAH-ree-yohs?

VOCABULARY ••••

PERSONAL INFORMATION

married	*casado(a)*	kah-SAH-doh(dah)
widower/widow	*viudo(a)*	VYOO-doh(dah)
divorced	*divorciado(a)*	dee-vohr-SYAH-doh(dah)
single	*soltero(a)*	sohl-TEH-roh(rah)
separated	*separado(a)*	seh-pah-RAH-doh(dah)
city	*ciudad*	syoo-DAHD
state	*estado*	ehs-TAH-doh
country	*país*	pah-EEHS
appointment	*cita*	SEE-tah
employment	*empleo*	EHM-pleh-oh

If a nurse will see the patient first and gather the preliminary data, say:

The nurse will take your vital signs.	*La enfermera le tomará sus signos vitales.*	Lah ehn-fehr-MEH-rah leh toh-mah-RAH soos SEEG-nohs vee-TAH-lehs.
Then, the doctor will see you.	*Luego la (lo) verá el (la) doctor(a).*	LWEH-goh lah (loh) veh-RAH ehl (lah) dohk-TOHR(TOH-rah).
Mr./Mrs. ____, the nurse is ready.	*Señor(a)* ____, la *enfermera está lista.*	Seh-NYOHR (NYOH-rah) ____, lah ehn-fehr-MEH-rah ehs-TAH LEES-tah.
Please follow me.	*Por favor, sígame.*	Pohr fah-VOHR, SEE-gah-meh.
Mr./Mrs. ____, please take a seat.	*Señor(a)* ____, *por favor siéntese.*	Seh-NYOHR (NYOH-rah) ____, pohr fah-VOHR SYEHN-teh-seh.
It will only be a moment.	*Esperará sólo un momento.*	Ehs-peh-rah-RAH SOH-loh oon moh-MEHN-toh.

GRAMMAR NOTE ••••

THE PRESENT TENSE In Spanish there are different verb endings for each of the subjects I, you, he, etc. performing an action. The present tense expresses actions that are occurring at the present moment. There are three sets of endings for the present tense of regular verbs in Spanish. One set of verb endings for infinitives ending in *-ar*, one set for those ending in *-er*, and another for *-ir* verbs.

TO WORK *TRABAJ-AR*

I	*yo*	*trabaj- o*
you (inf.)	*tú*	*trabaj- as*
he/she/you (form.)	*él/ella/usted*	*trabaj- a*
we	*nosotros*	*trabaj- amos*
you (inf.)	*vosotros*	*trabaj- áis*
they/you (form.)	*ellos/ellas/ustedes*	*trabaj- an*

TO UNDERSTAND *COMPREND-ER*

I	*yo*	*comprend- o*
you (inf.)	*tú*	*comprend- es*
he/she/you (form.)	*él/ella/usted*	*comprend- e*
we	*nosotros*	*comprend- emos*
you (inf.)	*vosotros*	*comprend- éis*
they/you (form.)	*ellos/ellas/ustedes*	*comprend- en*

TO LIVE *VIV-IR*

I	*yo*	*viv- o*
you (inf.)	*tú*	*viv- es*
he/she/you (form.)	*él/ellas/usted*	*viv- e*
we	*nosotros*	*viv- imos*
you (inf.)	*vosotros*	*viv- ís*
they/you (form.)	*ellos/ellas/ustedes*	*viv- en*

2. Preliminary Examination of a Patient (by a Nurse)

CULTURE NOTE ••••

THE ATTITUDE TOWARD NURSES AND DOCTORS
Often Latino patients feel more comfortable with the nurse than with the doctor. This is especially true if nurse and patient are of the same gender. Doctors are perceived to be authority figures, and therefore, Latino patients may feel more distanced toward them. Nurses, on the other hand, are perceived to be nurturing and caring, ready to make patients feel as comfortable as possible. Please note that Latino patients may not be used to working with male nurses. They may be very surprised, but will ultimately yield to their authority. In particular, male patients may end up feeling very comfortable with a male nurse.

NURSE	*ENFERMERA*	
Good...	*Buenos(as)...*	BWEH-nohs(nahs)...
• morning.	• *días.*	• DEE-ahs.
• afternoon.	• *tardes.*	• TAHR-dehs.
• evening.	• *noches.*	• NOH-chehs.
I am the nurse of Dr. _____.	*Soy la enfermera del (de la) Doctor(a)* _____.	Soy lah ehn-fehr-MEH-rah dehl (deh lah) Dohk-TOHR (TOH-rah) _____.
My name is _____.	*Me llamo* _____.	Meh YAH-moh _____.

I'm going to...	*Le voy a...*	Leh-voy ah...
• take your vital signs.	• *tomar los signos vitales.*	• toh-MAHR lohs SEEG-nohs vee-TAH-lehs.
• weigh you.	• *pesar.*	• peh-SAHR.
Follow me.	*Sígame.*	SEE-gah-meh.
Please get on the scale.	*Por favor, súbase a la báscula.*	Pohr fah-VOHR, SOO-bah-seh ah lah BAHS-koo-lah.
Very well.	*Muy bien.*	MOO-ee byehn.
Thank you.	*Gracias.*	GRAH-syahs.
I'm going to take your blood pressure.	*Le voy a tomar la presión.*	Leh voy ah toh-MAHR lah preh-SYOHN.
Please roll up your sleeves.	*Por favor, súbase la manga de la blusa/camisa.*	Pohr fah-VOHR, SOO-bah-seh lah MAHN-gah deh lah BLOO-sah/kah-MEE-sah.
Extend your arm and relax.	*Extienda su brazo y descánselo.*	Ehks-TYEHN-dah soo BRAH-soh ee dehs-KAHN-seh-loh.
I'm going to take your pulse.	*Le voy a tomar el pulso.*	Leh voy ah toh-MAHR ehl POOL-soh.
May I hold your wrist?	*¿Puedo tomar su muñeca?*	PWEH-doh toh-MAHR soo moo-NYEH-kah?
I'm going to...	*Le voy a...*	Leh voy ah...
• take your temperature.	• *tomar su temperatura.*	• toh-MAHR soo tehm-peh-rah-TOO-rah.
• put a thermometer in your mouth.	• *poner un termómetro en la boca.*	• poh-NEHR oon tehr-MOH-meh-troh ehn lah BOH-kah.
Please open/close your breathing.	*Por favor, abra/cierre la boca.*	Pohr fah-VOHR, AH-brah/SYEH-rreh lah BOH-kah.
I'm going to count your respirations.	*Voy a contar sus respiraciones.*	Voy ah kohn-TAHR soos rehs-pee-rah-SYOH-nehs.

If it is necessary to gown the patient:

The doctor will examine you.	*El (la) doctor(a) la (lo) va a examinar.*	Ehl (lah) dohk-TOHR (TOH-rah) lah (loh) vah ah eks-ah-mee-NAHR.
You need to take off your clothes and put this gown on.	*Necesita quitarse la ropa y ponerse esta bata.*	Neh-seh-SEE-tah kee-TAHR-seh lah ROH-pah ee poh-NEHR-seh EHS-tah BAH-tah.

If you have to draw blood:

I need to draw a blood sample.	*Necesito tomar una muestra de sangre.*	Neh-seh-SEE-toh toh-MAHR OO-nah MWEHS-trah deh SAHN-greh.
Please give me your arm.	*Por favor, déme el brazo.*	Pohr fah-VOHR, DEH-meh ehl BRAH-soh.
It may cause a little discomfort.	*Le puede causar alguna molestia.*	Leh PWEH-deh kahw-SAHR ahl-GOO-nah moh-LEHS-tyah.
I am going to put a tourniquet around your arm.	*Le voy a poner una liga alrededor del brazo.*	Leh voy ah poh-NEHR OO-nah LEE-gah ahl-reh-deh-DOHR dehl BRAH-soh.
I am going to draw blood from this vein.	*Voy a sacar la sangre de esta vena.*	Voy ah sah-KAHR lah SAHN-greh deh EHS-tah VEH-nah.

If you need to take a urine sample:

We also need a urine sample.	*También necesitamos una muestra de orina.*	Tahm-BYEHN neh-seh-see-TAH-mohs OO-nah MWEHS-trah deh oh-REE-nah.
It has to be from the middle of the stream.	*Tiene que ser de la mitad del chorro.*	TYEH-neh keh sehr deh lah mee-TAHD dehl CHOH-rroh.
Put the urine in this cup.	*Ponga la orina en este vaso.*	POHN-gah lah oh-REE-nah ehn EHS-teh VAH-soh.

The rest room is…	*El baño está…*	Ehl BAH-nyoh ehs-TAH…
• right here.	• *aquí.*	• ah-KEE.
• over there.	• *allá.*	• ah-YAH.
• at the end of the hall.	• *al final del pasillo.*	• ahl fee-NAHL dehl pah-SEE-yoh.
• the second door on the right/left.	• *en la segunda puerta a la derecha/izquierda.*	• ehn lah seh-GOON-dah PWEHR-tah ah lah deh-REH-chah/ees-KYEHR-dah.

GRAMMAR NOTE ••••

DIRECT COMMANDS If you give an order to an adult you don't know, use the formal command form.

(You) open your mouth! *¡Abra la boca!*

You can also include yourself when giving an order:

Let's open the mouth! *¡Abramos la boca!*

The command forms of *-ar* verbs use the present tense endings of *-er* and *-ir* verbs.

TO CALL *LLAM- AR*

(don't) call!	*¡(no) llam- e!*
you [pl.] (don't) call!	*¡(no) llam- en!*
let's (not) call!	*¡(no) llam- emos!*

-er and *-ir* verbs use *-ar* endings:

TO RUN *CORR- ER*

you (don't) run!	*¡(no) corr- a!*
you [pl.] (don't) run!	*¡(no) corr- an!*
let's (not) run!	*¡(no) corr- amos!*

TO WRITE *ESCRIB- IR*

you (don't) write!	*¡(no) escrib- a!*
let's (not) write!	*¡(no) escrib- amos!*
you [pl.] (don't) write!	*¡(no) escrib- an!*

THE PATIENT INTERVIEW

CULTURE NOTE ••••

MUTUAL RESPECT As with any other patient, it is very important to establish a relationship of mutual respect and trust with your Latino patient. Take the time to greet the patient, and if you haven't met him or her before, take the time to introduce yourself. If you have met the patient before, you may want to take a few moments to inquire about his/her family or work. To Latinos, a doctor is an authority figure whose expertise is beyond doubt. Return this respect, and treat your Latino patients with courtesy.

1. Beginning the Interview

DOCTOR	*DOCTOR*	
Good..., Mr./ Mrs. ____.	*Buenos(as)..., Señor/ Señora* ____.	BWEH-nohs(nahs)..., Seh-NYOHR/Seh-NYOH-rah ____.
• morning	• *días*	• DEE-ahs

• afternoon	• *tardes*	• TAHR-dehs
• evening	• *noches*	• NOH-chehs

If you have met the patient before:

How are you?	*¿Cómo está?*	¿KOH-moh ehs-TAH?
How is your family?	*¿Cómo está su familia?*	¿KOH-moh ehs-TAH soo fah-MEE-lyah?
And how is work?	*¿Y cómo le va en el trabajo?*	¿Ee, KOH-moh leh vah ehn ehl trah-BAH-hoh?
I am glad to see you again.	*Me da gusto verlo(la) de nuevo.*	Meh dah GOOS-toh VEHR-loh(lah) deh NWEH-voh.
You look very well.	*Se ve usted muy bien.*	Seh veh oos-TEHD MOO-ee byehn.
How have you been with the treatment?	*¿Cómo le ha ido con el tratamiento?*	¿KOH-moh leh ah EE-doh kohn ehl trah-tah-MYEN-toh?

If you have never met the patient before.

I am Doctor ____.	*Soy el (la) Doctor(a)* ____.	Soy ehl (lah) Dohk-TOHR(TOH-rah) ____.
I am going to ask you some questions.	*Le voy a hacer unas preguntas.*	Leh voy ah ah-SEHR OO-nahs pre-GOON-tahs.
Can you tell me why you came to see me?	*¿Me puede decir por qué vino a verme?*	¿Meh PWEH-deh deh-SEER-pohr KEH VEE-noh ah VEHR-meh?
Tell me...	*Dígame...*	DEE-gah-meh...
• how I can help you today.	• *cómo puedo ayudarla(lo) hoy.*	• KOH-moh PWEH-doh ah-YOO-DAHR-lah(loh) oy.
• what the problem is.	• *cuál es el problema.*	• KWAHL ehs ehl proh-BLEH-mah.

GRAMMAR NOTE ••••

ASKING QUESTIONS To ask questions in Spanish, reverse the order of verb and subject:

You have…	*Usted tiene…*
Do you have…?	*¿Tiene usted…?*

Just like English, Spanish uses question words:

What do you have?	*¿Qué tiene usted?*

Here's a list of important question words:

What?	*¿Qué?*
Of what?	*¿De qué?*
Which?	*¿Cuál?*
How?	*¿Cómo?*
Where?	*¿Dónde?*
From where?	*¿De dónde?*
To where?	*¿Adónde?*
When?	*¿Cuándo?*
How much?	*¿Cuánto?*
How many?	*¿Cuánto(a/os/as)?*
Why?	*¿Por qué?*
Who?	*¿Quién?*
With whom?	*¿Con quién?*
To whom?	*¿A quién?*
Whose?	*¿De quién?*

It is also possible to just allow your voice to rise in the end of the sentence, as you would in English.

You have…?	*¿Usted tiene…?*

In writing, use question marks at the beginning and at the end (*¿…?*). Please note that there is no equivalent for the auxiliary "do/does/did."

Do you have allergies?	*¿Tiene alergias?*

2. History of the Present Illness

CULTURE NOTE ••••

AVOIDING EMBARRASSMENT As other patients, Latinos may feel uncomfortable when speaking about certain symptoms and illnesses. Discussing sexually transmitted diseases or symptoms, and dealing with digestive and excretory functions may be especially embarrassing. Guide your patients gently through the questionnaire, and deal with your questions and their answers in a professional and factual manner. If you feel that you are not getting the answers you need, call in an interpreter who may be able to speak to your patients more freely.

DOCTOR	*DOCTOR*	
When did you notice that you were sick?	*¿Cuande se dio cuenta que está enferma(o)?*	¿KWAHN-doh seh dyoh KWEHN-tah keh ehs-TAH ehn-FEHR-mah(moh)?
PATIENT	***PACIENTE***	
This morning.	*Esta mañana.*	EHS-tah mah-NYAH-nah.
Yesterday.	*Ayer.*	Ah-YEHR.
A few days ago.	*Hace unos días.*	AH-seh OO-nohs DEE-ahs.
A week ago.	*Hace una semana.*	AH-seh OO-nah seh-MAH-nah.
DOCTOR	***DOCTOR***	
What was the first thing you noticed?	*¿Qué fue lo primero que notó?*	¿KEH fweh loh pree-MEH-roh keh noh-TOH?

PATIENT	*PACIENTE*	
A pain in my…	*Un dolor de/en…*	Oon doh-LOHR deh/ehn…
• head.	• *la cabeza.*	• lah kah-BEH-sah.
• throat.	• *la garganta.*	• lah ghar-GHAN-tah.
• ear.	• *el oído.*	• ehl oh-EE-doh.
• neck.	• *el cuello.*	• ehl KWEH-yoh.
• tooth.	• *un diente.*	• oon DYEHN-teh.
• chest.	• *el pecho.*	• ehl PEH-choh.
• abdomen.	• *el vientre.*	• ehl VYEHN-treh.
• back.	• *la espalda.*	• lah ehs-PAHL-dah.
Blood from/in my…	*Sangre de/en…*	SAHN-greh deh/ehn…
• nose.	• *la nariz.*	• lah nah-REES.
• sputum.	• *el esputo.*	• ehl ehs-POO-toh.
• vomit.	• *el vómito.*	• ehl VOH-mee-toh.
• stool.	• *la caca.*	• lah KAH-kah.
• urine.	• *la orina.*	• lah oh-REE-nah.
A discharge from my…	*Un desecho…*	Oon deh-SEH-choh…
• penis.	• *del pene.*	• dehl PEH-neh.
• vagina.	• *de la vagina.*	• deh lah vah-HEE-nah.
I have…	*Tengo…*	TEHN-goh…
• nausea.	• *mareo.*	• mah-REH-oh.
• vomiting.	• *vómito.*	• VOH-mee-toh.
• diarrhea/constipation.	• *diarrea/constipación.*	• dee-ah-REH-ah/kohn-stee-pah-SYOHN.
I am urinating a lot.	*Estoy orinando mucho.*	Ehs-TOY oh-ree-NAHN-doh MOO-choh.
I am not…	*No estoy…*	Noh ehs-TOY…
• urinating.	• *orinando.*	• oh-reen-NAHN-doh.
• walking well.	• *caminando bien.*	• kah-mee-NAHN-doh byehn.

• speaking well.	• *hablando bien.*	• ah-BLAHN-doh byehn.
• seeing well.	• *viendo bien.*	• VYEHN-doh byehn.
I have a lump in…	*Tengo una bola en…*	TEHN-goh OO-nah BOH-lah ehn…
• my breast.	• *el pecho.*	• ehl PEH-choh.
• my armpit.	• *el sobaco.*	• ehl soh-BAH-koh.
I get tired easily.	*Me canso fácilmente.*	Meh KAHN-soh FAH-seel-mehn-teh.
My feet are swollen.	*Se me hinchan los pies.*	Seh meh EEN-chan lohs pyehs.
DOCTOR	***DOCTOR***	
Point to the part of your body where…	*Señale la parte de su cuerpo donde…*	Seh-NYAH-leh lah PAHR-teh deh soo KWEHR-poh DOHN-deh…
• it began.	• *empezó.*	• ehm-peh-SOH.
• it is now.	• *está ahora.*	• ehs-TAH ah-OH-rah.
Tell me if it comes and goes.	*Dígame si lo que siente va y viene.*	DEE-gah-meh see loh keh SYEHN-teh vah ee VYEH-neh.
Do you feel it all the time?	*¿Lo siente todo el tiempo?*	¿Loh SYEHN-teh TOH-doh ehl TYEHM-poh?
How often does it occur?	*¿Cada cuándo le ocurre?*	¿KAH-dah KWAHN-doh leh oh-KOO-rreh?
How sick do you feel now?	*¿Cuán enferma(o) se siente ahora?*	¿Kwahn ehn-FEHR-mah(moh) seh SYEHN-teh ah-OH-rah?
PATIENT	***PACIENTE***	
I feel…	*Me siento…*	Meh SYEHN-toh…
• very sick.	• *muy enfermo(a).*	• MOO-ee ehn-FEHR-moh(mah).
• so, so.	• *más o menos.*	• mahs oh MEH-nohs.
• bad.	• *mal.*	• mahl.
• well.	• *bien.*	• byehn.

DOCTOR	*DOCTOR*	
What brings it on?	*¿Qué es lo que se lo provoca?*	¿Keh ehs loh keh seh loh proh-VOH-kah?
PATIENT	*PACIENTE*	
Nothing in particular.	*Nada en particular.*	NAH-dah ehn pahr-tee-koo-LAHR.
It starts by itself.	*Empieza solo.*	Ehm-PYEH-sah SOH-loh.
Work.	*El trabajo.*	Ehl trah-BAH-hoh.
Walking.	*Caminar.*	Kah-mee-NAHR.
Reading.	*Leer.*	Leh-EHR.
DOCTOR	*DOCTOR*	
What do you do when you feel it coming?	*¿Qué es lo que usted hace cuando lo siente venir?*	¿Keh ehs loh keh oos-TEHD AH-seh KWAHN-doh loh SYEHN-teh veh-NEER?
How does it affect you when it occurs?	*¿Cómo le afecta cuando eso le ocurre?*	¿KOH-moh leh ah-FEHK-tah KWAHN-doh EH-soh leh oh-KOO-rreh?
PATIENT	*PACIENTE*	
I cannot…	*No puedo…*	Noh PWEH-doh…
• breathe.	• *respirar.*	• rehs-pee-RAHR.
• work.	• *trabajar.*	• trah-bah-HAHR.
• walk.	• *caminar.*	• kah-mee-NAHR.
I have to…	*Tengo que…*	TEHN-goh keh…
• sit down.	• *sentarme.*	• sehn-TAHR-meh.
• lie down.	• *acostarme.*	• ah-kohs-TAHR-meh.
• rest.	• *descansar.*	• dehs-kahn-SAHR.
• stop working.	• *dejar de trabajar.*	• deh-HAHR deh trah-bah-HAHR.
• take an aspirin.	• *me tomar una aspirina.*	• meh toh-MAHR OO-nah ahs-pee-REE-nah.

DOCTOR	***DOCTOR***	
Can you still do everything you used to do?	*¿Puede hacer lo que siempre hacía?*	¿PWEH-deh ah-SEHR loh keh SYEHM-preh ah-SEE-ah?
What are you no longer able to do?	*¿Qué es lo que ya no puede hacer?*	¿Keh ehs loh keh yah noh PWEH-deh ah-SEHR?
PATIENT	***PACIENTE***	
I can no longer…	*Ya no puedo…*	Yah noh PWEH-doh…
• enjoy life/food/beer/smoking.	• *gozar de la vida/comida/cerveza/fumar.*	• goh-SAHR deh lah VEE-dah/koh-MEE-dah/sehr-VEH-sah/foo-MAHR.
• sleep well.	• *dormir bien.*	• dohr-MEER byehn.
• exercise.	• *hacer ejercicio.*	• ah-SEHR eh-hehr-SEE-syoh.
• work.	• *trabajar.*	• trah-bah-HAHR.
I feel…	*Me siento…*	Meh SYEHN-toh…
• very old.	• *muy vieja(o).*	• MOO-ee VYEH-hah(hoh).
• anxious.	• *ansiosa(o).*	• ahn-SYOH-sah(soh).
• unhappy.	• *infeliz.*	• een-feh-LEES.
• scared.	• *asustada(o).*	• ah-soos-TAH-dah(doh).
• as if I were a failure.	• *como si fuera un fracaso.*	• KOH-moh see FWEH-rah oon frah-KAH-soh.
DOCTOR	***DOCTOR***	
Do the people you deal with treat you differently?	*La gente con quien usted tiene que tratar la (lo) tratan distinto?*	Lah HEHN-teh kohn KYEHN oos-TEHD TYEH-neh keh trah-TAHR lah (loh) TRAH-tahn dees-TEEN-toh?
How?	*¿Cómo?*	¿KOH-moh?
PATIENT	***PACIENTE***	
As if I were…	*Como si fuera…*	KOH-moh see FWEH-rah…

English	Spanish	Pronunciation
• disabled.	• *un inválido.*	• oon een-VAH-lee-doh.
• an outcast.	• *un paria.*	• oon PAH-ryah.
• a failure.	• *un fracaso.*	• oon frah-KAH-soh.
• going to die.	• *a morirme.*	• ah moh-REER-meh.
My spouse no longer wants to make love.	*Mi esposo(a) ya no quiere hacer el amor.*	Mee ehs-POH-soh (sah) yah noh KYEH-reh ah-SEHR ehl ah-MOHR.
DOCTOR	***DOCTOR***	
How have you tried to alleviate the problem?	*¿Con qué ha tratado de aliviar el problema?*	¿Kohn keh ah trah-TAH-doh deh ah-lee-vee-AHR ehl proh-BLEH-mah?
PATIENT	***PACIENTE***	
I have done nothing.	*No he hecho nada.*	Noh eh EH-choh NAH-dah.
With household remedies.	*Con unos remedios caseros.*	Kohn OO-nohs reh-MEH-dyohs kah-SEH-rohs.
DOCTOR	***DOCTOR***	
Have you seen another doctor?	*¿Ha visto otro(a) doctor(a)?*	¿Ah VEES-toh OH-troh(trah) dohk-TOHR(TOH-rah)?
What treatment did the doctor prescribe?	*¿Qué tratamiento le dio el (la) doctor(a)?*	¿KEH trah-tah-MYEHN-toh leh dyoh ehl (lah) dohk-TOHR (TOH-rah)?
PATIENT	***PACIENTE***	
She/he prescribed medicines.	*Me recetó unas medicinas.*	Meh reh-seh-TOH OO-nahs meh-dee-SEE-nahs.
She/he said she/he would have to operate on me.	*Me dijo que tenía que operarme.*	Meh DEE-hoh keh teh-NEE-ah keh oh-peh-RAHR-meh.
She/he said I had to change my lifestyle.	*Me dijo que tenía que cambiar mi estilo de vida.*	Meh DEE-hoh keh teh-NEE-ah keh kahm-BYAHR mee ehs-TEE-loh deh VEE-dah.

DOCTOR	*DOCTOR*	
What medicines did she/he prescribe?	*¿Qué medicinas le recetó?*	¿Keh meh-dee-SEE-nahs leh reh-seh-TOH?
PATIENT	*PACIENTE*	
Some pills/capsules that are ____ in color.	*Unas pastillas/cápsulas de color ____.*	Oo-nahs pahs-TEE-yahs/KAHP-soo-lahs deh koh-LOHR ____.

VOCABULARY ••••

COLORS

black	*negro*	NEH-groh
brown	*café*	kah-FEH
blue	*azul*	ah-SOOL
orange	*anaranjado*	ah-nah-rahn-HAH-doh
grey	*gris*	grees
green	*verde*	VEHR-deh
maroon	*morado*	moh-RAH-doh
red	*rojo*	ROH-hoh
yellow	*amarillo*	ah-mah-REE-yoh
pink	*rosa*	ROH-sah
white	*blanco*	BLAHN-koh

DOCTOR	*DOCTOR*	
Did you take the medications as prescribed?	*¿Tomó las medicinas como le dijo?*	¿Toh-MOH lahs meh-dee-SEE-nahs KOH-moh leh DEE-hoh?
What operation did the doctor recommend?	*¿Qué operación le recomendó el (la) doctor(a)?*	¿KEH opeh-rah-SYOHN leh reh-koh-mehn-DOH ehl (lah) dohk-TOHR(TOH-rah)?

PATIENT	*PACIENTE*	
A(n)...	*Una...*	OO-nah...
• appendectomy.	• *apendicectomía.*	• ah-pehn-dee-sehk-toh-MEE-ah.
• coronary bypass.	• *bypass de las coronarias.*	• BEE-pahs deh lahs koh-roh-NAH-ryahs.
• hernia repair.	• *reparación de hernia.*	• reh-pah-rah-SYOHN deh EHR-nyah.
• spinal surgery.	• *cirugía de la columna.*	• see-roo-HEE-ah deh lah koh-LOOM-nah.
DOCTOR	*DOCTOR*	
Did you have an operation?	*¿Se operó?*	¿Seh opeh-ROH?
When?	*¿Cuándo?*	¿KWAHN-doh?
Where?	*¿Dónde?*	¿DOHN-deh?
PATIENT	*PACIENTE*	
I was operated...	*Me operó...*	Meh opeh-ROH...
• by Dr. ____.	• *el (la) Doctor(a)* ____.	• ehl (lah) Dohk-TOHR (TOH-rah) ____.
• ____ years ago.	• *hace* ____ *años.*	• AH-seh ____ AH-nyohs.
• here.	• *aquí.*	• ah-KEE.
DOCTOR	*DOCTOR*	
How did he/she recommend you change your lifestyle?	*¿Cómo le recomendó que cambiara su estilo de vida?*	¿KOH-moh leh reh-koh-mehn-DOH keh KAHM-byah-rah soo ehs-TEE-loh deh VEE-dah?
PATIENT	*PACIENTE*	
She/he recommended that I...	*Me recomendó que...*	Meh reh-kohm-DOH keh...
• lose weight.	• *perdiera peso.*	• pehr-DYEH-rah PEH-soh.
• exercise.	• *hiciera ejercicio.*	• hee-SYEH-rah eh-hehr-SEE-syoh.

• follow a diet.	• *siguiera una dieta.*	• see-GYEH-rah OO-nah DYEH-tah.
• stop smoking.	• *dejara de fumar.*	• deh-HAH-rah deh foo-MAHR.
• stop drinking.	• *dejara de tomar.*	• deh-HAH-rah deh toh-MAHR.
• stop using drugs.	• *dejara de usar drogas.*	• deh-HAH-rah deh oo-SAHR DROH-gahs.
DOCTOR	***DOCTOR***	
Did you follow the recommendations?	*¿Siguió las recomendaciones?*	¿See-GYOH lahs reh-koh-mehn-dah-SYOH-nehs?
Why not?	*¿Por qué no?*	¿Pohr KEH noh?
PATIENT	***PACIENTE***	
Because…	*Porque…*	POHR-keh…
• it is too expensive.	• *es muy caro.*	• ehs MOO-ee KAH-roh.
• I did not want to.	• *no quise.*	• no KEE-seh.
• it's too difficult.	• *es muy difícil.*	• ehs MOO-ee dee-FEE-seel.
• I don't have the time.	• *no tengo tiempo.*	• noh TEHN-goh TYEHM-poh.
DOCTOR	***DOCTOR***	
Did you improve with the treatment?	*¿Mejoró con el tratamiento?*	¿Meh-hoh-ROH kohn ehl trah-tah-MYEHN-toh?
Why do you think you did not improve?	*¿Por qué cree que no mejoró?*	¿Pohr KEH kreh-EH keh noh meh-hoh-ROH?
PATIENT	***PACIENTE***	
Because…	*Porque…*	POHR-keh…
• the treatment was useless.	• *el tratamiento no servía.*	• ehl trah-tah-MYEHN-toh noh sehr-VEE-ah.
• I did not follow the treatment.	• *no seguí el tratamiento.*	• Noh seh-GEE ehl trah-tah-MYEHN-toh.

DOCTOR	***DOCTOR***	
What else do you want to tell me about this problem?	*¿Qué más me quiere decir de este problema?*	¿Keh mahs meh KYEH-reh deh-SEER deh EHS-teh proh-BLEH-mah?
PATIENT	***PACIENTE***	
Nothing else.	*Nada más.*	NAH-dah mahs.
That's all.	*Es todo.*	Ehs TOH-doh.
DOCTOR	***DOCTOR***	
What do you think is the cause of the problem?	*¿Cuál cree usted que es la causa del problema?*	¿Kwahl KREH-eh oos-TEHD keh ehs lah KAHW-sah dehl proh-BLEH-mah?
PATIENT	***PACIENTE***	
I have been...	*He estado...*	Eh ehs-TAH-doh...
• eating badly.	• *comiendo mal.*	• koh-MYEHN-doh mahl.
• working too much.	• *trabajando mucho.*	• trah-bah-HAHN-doh MOO-choh.
Maybe I have...	*Tal vez tengo...*	Tahl vehs TEHN-goh...
• cancer.	• *cáncer.*	• KAHN-sehr.
• diabetes.	• *diabetes.*	• dyah-BEH-tes.
• high blood pressure.	• *alta presión de la sangre.*	• AHL-tah preh-SYOHN deh lah SAHN-greh.
• an ulcer.	• *una úlcera.*	• OO-nah OOL-sehr-ah.
• heart disease.	• *una enfermedad del corazón.*	• OO-nah ehn-fehr-meh-DAHD dehl koh-rah-SOHN.
DOCTOR	***DOCTOR***	
Do you believe your problem is curable?	*¿Cree usted que su problema es curable?*	¿Kreh-EH oos-TEHD keh soo proh-BLEH-mah ehs koo-RAH-bleh?
PATIENT	***PACIENTE***	
I sure hope so.	*Ojalá que sí.*	Oh-hah-LAH keh SEE.

Perhaps not.	*Tal vez no.*	Tahl vehs noh.
DOCTOR	***DOCTOR***	
What worries you most about your problem?	*¿Qué es lo que más le preocupa de su problema?*	¿Keh ehs loh keh mahs leh preh-oh-KOO-pah deh soo proh-BLEH-mah?
PATIENT	***PACIENTE***	
I want to know…	*Quiero saber…*	KYEH-roh sah-BEHR…
• if my disease is curable.	• *si mi enfermedad es curable.*	• see mee ehn-fehr-meh-DAHD ehs koo-RAH-bleh.
• what do I have to do to be cured.	• *qué tengo que hacer para curarme.*	• keh TEHN-goh keh ah-SEHR PAH-rah koo-RAHR-meh.
• if the treatment is expensive.	• *si el tratamiento es caro.*	• see ehl trah-tah-MYEHN-toh ehs KAH-roh.
• if I will be able to work.	• *si voy a poder trabajar.*	• see voy ah poh-DEHR trah-bah-HAHR.
• if I will be able to continue with my house chores.	• *si voy a poder seguir con mi trabajo en la casa.*	• see voy a poh-DEHR seh-GEER kohn mee trah-BAH-hoh ehn lah KAH-sah.
• if I will have to go to the hospital.	• *si voy a tener que ir al hospital.*	• see voy ah teh-NEHR keh eer ahl ohs-pee-TAHL.
• what will happen to me.	• *qué me va a pasar.*	• keh meh vah ah pah-SAHR.
• if I am dying.	• *si me estoy muriendo.*	• see meh ehs-TOY moo-RYEHN-doh.
• if I will die.	• *si me voy a morir.*	• see meh voy ah moh-REER.
• how am I going to tell my spouse and children what I have.	• *cómo le voy a decir a mi esposo(a) y mis hijos qué es lo que tengo.*	• KOH-moh leh voy ah deh-SEER ah mee ehs-POH-soh(sah) ee mees EE-hohs keh ehs loh keh TEHN-goh.

VOCABULARY ••••

BODY PARTS

head	*cabeza*	kah-BEH-sah
hair	*pelo*	PEH-loh
face	*cara*	KAH-rah
eyes	*ojos*	OH-hohs
nose	*nariz*	nah-REES
ears	*orejas*	oh-REH-hahs
mouth	*boca*	BOH-kah
teeth	*dientes*	DYEHN-tehs
tongue	*lengua*	LEHN-gwah
beard	*barba*	BAHR-bah
moustache	*bigote*	bee-GOH-teh
neck	*cuello*	KWEH-yoh
shoulders	*hombros*	OHM-brohs
arms	*brazos*	BRAH-sohs
hands	*manos*	MAH-nohs
fingers	*dedos*	DEH-dohs
wrist	*muñeca*	moo-NYEH-kah
elbow	*codo*	KOH-doh
chest	*pecho*	PEH-choh
back	*espalda*	ehs-PAHL-dah
hip	*cadera*	kah-DEH-rah
stomach	*estómago*	ehs-TOH-mah-goh
legs	*piernas*	PYEHR-nahs
knees	*rodillas*	rroh-DEE-yahs
feet	*pies*	pyehs
toes	*dedos*	DEH-dohs
ankles	*tobillos*	toh-BEE-yohs

3. Medical History of the Patient

GRAMMAR NOTE ••••

THE PRETERITE The preterite is one of the three different past tenses (the others are the perfect tense and the imperfect tense) in Spanish. It indicates that an action began and ended at a specific time in the past.

TO TAKE, TO WEAR *LLEVAR*

I took	*llev- é*
you took (inf.)	*llev- aste*
you (form.)/he/she took	*llev- ó*
we took	*llev- amos*
you all took (inf.)	*llev- asteis*
you all (form.)/they took	*llev- aron*

-er and *-ir* verbs have the same endings.

TO SEE *VER*

I saw	*v- i*
you saw (inf.)	*v- iste*
you (form.)/he/she saw	*v- io*
we saw	*v- imos*
you all saw (inf.)	*v- isteis*
you all (form.)/they saw	*v- ieron*

TO LIVE *VIVIR*

I lived	*viv- í*
you lived (inf.)	*viv- iste*
you (form.)/he/she lived	*viv- ió*
we lived	*viv- imos*
you all lived (inf.)	*viv- isteis*
you all (form.)/they lived	*viv- ieron*

DOCTOR	*DOCTOR*	
Have you had any serious diseases?	*¿Ha tenido enfermedades graves?*	¿Ah teh-NEE-doh ehn-fehr-meh-DAH-dehs GRAH-vehs?
Which?	*¿Cuáles?*	¿KWAH-lehs?

The patient may name ailments that are not strictly medical.

PATIENT	*PACIENTE*	
Indigestion.	*Empacho.*	Ehm-PAH-choh.
Fear.	*Susto.*	SOOS-toh.
Attacks.	*Ataques.*	Ah-TAH-kehs.
An ulcer.	*Úlcera.*	OOL-seh-rah.
Cancer.	*Cáncer.*	KAHN-sehr.
Diabetes.	*Diabetes.*	Dee-ah-BEH-tehs.
DOCTOR	*DOCTOR*	
Who diagnosed these diseases?	*¿Quién le diagnosticó esas enfermedades?*	KYEHN leh dee-ahg-nohs-tee-KOH EH-sahs ehn-fehr-meh-DAH-dehs?
PATIENT	*PACIENTE*	
A doctor.	*Un(a) doctor(a).*	Oon (OO-nah) dohk-TOHR (TOH-rah).
A nurse.	*Una enfermera.*	OO-nah ehn-fehr-MEH-rah.
A folk-healer.	*Un(a) curandero(a).*	Oon (OO-nah) koo-rahn-DEH-roh(rah).
DOCTOR	*DOCTOR*	
What treatment did they give you?	*¿Qué tratamiento le dieron?*	¿KEH trah-tah-MYEHN-toh leh DYEH-rohn?
PATIENT	*PACIENTE*	
Household remedies.	*Unos remedios caseros.*	OO-nohs reh-MEH-dyohs kah-SEH-rohs.
Medications.	*Unas medicinas.*	OO-nahs meh-dee-SEE-nahs.

I had an operation.	*Me operaron.*	Meh opeh-RAH-rohn.
DOCTOR	**DOCTOR**	
Did you have go to the hospital?	*¿Tuvo que ir al hospital?*	¿TOO-voh keh eer ahl ohs-pee-TAHL?
Have you ever been operated on?	*¿Lo han tenido que operar alguna vez?*	¿Loh ahn teh-NEE-doh keh oh-peh-RAHR ahl-GOO-nah vehs?
Why?	*¿Por qué?*	¿Pohr keh?
PATIENT	**PACIENTE**	
I broke my…	*Me quebré…*	Meh keh-BREH…
• arm.	• *el brazo.*	• ehl BRAH-soh.
• wrist.	• *la muñeca.*	• lah moo-NYEH-kah.
• leg.	• *la pierna.*	• lah PYEHR-nah.
• ankle.	• *el tobillo.*	• ehl toh-BEE-yoh.
• back.	• *la espalda.*	• lah ehs-PAHL-dah.
I had…	*Tenía…*	Teh-NEE-ah…
• apendicitis.	• *apendicitis.*	• ah-pehn-dee-SEE-tees.
• gastric ulcer.	• *úlcera del estómago.*	• OOL-seh-rah dehl ehs-TOH-mah-goh.
• gall bladder stones.	• *piedras en la vesícula.*	• PYEH-drahs ehn lah veh-SEE-koo-lah.
• kidney stones.	• *piedras en el riñón.*	• PYEH-drahs ehn ehl ree-NYOHN.
• cancer of the…	• *cáncer…*	• KAHN-sehr…
• prostate.	• *del la próstata.*	• deh lah PROHS-tah-tah.
• lung.	• *del pulmón.*	• dehl pool-MOHN.
DOCTOR	**DOCTOR**	
Have you ever had an accident?	*¿Ha sufrido algún accidente?*	¿Ah soo-FREE-doh ahl-GOON ahks-ee-DEHN-teh?
How did the accident happen?	*¿Cómo ocurrió el accidente?*	¿KOH-moh oh-koo-RYOH ehl ahk-see-DEHN-teh?

PATIENT	*PACIENTE*	
There was an explosion/fire where I work.	*Hubo una explosión/ incendio donde trabajo.*	OO-boh OO-nah ehks-ploh-SYOHN/een-SEHN-dyoh DOHN-deh trah-BAH-hoh.
I fell asleep driving.	*Me quedé dormido manejando.*	Meh keh-DEH dohr-MEE-doh mah-neh-HAHN-doh.
I fell…	*Me caí…*	Meh kah-EE…
• down some stairs.	• *al piso de abajo.*	• ahl PEE-soh deh ah-BAH-hoh.
• off a ladder.	• *de la escalera.*	• deh lah ehs-kah-LEH-rah.
• from a tree.	• *de un árbol.*	• deh oon AHR-bohl.
I was hit by…	*Me atropelló…*	Meh ah-troh-peh-YOH…
• a car.	• *un carro.*	• oon KAH-rroh.
• a tractor.	• *un tractor.*	• oon trahk-TOHR.
• a piece of machinery.	• *una máquina.*	• OO-nah MAH-kee-nah.
DOCTOR	***DOCTOR***	
Were you injured?	*¿Resultó herida(o)?*	¿Reh-sool-TOH eh-REE-dah (doh)?
PATIENT	***PACIENTE***	
I burnt my…	*Me quemé…*	Meh keh-MEH…
• face.	• *la cara.*	• lah KAH-rah.
• hands.	• *las manos.*	• lahs MAH-nohs.
• back.	• *la espalda.*	• la ehs-PAHL-dah.
• legs.	• *las piernas.*	• lahs PYEHR-nahs.
• feet.	• *los pies.*	• lohs pyehs.
I broke my…	*Me quebré…*	Meh keh-BREH…
• neck.	• *el cuello.*	• ehl KWEH-yoh.
• arm.	• *el brazo.*	• ehl BRAH-soh.

• leg.	• *la pierna.*	• lah PYEHR-nah.
• back.	• *la espalda.*	• lah ehs-PAHL-dah.

If the patient is a woman:

DOCTOR	*DOCTOR*	
Have you ever been pregnant?	*¿Ha estado usted embarazada?*	¿Ah ehs-TAH-doh oos-TEHD ehm-bah-rah-SAH-dah?
How many times?	*¿Cuántas veces?*	¿KWAHN-tahs VEH-sehs?
Have you had any complications during pregnancy?	*¿Ha tenido alguna complicación durante el embarazo?*	¿Ah teh-NEE-doh ahl-GOO-nah kohm-plee-kah-SYOHN doo-RAHN-teh ehl ehm-bah-RAH-soh?
Which?	*¿Cuál(es)?*	¿Kwahl(es)?
PATIENT	***PACIENTE***	
I gained a lot of weight.	*Aumenté mucho de peso.*	Ah-oo-mehn-TEH MOO-choh deh PEH-soh.
My feet and face were swollen.	*Se me hincharon los pies y la cara.*	Seh meh een-CHAH-rohn lohs pyehs ee lah KAH-rah.
My blood pressure was very high.	*Me subió mucho la presión de la sangre.*	Meh soo-BYOH MOO-choh lah preh-SYOHN deh lah SAHN-greh.
I had attacks/seizures.	*Tuve ataques/ convulsiones.*	TOO-veh ah-TAH-kehs/kohn-vool-SYOHN-ehs.
I lost the child.	*Perdí el niño.*	Pehr-DEE ahl NEEN-yoh.
DOCTOR	***DOCTOR***	
How many miscarriages have you had?	*¿Cuántos abortos ha sufrido?*	¿KWAHN-tohs ah-BOHR-tohs ah soo-FREE-doh?
What was the cause of the miscarriage?	*¿Cuál fue la causa del aborto?*	¿Kwahl fweh lah KAHW-sah-dehl ah-BOHR-toh?

DOCTOR	***DOCTOR***	
How many deliveries have you had?	*¿Cuántos partos ha tenido?*	¿KWAHN-tohs PAHR-tohs ah teh-NEE-doh?
Are the children…	*¿Están…los niños?*	¿Ehs-TAHN…lohs NEEN-yohs.
• alive?	• *vivos*	• VEE-vohs
• healthy?	• *sanos*	• SAH-nohs
PATIENT	***PACIENTE***	
One of the children has…	*Uno de los niños está enfermo…*	OO-noh deh lohs NEEN-yohs- ehs-TAH ehn-FEHR-moh…
• heart disease.	• *del corazón.*	• dehl koh-rah-SOHN.
• kidney disease.	• *de los riñones.*	• deh lohs ree-NYOO-nehs.
• pneumonia.	• *de pulmonía.*	• deh pool-moh-NEE-ah.
• cerebral palsy.	• *de parálisis cerebral.*	• pah-RAH-lee-sees seh-reh-BRAHL.
• epilepsy.	• *de epilepsia.*	• deh eh-pee-LEHP-syah.
• a cold.	• *de un resfriado.*	• deh oon rehs-free-AH-doh.
• diarrhea.	• *de diarrea.*	• deh dyah-RREH-ah.
DOCTOR	***DOCTOR***	
What did the(se) child(ren) die from?	*¿De qué murió(eron) ese (esos) niño(s)?*	• Deh KEH moo-RYOH (YEH-rohn) EH-seh (EH-sohs) NEEN-yoh(s)?
PATIENT	***PACIENTE***	
Diarrhea.	*Diarrea.*	Dyah-RREH-ah.
Measles.	*Sarampión.*	Sah-rahm-PYOHN.
Pneumonia.	*Pulmonía.*	Pool-moh-NEE-ah.
An accident.	*Un accidente.*	Oon ahk-see-DEHN-teh.

DOCTOR	***DOCTOR***	
What diseases are you vaccinated against?	*¿Contra qué enfermedades está vacunada?*	¿KOHN-trah KEH ehn-fehr-meh-DAH-dehs ehs-TAH vah-koo-NAH-dah?
PATIENT	***PACIENTE***	
I am vaccinated...	*Estoy vacunado(a)...*	Ehs-TOY vah-koo-NAH-doh (dah)...
• with DPT.	• *con DPT.*	• kohn Deh-peh-teh.
• against measles.	• *contra el sarampión.*	• KOHN-trah ehl sah-rahm-PYOHN.
• against polio.	• *contra la polio.*	• KOHN-trah lah POH-yoh.
DOCTOR	***DOCTOR***	
What was the date of your last vaccination?	*¿Cuál es la fecha de su última vacunación?*	¿Kwahl ehs lah FEH-chah deh soo OOL-tee-mah vah-koo-nah-SYOHN?
Do you have any allergies?	*¿Tiene alergias?*	¿TYEH-neh ah-LEHR-hee-ahs?
What complaints do you have?	*¿Qué molestias tiene?*	¿Keh moh-LEHS-tee-ahs YEH-neh?
PATIENT	***PACIENTE***	
I sneeze a lot.	*Estornudo mucho.*	Ehs-tohr-NOO-doh MOO-choh.
My eyes itch.	*Comezón en los ojos.*	Koh-meh-SOHN ehn lohs OH-hohs.
I run out of breath.	*Me falta la respiración.*	Meh FAHL-tah lah rehs-pee-rah-SYOHN.
My head aches.	*Me duele la cabeza.*	Meh DWEH-leh lah kah-BEH-sah.
DOCTOR	***DOCTOR***	
What are you allergic to?	*¿A qué cosas es alérgica(o)?*	¿Ah keh KOH-sahs ehs ah-LEHR-heh-kah(koh)?
PATIENT	***PACIENTE***	
Pollen.	*Polen.*	POH-lehn.

Dust.	*Polvo.*	POHL-voh.
Mosquitos.	*Mosquitos.*	Mohs-KEE-tohs.
Bees.	*Abejas.*	Ah-BEH-has.
Smoke.	*Humo.*	OO-moh.
Ants.	*Hormigas.*	Ohr-MEE-gahs.
Peanuts.	*Cacahuates/maní.*	Kah-kah-WAH-tehs/mah-NEE.
Chocolate.	*Chocolate.*	Choh-koh-LAH-teh.
Strawberries.	*Fresas.*	FREH-sahs.
Eggs.	*Huevos.*	WEH-vohs.
DOCTOR	**DOCTOR**	
What medications are you taking for your allergies?	*¿Qué medicinas está tomando para sus alergias?*	¿KEH meh-dee-SEE-nahs ehs-TAH toh-MAHN-doh PAH-rah soos ah-LEHR-hee-ahs?
PATIENT	**PACIENTE**	
Some medicines that…	*Unas medicinas que…*	OO-nahs meh-dee-SEE-nahs keh…
• a doctor prescribed.	• *me recetó un(a) doctor(a).*	• meh reh-seh-TOH oon (OO-nah) dohk-TOHR(TOH-rah).
• a friend recommended.	• *me recomendó un(a) amigo(a).*	• meh reh-koh-mehn-DOH oon (OO-nah) ah-MEE-goh(gah).
• I bought at the drugstore.	• *compré en la farmacia.*	• kohm-PREH ehn lah fahr-MAH-syah.

VOCABULARY ••••

COMMON ILLNESSES

allergy	*alergia*	ah-LEHR-hee-ah
anemia	*anemia*	ah-NEH-mee-ah
angina	*angina*	ahn-HEE-nah
arthritis	*artritis*	ahr-TREE-tees
cancer	*cancer*	KAHN-sehr
common cold	*resfriado*	rehs-free-AH-doh
diabetes	*diabetes*	dyah-BEH-tehs
diarrhea	*diarrea*	dyah-RREH-ah
stroke	*embolia*	ehm-BOH-lee-ah
epilepsy	epilepsia	eh-pee-LEHP-syah
gallstones	*piedras en la vesícula*	pyeh-drahs ehn lah VEH-see-koo-lah
heart murmur	*murmullo en el corazón/soplo cardíaco*	moor-MOO-yoh ehn ehl koh-rah-SOHN/SOH-ploh kahr-dee-AH-koh
high blood pressure	*presión alta de la sangre*	preh-SYOHN AHL-tah deh lah SAHN-greh
infarct	*infarto*	een-FAHR-toh
kidney disease	*enfermedad del riñón*	ehn-FEHR-meh-dahd dehl ree-NYOHN
measles	*sarampión*	sah-rahm-PYOHN
mumps	*papéras*	pah-PEH-rahs
pneumonia	*pulmonía*	pool-moh-NEE-ah
prostate cancer	*cáncer de la próstata*	KAHN-sehr deh lah PROH-stah-tah
rheumatism	*reumatismo*	reh-oo-mah-TEEHS-moh
tuberculosis	*tuberculosis*	too-behr-koo-LOH-sees
ulcer	*úlcera*	OOL-seh-rah

4. General Family History

CULTURE NOTE ••••

FAMILY VALUES The family and its history is one of the pillars of Latino culture. In most Hispanic countries, large extended families—children, parents, grandparents—live under one roof, and therefore know each other rather well. The elderly are very well respected in Hispanic communities, and they have a rather strong influence on family decisions. Children are adored and raised by the entire family. Getting a rather complete and accurate family history should not be any problem at all.

DOCTOR	*DOCTOR*	
Are your parents alive?	*¿Viven sus padres?*	¿VEE-vehn soos PAH-drehs?
PATIENT	***PACIENTE***	
Yes, they are alive.	*Sí, viven.*	See, VEE-vehn.
My mom/dad is alive.	*Mi mamá/papá vive.*	Mee mah-MAH/ pah-PAH VEE-veh.
My mom/dad has died.	*Mi papá/mamá ya murió.*	Mee pah-PAH/mah-MAH yah moo-RYOH.
Both are dead.	*Están muertos los dos.*	Ehs-TAHN MWEHR-tohs lohs dohs.

GRAMMAR NOTE ••••

SUBJECT PRONOUNS

I	*yo*
you (inf.)	*tú*
you (form.)	*usted*
he, she	*él, ella*
we	*nosotros*
you all (pl.)	*ustedes*
they	*ellos/ellas*
I work.	*Yo trabajo.*
I am working.	*Yo trabajo./Yo estoy trabajando.*

DOCTOR	***DOCTOR***	
How old is he/she?	*¿Qué edad tiene él/ella.*	¿Keh eh-DAHD TYEH-neh EHL/EH yah?
Is she/he/are they healthy?	*¿Está/están sana/ sano/sanos?*	¿Ehs-TAH/Ehs-TAHN SAH-nah (SAH-noh/SAN-nohs)?
Is she/he/are they sick?	*¿Está/están enferma/ enfermo/enfermos?*	¿Ehs-TAH/ehs-TAHN ehn-FEHR-mah/ehn-FEHR-moh/ehn-FEHR/mohs?
DOCTOR	***DOCTOR***	
What problem do they/does he/she have?	*¿Qué problema tienen/tiene él/ella?*	¿KEH proh-BLEH-mah TYEH-nehn/TYEH-neh EHL/EH-yah?
What is the matter with them/him/her?	*¿Qué les/le pasa?*	¿Keh lehs/leh PAH-sah?
PATIENT	***PACIENTE***	
They just have aches and pains.	*Sólo tienen achaques.*	SOH-loh TYEHN-ehn ah-CHAH-kehs.

She/he has/they have…	*¿Está/están enferma/ enfermo/enfermos de…*	Ehs-TAH/ehs-TAHN ehn-FEHR-mah/ehn-FEHR-moh/ehn-FEHR-mohs deh…
• a cold.	• *un resfriado.*	• oon rehs-free-AH-doh.
• high blood pressure.	• *alta presión.*	• AHL-tah preh-SYOHN.
• diabetes.	• *diabetes.*	• dyah-BEH-tehs.
• arthritis.	• *artritis.*	• ahr-TREE-tees.
• cancer.	• *cáncer.*	• KAHN-sehr.
DOCTOR	DOCTOR	
How have they/ has she/he been treated?	*¿Qué tratamiento están/está recibiendo?*	¿KEH trah-tah-MYEHN-toh ehs-TAHN/ehs-TAH reh-see-BYEHN-doh?
PATIENT	PACIENTE	
They are/she/he is…	*Están/está…*	Ehs-TAHN/ehs-TAH…
• taking medications.	• *tomando medicinas.*	• toh-MAHN-doh meh-dee-SEE-nahs.
• on a diet without sugar/salt/coffee.	• *en una dieta sin azúcar/sal/café.*	• ehn OO-nah DYEH-tah seen ah-SOO-kahr/sahl/kah-FEH.
• exercising more.	• *haciendo más ejercicio.*	• ah-SYEHN-doh MAHS eh-hehr-SEE-syoh.
• resting.	• *descansando.*	• dehs-kahn-SAHN-doh.
• on chemotherapy.	• *en quimioterapia.*	• ehn kee-myoh teh-RAH-pyah.
• on radiotherapy.	• *en radioterapia.*	• ehn rah-dyoh-teh-RAH-pyah.
• getting insulin/ hormones.	• *recibiendo insulina/hormonas.*	• reh-see-BYEHN-doh een-soo-LEE-nah/ ohr-MOH-nahs.
She/he…	*La/lo…*	Lah/loh…
• will have to be operated on.	• *van a tener que operar.*	• vahn ah teh-NEHR keh oh-peh-RAHR.
• was just operated on.	• *acaban de operar.*	• ah-KAH-bahn deh oh-peh-RAHR.

GRAMMAR NOTE ••••

OBJECT PRONOUNS The direct object pronoun refers to objects or people directly relating to the action of the verb. It usually precedes the verb, but is attached to the affirmative command.

me	*me*
you (inf.)	*te*
him/her/it/you (form.)	*lo/la*
us	*nos*
you (inf.)	*os*
them/you (form.)	*los/las*

Do you know Jim?	*¿Conoces a Jim?*
Yes, I know him.	*Sí, lo conozco.*
The number? He has it.	*¿El número? Lo tiene él.*
Bring it.	*Tráigalo.*
Call us.	*Llámenos.*

The indirect object pronoun refers to the person or thing receiving the action. It precedes the verb and the direct object pronoun, and is attached to the affirmative command.

to me	*me*
to you (inf.)	*te*
to you (form.)/to him/to her	*le*
to us	*nos*
to you all (inf.)	*os*
to them/to you all (form.)	*les*

He gave the medicine to us.	*Él nos dio la medicina.*
Tell me the truth.	*Dígame la verdad.*

DOCTOR	***DOCTOR***	
Does she/he/do they live alone?	*¿Vive/viven sola/solo/ solos?*	¿VEE-veh/VEE-vehn SOH-lah/SOH-loh/SOH-lohs?
Who takes care of her/him/them?	*¿Quién la/lo/los cuida?*	¿Kyehn lah/loh/ los KWEE-dah?
PATIENT	***PACIENTE***	
Yes.	*Sí.*	SEE.
They live…	*Viven…*	VEE-vehn…
• with me.	• *conmigo.*	• kohn-MEE-goh.
• with one of my sisters/brothers.	• *con una(o) de mis hermanas/hermanos.*	• kohn OO-nah(noh) deh mees ehr-MAH-nahs/ehr-MAH-nohs.
• with relatives.	• *con unos parientes.*	• kohn OO-nohs pah-RYEHN-tehs.
• in a retirement home.	• *en una casa de retiro.*	• ehn OO-nah KAH-sah deh reh-TEE-roh.
DOCTOR	***DOCTOR***	
How old was she/he/ were they when she/he/they died?	*¿Qué edades tenía/ tenían cuando murió/ murieron?*	¿Keh eh-DAHD-ehs teh-NEE-ah/teh-NEE-ahn KWAHN-doh moo-RYOH/moo-RYEH-rohn
Of what disease did she/he/they die?	*¿De qué enfermedad murió/murieron?*	¿Deh KEH ehn-fehr-meh-DAHD moo-RYOH/moo-RYEH-rohn?
PATIENT	***PACIENTE***	
She/he/they died from…	*Murió/murieron de/del…*	Moo-RYOH/moo-RYEH-rohn deh/ dehl…
• old age.	• *vejez.*	• VEH-hehs.
• diabetes.	• *diabetes.*	• dyah-BEH-tehs.
• cancer.	• *cáncer.*	• KAHN-sehr.
• heart disease.	• *una enfermedad del corazón.*	• OO-nah ehn-fehr-meh-DAHD dehl koh-rah-SOHN.

• a stroke.	• *embolio.*	• ehm-BOH-lyoh.
• kidney disease.	• *una enfermedad del riñón.*	• OO-nah ehn-fehr-meh-DAHD dehl ree-NYOHN.
• liver disease.	• *una enfermedad del hígado.*	• OO-nah ehn-fehr-meh-DAHD dehl EE-gah-doh.
• tuberculosis.	• *tuberculosis.*	• too-behr-koo-LOH-sees.
• an accident.	• *un accidente.*	• oon ahk-see-DEHN-teh.
DOCTOR	***DOCTOR***	
How many brothers and sisters/sons and daughters do you have?	*¿Cuántos hermanos y hermanas/hijos y hijas tiene?*	¿KWAHN-tohs ehr-MAH-nohs ee ehr-MAH-nahs/EE-hohs ee EE-hahs TYEH-neh?
What are their ages?	*¿Qué edad tienen?*	¿KEH eh-DAHD TYEH-nehn?
Are they healthy?	*¿Están sanos?*	¿Ehs-TAHN SAH-nohs?
Is there a health problem that runs in your family?	*¿Hay algún problema de salud que ocurre en su familia?*	¿Ay ahl-GOON proh-BLEH-mah deh sah-LOOD keh oh-KOO-reh ehn soo fah-MEE-lyah?
What problem is it?	*¿Qué problema es?*	¿Keh proh-BLEH-mah ehs?
PATIENT	***PACIENTE***	
Diabetes.	*Diabetes.*	Dyah-BEH-tehs.
High blood pressure.	*Presión alta.*	Preh-SYOHN AHL-tah.
Obesity.	*Gordura.*	Gohr-DOO-rah.
Mental diseases.	*De la mente.*	Deh lah MEHN-teh.
Cancer.	*Cáncer.*	KAHN-sehr.
Heart disease.	*Del corazón.*	Dehl koh-rah-SOHN.
Seizures.	*Ataques.*	Ah-TAH-kehs.
We die young.	*Nos morimos jóvenes.*	Nohs moh-REE-mohs HOH-veh-nehs.

DOCTOR	*DOCTOR*	
Does anyone else in your family have the same problem?	*¿Alguien en su familia tiene el mismo problema?*	¿AHL-gyehn ehn soo fah-MEE-lyah TYEH-neh ehl MEES-moh proh-BLEH-mah?
Who?	*¿Quién?*	¿Kyehn?
PATIENT	*PACIENTE*	
My...	*Mi(s)...*	Mee(s)...
• mother/father.	• *mamá/papá.*	• mah-MAH/pah-PAH.
• brothers/sisters.	• *hermanos/hermanas.*	• ehr-MAH-nohs/ehr-MAH-nahs.
• aunts/uncles.	• *tías/tíos.*	• TEE-ahs/TEE-ohs.
• cousins.	• *primas/primos.*	• PREE-mahs/PREE-mohs.
• grandmother/grandfather.	• *abuela/abuelo.*	• ah-BWEH-lah/ah-BWEH-loh.
DOCTOR	*DOCTOR*	
Does anyone in your family have...	*¿Alguien en su familia tiene...*	¿AHL-gyehn ehn soo fah-MEE-lyah TYEH-neh...
• anemia or blood problems?	• *anemia o problemas de la sangre?*	• ah-NEH-myah oh proh-BLEH-mahs deh lah SAHN-greh?
• heart diseases, like angina or infarcts?	• *enfermedades del corazón, como angina o infartos?*	• Ehn-fehr-meh-DAH-dehs dehl koh-rah-SOHN, KOH-moh ahn-HEE-nah o een-FAHR-tohs?
• high blood pressure?	• *presión alta de la sangre?*	• preh-SYOHN AHL-tah deh lah SAHN-greh?
• tuberculosis or emphysema?	• *tuberculosis o enfisema?*	• too-behr-koo-LOH-sees oh ehn-fee-SEH-mah?
• diseases of the kidney?	• *enfermedades del riñón?*	• ehn-fehr-meh-DAH-dehs dehl ree-NYOHN?

• arthritis or rheumatism?	• *artritis o reumatismo?*	• ahr-TREE-tees o reh-oo-mah-TEES-moh?
• goiter or thyroid problems?	• *problemas de bocio o la glándula tiroides?*	• proh-BLEH-mahs deh BOH-see-oh lah GLAHN-doo-lah tee-ROY-dehs?
• cancer?	• *cáncer?*	• KAHN-sehr?
• problems with...	• *problemas con...*	• proh-BLEH-mahs kohn...
• alcohol?	• *alcohol?*	• ahl-koh-OHL?
• tobacco?	• *tabaco?*	• tah-BAH-koh?
• other substances?	• *otras substancias?*	• OH-trahs soobs-TAHN-syahs?
Which substance?	*¿Qué substancia?*	¿Keh soobs-TAHN-syah?
PATIENT	**PACIENTE**	
Marijuana.	*Marijuana.*	Mah-ree-WAH-nah.
Cocaine.	*Cocaína.*	Koh-kah-EE-nah.
Morphine.	*Morfina.*	Mohr-FEE-nah.
Heroin.	*Heroína.*	Eh-roh-EE-nah.
Tranquilizers.	*Tranquilizantes.*	Trahn-kee-lee-SAHN-tehs.
Sleeping pills.	*Pastillas para dormir.*	Pahs-TEE-yahs pah-rah dohr-MEER.
Cigarettes.	*Cigarillas.*	See-gah-REE-yahs.
DOCTOR	**DOCTOR**	
Does anyone in your family have...	*¿Alguien en su familia tiene...*	¿AHL-gyehn ehn soo fah-MEE-lyah TYEH-neh...
• weight problems?	• *problemas con el peso?*	• proh-BLEH-mahs kohn ehl PEH-soh?
• nerve problems?	• *problemas de los nervios?*	• proh-BLEH-mahs deh lohs NEHR-vyohs?
• mental problems?	• *problemas mentales?*	• proh-BLEH-mahs mehn-TAH-lehs?

DOCTOR	*DOCTOR*	
Who?	*¿Quién?*	¿Kyehn?
What did she/he suffer from?	*¿Qué tuvo?*	¿Keh TOO-voh?
PATIENT	*PACIENTE*	
He/she was…	*Estaba…*	Ehs-TAH-bah…
• very nervous.	• *muy nervioso.*	• moo-ee NEHR-vyoh-soh.
• very sad.	• *muy triste.*	• moo-ee TREES-teh.
• suicidal.	• *suicido(a).*	• soo-ee-SEE-doh(dah).
• manic.	• *maníaco(a).*	• mah-NEE-ah-koh (kah).
• depressed.	• *deprimido(a).*	• deh-pree-MEE-doh (dah).
• psychotic.	• *psicótico(a).*	• psee-KOH-tee-koh (kah).
DOCTOR	*DOCTOR*	
How old was he/she/were they when this/these problem(s) began?	*¿Qué edad tenía/tenían cuando este (estos) problema(s) empezó(aron)?*	¿Keh eh-DAHD teh-NEE-ah/teh-NEE-ahn KWAHN-doh EHS-teh(tohs) proh-BLEH-mah(mahs) ehm-peh-SOH(SAH-rohn)?
What treatment did she/he/they get?	*¿Qué tratamiento recibió/recibieron?*	¿Keh trah-tah-MYEHN-toh reh-see-BYOH/reh-see-BYEH-rohn?
PATIENT	*PACIENTE*	
Counseling.	*Consejería.*	Kohn-seh-heh-REE-ah.
Psychotherapy.	*Psicoterapia.*	Psee-koh-teh-RAH-pyah.
Medications.	*Medicamentos.*	Meh-dee-kah-MEHN-tohs.
Electroshocks.	*Electrochoques.*	Eh-lehk-troh-CHOH-kehs.
He/she was/they were…	*Él/ella/ellos/ellas fue/fueron…*	Ehl/EH-yah/EH-yohs/EH-yahs fweh/fweh-rohn…

• hospitalized.	• *hospitalizado(a/os/as).*	• ohs-pee-tah-lee-SAH-doh(dah/dohs/dahs).
• institutionalized.	• *institucionalizado (a/os/as).*	• een-stee-too-syoh-nah-lee-SAH-doh (dah/dohs/dahs).

VOCABULARY ••••

FAMILY RELATIONS

relatives	*parientes*	pah-RYEHN-tehs
parents	*padres*	PAH-drehs
father	*padre*	PAH-dreh
mother	*madre*	MAH-dreh
husband	*esposo/marido*	ehs-POH-soh/mah-REE-doh
wife	*esposa/mujer*	ehs-POH-sah/moo-HEHR
son	*hijo*	EE-hoh
daughter	*hija*	EE-hah
children	*niños*	NEE-nyohs
brother	*hermano*	ehr-MAH-noh
sister	*hermana*	ehr-MAH-nah
nephew	*sobrino*	soh-BREE-noh
niece	*sobrina*	soh-BREE-nah
grandmother	*abuela*	ah-BWEH-lah
grandfather	*abuelo*	ah-BWEH-loh
uncle	*tío*	TEE-oh
aunt	*tía*	TEE-ah
cousin	*primo(a)*	PREE-moh(mah)
man	*hombre*	OHM-breh
woman	*mujer*	moo-HEHR

5. Life and Lifestyle History

CULTURE NOTE ••••

DISCRETION AND LOYALTY Your Latino patient may not be quite sure why personal and social circumstances are important to a medical doctor, and therefore may be reluctant to answer your questions. Family and friends are a source of pride and honor, and therefore many Latinos exhibit a strong sense of loyalty. If there are any problems in your patient's family, he or she may not want to share them with you in order not to betray the family's honor. Make sure that your patient understands that you will not disclose this information to anyone without the patient's consent, and that you will treat anything shared with you with respect.

DOCTOR	*DOCTOR*	
I am going to ask you a few personal questions.	*Le voy a hacer unas preguntas privadas.*	Leh voy ah ah-SEHR OO-nahs preh-GOON-tahs pree-VAH-dahs.
Your answers will help me…	*Sus respuestas me ayudarán a…*	Soos rehs-PWEHS-tahs meh ah-yoo-dah-RAHN ah…
• make a better diagnosis.	• *hacer un mejor diagnóstico.*	• ah-SEHR oon meh-HOHR dyahg-NOHS-tee-koh.
• choose a better treatment.	• *escoger un tratamiento mejor.*	• ehs-koh-HEHR oon trah-tah-MYEHN-toh meh-HOHR.
I will not disclose any information without your consent.	*No informaré a nadie sin su consentimiento.*	Noh een-fohr-mah-REH ah nah-DYEH seen soo kohn-SEHN-tee-MYEHN-toh.

Anything you tell me will be confidential.	*Cualquier cosa que me diga será confidencial.*	Kwahl-KYEHR KOH-sah keh meh DEE-gah SEH-rah kohn-fee-dehn-SYAHL.

A. SOCIAL HISTORY

GRAMMAR NOTE ••••

POSSESSIVE There are short and long forms of possessive adjectives. The short forms precede the noun. The long forms are placed after the noun.

SHORT FORMS

my	*mi/s*
your (fam.)	*tu/s*
your/his/her/its/their	*su/s*
ours	*nuestro/a/os/as*
your (fam.)	*vuestro/a/os/as*

LONG FORMS

mine	*mío*
yours (fam.)	*tuyo*
yours/his/hers/its/theirs	*suyo/a/os/as*
ours	*nuestro/a/os/as*
yours	*vuestro/a/os/as*
The medication is not mine.	*La medicina no es mía.*
It's John's. It's his medication.	*Es de Juan. Es su medicina.*

The preposition *de* (of) is used to indicate possession.

This is John's medication. *La medicina es de Juan.*

The possessive pronouns stand alone in the sentence because they substitute the nouns they refer to. Their forms are the same as the long forms of the possessive adjective.

The medication? It's mine. *¿La medicina? Es la mía.*

DOCTOR	*DOCTOR*	
Where…	*¿Dónde…*	¿DOHN-deh…
• were you born?	• *nació?*	• nah-SYOH?
• did you grow up?	• *creció?*	• kreh-SYOH?
• have you lived the longest?	• *ha vivido más?*	• ah vee-VEE-doh MAHS?
How old were you when you came to the United States?	*¿Qué edad tenía cuando vino a los Estados Unidos?*	¿Keh eh-DAHD teh-NEE-ah KWAHN-doh VEE-noh ah lohs ehs-TAH-dohs oo-NEE-dohs?
Where are your parents from?	*¿De dónde son sus padres?*	¿Deh DOHN-deh sohn soos PAH-drehs?
Who are the important persons in your life?	*¿Quiénes son las personas importantes en su vida?*	¿KYEH-nehs sohn lahs pehr-SOH-nahs eem-pohr-TAHN-tehs ehn soo VEE-dah?
Are they healthy?	*¿Están sanos(as)?*	¿Ehs-TAHN SAH-nohs(nahs)?
What is the problem?	*¿Cuál es el problema?*	¿Kwahl ehs ehl proh-BLEH-mah?
Do you get along well with them?	*¿Se lleva bien con ellos(as)?*	¿Seh YEH-vah byehn kohn EH-yohs(yahs)?
PATIENT	*PACIENTE*	
Yes.	*Sí.*	SEE.
Almost always.	*Casi siempre.*	KAH-see SYEHM-preh.
Sometimes.	*A veces.*	Ah VEH-sehs.
Almost never.	*Casi nunca.*	KAH-see NOON-kah.
Not at all.	*De plano, no.*	Deh PLAH-noh, noh.
DOCTOR	*DOCTOR*	
Are you single or married?	*¿Es usted soltera(o) o casada(o)?*	¿Ehs oos-TEHD sohl-TEH-rah(roh) oh kah-SAH-dah(doh)?
Have you been married?	*¿Ha estado casada(o)?*	¿Ah ehs-TAH-doh kah-SAH-dah(doh)?
How long?	*¿Cuánto tiempo?*	¿KWAHN-toh TYEHM-poh?

How many times have you been married?	*¿Cuántes veces ha estado casada(o)?*	¿KWAHN-tahs VEH-sehs ah ehs-TAH-doh kah-SAH-dah(doh)?
Do you get along with your spouse?	*¿Se lleva bien con su esposo(a)?*	¿Seh YEH-vah byehn kohn soo ehs-POH-soh(sah)?
Do you have children?	*¿Tiene hijos?*	¿TYEH-neh EE-hohs?
How many?	*¿Cuántos?*	¿KWAHN-tohs?
How often do you see your son(s)/ daughter(s)?	*¿Cada cuánto ve a su(s) hijo(s)/ hija(s)?*	¿KAH-dah KWAHN-toh veh ah soo(s) EE-hoh(hohs)/EE-hah(hahs)?

B. OCCUPATIONAL HISTORY

CULTURE NOTE ••••

EDUCATIONAL BACKGROUNDS While it is true that Latinos from middle and upper classes who live in the U.S. are rather well educated, speak English well and are assimilated to American culture, it is not necessarily true that those who don't speak English well are from lower classes, uneducated and unassimilated illegal aliens. Please bear in mind that your Latino patients are not only from a variety of national and cultural backgrounds, but from a variety of socio-economic backgrounds as well. While most of your patients probably reside in the U.S. and will be able to speak at least some English, you may find yourself treating a tourist or business traveler who doesn't speak English at all. Always remember that a patient's inability to answer your questions and provide you with valuable information is due only to a lack of English skills, not a lack of knowledge, education or sophistication. Therefore, if you are experiencing trouble communicating with your Latino patient, don't dismiss the answers, but call in an interpreter instead.

DOCTOR	***DOCTOR***	
How many years did you go to school?	*¿Cuántos años fué a la escuela?*	¿KWAHN-tohs AH-NYOHS fweh ah lah ehs-KWEH-lah?
What is your profession?	*¿Qué profesión tiene?*	¿Keh proh-feh-SYOHN TYEH-neh?
PATIENT	***PACIENTE***	
I am a…	*Soy…*	Soy…
• physician.	• *doctor(a).*	• dohk-TOHR(TOH-rah).
• lawyer.	• *abogado(a).*	• ah-boh-GAH-doh(dah).
• editor.	• *editor(a).*	• eh-dee-TOHR (TOH-rah).
• actor.	• *actor(actriz).*	• ahk-TOHR(ahk-TREES).
• photographer.	• *fotógrafo(a).*	• foh-TOH-grah-foh(fah).
• journalist.	• *periodista.*	• peh-ryoh-DEES-tah.
• airline pilot.	• *piloto de aerolínea.*	• pee-LOH-toh deh ay-roh-LEE-neh-ah.
• teacher/professor.	• *maestro(a)/ profesor(a).*	• mah-EHS-troh(trah)/ proh-feh-SOHR (SOH-rah).
• dentist.	• *dentista.*	• dehn-TEES-tah.
• engineer.	• *ingeniero(a).*	• een-heh-NYEH-roh(rah).
• architect.	• *arquitecto(a).*	• ahr-kee-TEHK-toh(tah).
• accountant.	• *contador(a).*	• kohn-tah-DOHR (DOH-rah).
• administrator.	• *administrador(a).*	• ahd-mee-nees-trah-DOHR(DOH-rah).

GRAMMAR NOTE ••••

THE GENDER AND NUMBER OF NOUNS In Spanish every noun has a gender. In some cases, as with people, the gender is obvious: man, brother, father, etc., are masculine, while mother, sister, woman, etc., are feminine. However, with most other nouns, the gender and meaning are unrelated.

Nouns ending in *-o,* most words ending in *-e* or in a consonant other than *-d* are masculine:

> *el libro* (book), *el profesor* (professor), *el árbol* (tree), *el aire* (air).
> exception: *el día* (day), *el mapa* (map), *el problema* (problem), *el sistema* (system).

Nouns ending in *-a, -d, -ción, -sión,* and many that end in *-e,* are feminine.

> *la casa* (house), *la ciudad* (city), *la situación* (situation), *la leche* (milk).
> exception: *la mano* (hand).

In order to form the plural of nouns and adjectives add *-es* if the word ends in a consonant:

the blue uniform	*el uniforme azul*
the blue uniforms	*los uniformes azules*

Add *-s* if the noun or adjective ends in a vowel:

the black dress	*la ropa negra*
the black dresses	*las ropas negras*

El (the), and *un* (a/an) are the articles for masculine nouns. *La* (the) and *una* (a/an) are the articles for feminine nouns. The plural of *el/la* is *los/las.* The plural of *un/una* is *unos/unas.*

DOCTOR	*DOCTOR*	
Where did you study?	*¿Dónde estudió?*	¿DOHN-deh ehs-too-DYOH?
What degrees do you have?	*¿Qué títulos tiene?*	¿Keh TEE-too-lohs TYEH-neh?
PATIENT	*PACIENTE*	
I have...	*Tengo...*	TEHN-goh...
• a high school diploma.	• *diploma de bachiller/ preparatoria.*	• dee-PLOH-mah deh bah-chee-YEHR/ PREH-pah-rah-TOH-ryah.
• a BA/BS.	• *una licenciatura en artes/ciencias.*	• OO-nah lee-sehn-syah-TOO-rah ehn AHR-tehs/SYEHN-syahs.
• a masters.	• *una maestría.*	• OO-nah mah-ehs-TREE-ah.
• a doctorate.	• *un doctorado.*	• oon dohk-toh-RAH-doh.
• an MD.	• *título de médico.*	• TEE-too-loh de MEH-dee-koh.
• a DDS.	• *título de dentista.*	• TEE-too-loh deh dehn-TEES-tah.
• a JD.	• *título de abogado.*	• TEE-too-loh deh ah-boh-GAH-doh.
DOCTOR	*DOCTOR*	
Have you been in the armed forces of the United States?	*¿Ha estado usted en las fuerzas armadas de los Estados Unidos?*	¿Ah ehs-TAH-doh oos-TEHD ehn lahs FWEHR-sahs ahr-MAH-dahs deh lohs ehs-TAH-dohs oo-NEE-dohs?
PATIENT	*PACIENTE*	
I have been in...	*Estuve en...*	Ehs-TOO-veh ehn...
• the army.	• *el ejército.*	• ehl eh-HEHR-see-toh.
• the air force.	• *la fuerza aérea.*	• lah FWEHR-sah ah-EH-reh-ah.

• the marines.	• *los marines.*	• lohs mah-REE-nehs.
• the navy.	• *la marina.*	• lah mah-REE-nah.
• the coast guard.	• *los guardacostas.*	• lohs gwahr-dah-KOHS-tahs.
DOCTOR	*DOCTOR*	
How long did you serve?	*¿Cuánto tiempo estuvo enlistado(a)?*	¿KWAHN-toh TYEHM-poh ehs-TOO-voh ehn-lees-TAH-doh(dah)?
Did you go to war?	*¿Fue a la guerra?*	¿Fweh ah lah GHEH-rrah?
Which war?	*¿Qué guerra?*	¿KEH GHEH-rrah?
PATIENT	*PACIENTE*	
WW II.	*La segunda guerra mundial.*	Lah seh-GOON-dah GHEH-rrah moon-DYAHL.
Korea.	*Corea.*	Koh-REH-ah.
Vietnam.	*Vietnam.*	Vee-eht-NAHM.
Panama.	*Panamá.*	Pah-nah-MAH.
Desert Storm.	*Desert Storm.*	DEH-sehrt stohrm.
Persian Gulf.	*Golfo Pérsico.*	GOHL-foh PEHR-see-koh.
Somalia.	*Somalia.*	Soh-MAH-lyah.
Bosnia.	*Bosnia.*	BOHS-nyah.
DOCTOR	*DOCTOR*	
Were you injured in combat?	*¿Fue herida(o) en combate?*	¿Fweh eh-REE-dah(doh) ehn kohm-BAH-teh?
What type of injury?	*¿Qué tipo de herida sufrió?*	¿Keh TEE-poh deh eh-REE-dah soo-FRYOH?
PATIENT	*PACIENTE*	
I had...	*Sufrí una...*	Soo-FREE OO-nah...
• a bullet wound.	• *herida de bala.*	• eh-REE-dah deh BAH-lah.

• a stab wound.	• *herida de cuchillo.*	• eh-REE-dah deh koo-CHEE-yoh.
• a first/second/third degree burn.	• *quemadura de primer/segundo/ tercer grado.*	• keh-mah-DOO-rah deh pree-MEHR/seh-GOON-doh/tehr-SEHR GRAH-doh.
I was injured with...	*Me hirieron con...*	Meh ee-RYEH-rohn kohn...
• a hand grenade.	• *una granada de mano.*	• OO-nah grah-NAH dah deh MAH-noh.
• a cannon bullet.	• *una bala de cañón.*	• OO-nah BAH-lah deh kah-NYOHN.
• a chemical substance.	• *una substancia química.*	• OO-nah soob-STAHN-syah KEE-mee-kah.
DOCTOR	***DOCTOR***	
Were you exposed to any chemicals?	*¿Estuvo expuesto a alguna substancia química?*	¿Ehs-TOO-voh ehks-PWEHS-toh ah ahl-GOO-nah soob-STAHN-syah KEE-mee-kah?
Which?	*¿Cuál?*	¿Kwahl?
PATIENT	***PACIENTE***	
Nerve gas.	*Gas para los nervios.*	Gahs PAH-rah lohs NEHR-vyohs.
Toxic fumes.	*Humos tóxicos.*	OO-mohs TOKS-ee-kohs.
DOCTOR	***DOCTOR***	
When were you discharged?	*¿Cuándo fue dado de baja?*	¿KWAHN-doh fweh DAH-doh deh BAH-hah?
What other jobs have you had?	*¿Qué otros trabajos ha tenido?*	¿Keh OH-trohs trah-BAH-hohs ah teh-NEE-doh?
What do you do now?	*¿En qué trabaja ahora?*	¿Ehn keh trah-BAH-hah ah-OH-rah?
Do you like your work?	*¿Le gusta a usted su trabajo?*	¿Leh GOOS-tah ah oos-TEHD soo trah-BAH-hoh?

VOCABULARY ••••

PROFESSIONS

accountant	*contador(a)*	kohn-tah-DOHR (DOH-rah)
actor	*actor*	AHK-tohr
actress	*actriz*	ahk-TREES
administrator	*administrador(a)*	ahd-mee-nees-trah-DOHR(DOH-rah)
architect	*arquitecto(a)*	ahr-kee-TEHK-toh(tah)
businessman/ businesswoman	*comerciante*	koh-mehr-SYAHN-teh
coast guard	*guardacostas*	gwahr-dah-KOHS-tahs
chemist	*químico(a)*	KEE-mee-koh(kah)
cleaning personnel	*personal de limpieza*	pehr-soh-NAHL deh leem-PYEH-sah
construction worker	*obrero(a) en la construcción*	oh-BREH-roh(rah) ehn lah kohn-strook-SYOHN
cook	*cocinero(a)*	koh-see-NEH-roh(rah)
dentist	*dentista*	dehn-TEES-tah
doctorate	*doctorado(a)*	dohk-toh-RAH-doh(dah)
editor	*editor(a)*	eh-DEE-tohr(rah)
factory worker	*obrero(a)*	oh-BREH-roh(rah)
gardner	*jardinero(a)*	hahr-dee-NEH-roh(rah)
high school graduate	*bachiller*	bah-chee-LEHR
household help	*empleado(a) doméstico(a)*	ehm-pleh-AH-doh (dah) doh-MEHS-tee-koh(kah)

(cont'd.)

Professions *(cont'd.)*

journalist	*periodista*	peh-ree-oh-DEES-tah
lawyer	*abogado(a)*	ah-boh-GAH-doh(dah)
photographer	*fotógrafo(a)*	foh-TOH-grah-foh(fah)
physician	*médico(a)*	MEH-dee-koh(kah)
pilot	*piloto(a)*	pee-loh-toh(tah)
street cleaning personnel	*personal de limpieza pública*	pehr-soh-NAHL deh leem-PYEH-sah POO-blee-kah
unemployed	*desempleado(a)*	dehs-ehm-plee-AH-doh(dah)
waiter	*camarero(a)* *mesero(a)*	kah-mah-REH-roh (rah) meh-SEH-roh(rah)

C. RECREATIONAL HISTORY

What do you do when you relax?	*¿Qué hace cuando descansa?*	¿Keh AH-seh KWAHN-doh dehs-KAHN-sah?
PATIENT	PACIENTE	
I play…	*Juego…*	HWEH-goh…
• football.	• *fútbol americano.*	• FOOT-bohl ah-meh-ree-KAH-noh.
• soccer.	• *fútbol.*	• FOOT-bohl.
• volleyball.	• *vóleibol.*	• VOH-leh-ee-BOHL.
• baseball.	• *béisbol.*	• behs-BOHL.
• billiards.	• *al billar.*	• ahl bee-YAHR.
I…	*Yo…*	Yoh…
• read.	• *leo.*	• LEH-oh.
• watch television.	• *veo televisión.*	• VEH-oh teh-leh-vee-SYOHN.

• go to the movies.	• *voy al cine.*	• voy ahl SEE-neh.
• go to a game.	• *voy a un juego.*	• voy ah oon HWEH-goh.
• sew.	• *coso.*	• KOH-soh.
• visit my friends.	• *visito a mis amistades.*	• vee-SEE-toh ah mees-TAH-dehs.
• drink beer.	• *tomo cerveza.*	• TOH-moh sehr-VEH-sah.
Do you play any sports?	*¿Juega usted algún deporte?*	¿HWEH-gah oos-TEHD ahl-GOON deh-POHR-teh?
Which one?	*¿Cuál?*	¿Kwahl?
How frequently do you exercise?	*¿Con qué frecuencia hace ejercicio?*	¿Kohn KEH freh-KWEHN-syah AH-seh eh-her-SEE-syoh?
PATIENT	***PACIENTE***	
Every day.	*Todos los días.*	TOH-dohs lohs DEE-ahs.
Every other day.	*Cada otro día.*	KAH-dah OH-troh DEE-ah.
Once a week.	*Una vez por semana.*	OO-nah vehs pohr seh-MAH-nah.
Once in a while.	*De vez en cuando.*	Deh vehs ehn KWAHN-doh.
DOCTOR	***DOCTOR***	
How often do you take vacations?	*¿Con qué frecuencia toma vacaciones?*	¿Kohn keh free-KWEHN-syah TOH-mah vah-kah-SYOH-nehs?
PATIENT	***PACIENTE***	
Never.	*Nunca.*	NOON-kah.
Once a year.	*Una vez al año.*	OO-nah vehs ahl ah-NYOH.
Every six months.	*Cada seis meses.*	KAH-dah sehs MEHS-ehs.
Whenever I can.	*Cuando puedo.*	KWAHN-doh PWEH-doh.

DOCTOR	*DOCTOR*	
What do you do during your vacations?	*¿Qué hace durante sus vacaciones?*	¿Keh AH-seh doo-RAHN-teh soos vah-kah-SYOH-nehs?
PATIENT	*PACIENTE*	
I relax.	*Descanso.*	Dehs-KAHN-soh.
I go back home.	*Voy a mi tierra.*	Voy ah mee TYEH-rah.
I visit my parents/ children.	*Visito a mis padres/ hijos.*	Vee-SEE-toh ah mees PAH-drehs/EH-hohs.
I travel.	*Viajo.*	VYAH-hoh.

D. ENVIRONMENTAL HISTORY

DOCTOR	*DOCTOR*	
Where do you live?	*¿Dónde vive?*	¿DOHN-deh VEE-veh?
PATIENT	*PACIENTE*	
I live in a(n)...	*Vivo en un(a)...*	VEE-voh ehn oon(OO-nah)...
• apartment.	• *apartamento.*	• ah-pahr-tah-MEHN-toh.
• house.	• *casa.*	• KAH-sah.
• condominium.	• *condominio.*	• kohn-doh-MEE-nyoh.
It is in _____.	*Está en _____.*	Ehs-TAH ehn_____.
DOCTOR	*DOCTOR*	
With whom do you live?	*¿Con quién(es) vive?*	¿Kohn KYEHN (KYEH-nehs) VEE-veh?
PATIENT	*PACIENTE*	
I live alone.	*Vivo solo(a).*	VEE-voh SOH-loh(lah).
I live with...	*Vivo con...*	VEE-voh kohn...
• my parents.	• *mis papás.*	• mees pah-PAHS.
• my children.	• *mis hijos.*	• mees EE-hohs.
• my family.	• *mi familia.*	• mee fah-MEE-lyah.

• my spouse and children.	• *mi esposa(o) y mis hijos.*	• mee ehs-POH-sah (soh) ee mees EE-hohs.
• a companion.	• *un(a) compañero(a).*	• oon (OO-nah) kohm-pah-NYEH-roh(rah).
• a roommate.	• *un(a) compañero(a) de cuarto.*	• oon (OO-nah) kohm-pah-NYEH-roh(rah) deh KWAHR-toh.
• some friends.	• *unas(os) amigas(os).*	• OO-nahs(nohs) ah-MEE-gahs(gohs).
DOCTOR	***DOCTOR***	
How long have you…	*¿Cuánto tiempo…*	¿KWAHN-toh TYEHM-poh…
• lived there?	• *ha vivido ahí?*	• ah vee-VEE-doh ah-EE?
• lived with them?	• *ha vivido con ellos?*	• ah vee-VEE-doh kohn EH-yohs?
Do you like your…	*¿Le gusta su…*	¿Leh GOOS-tah soo…
• apartment/house?	• *apartamento/casa?*	• ah-pahr-tah-MEHN-toh/KAH-sah.
• neighborhood?	• *vecindario?*	• veh-seen-DAH-ryoh?
Why not?	*¿Por qué no?*	¿Pohr-KEH noh?
PATIENT	***PACIENTE***	
It's…	*Es…*	Ehs …
• a poor neighborhood.	• *un barrio pobre.*	• oon BAH-ryoh POH-breh.
• far from everything.	• *muy lejos de todo.*	• MOO-ee LEH-hohs deh TOH-doh.
• very violent.	• *un lugar muy violento.*	• oon loo-GAHR moo-ee vyoh-LEHN-toh.
There are many…	*Hay muchos(as)…*	Ay MOO-chohs (chahs)…
• drug dealers.	• *vendedores de drogas.*	• vehn-deh-DOHR-ehs deh DROH-gahs.
• gangs.	• *pandillas.*	• pahn-DEE-yahs.
• shootings.	• *balaceras.*	• bah-lah-SEH-rahs.
• muggings.	• *asaltos.*	• ah-SAHL-tohs.

E. VALUES AND PLANS

GRAMMAR NOTE ••••

THE FUTURE TENSE The future tense describes events that will take place in the future. There is only one set of endings for all verbs. These endings are attached to the infinitive forms as in the model below.

TO HELP *AYUDAR*

I will help	*yo*	*ayudar- é*
you will help (inf.)	*tú*	*ayudar- ás*
you (form.)/he/she will help	*usted/él/ella*	*ayudar- a*
we will help	*nosotros*	*ayudar- emos*
you all will help (inf.)	*vosotros*	*ayudar- éis*
you all (form.)/they will help	*ustedes/ellos/ellas*	*ayudar- án*

We will help you. *Nosotros te ayudaremos.*

Another way to express the future is to use the verb *ir* + *a* + infinitive of another verb. First, here's the verb *ir*.

I go	*yo*	*voy*
you go (inf.)	*tú*	*vas*
you go (form.)/ he/she goes	*usted/él/ella*	*va*
we go	*nosotros*	*vamos*
you all go (inf.)	*vosotros*	*váis*
you all (form.)/they go	*ustedes/ellos/ellas*	*van*

Where are you going? *¿Adónde van ustedes?*
We are going home. *Vamos a casa.*

I'm going to help you. *Voy a ayudarlo.*
You are not going to do this again. *Tú no vas a hacer esto otra vez.*

DOCTOR	*DOCTOR*	
What religion do you practice?	*¿Qué religión tiene?*	¿Keh reh-lee-HYOHN TYEH-neh?
PATIENT	*PACIENTE*	
I am…	*Soy…*	Soy…
• Catholic.	• *católico(a).*	• kah-TOH-lee-koh (kah).
• Protestant.	• *protestante.*	• proh-tehs-TAHN-teh.
• a Jehova's Witness.	• *Testigo de Jehová.*	• TEHS-tee-goh deh heh-oh-VAH.
• Jewish.	• *judío(a).*	• hoo-DEE-oh(ah).
• an agnostic.	• *agnóstico(a).*	• ahg-NOHS-tee-koh (kah).
• an atheist.	• *ateo(a).*	• ah-TEH-oh(ah).
DOCTOR	*DOCTOR*	
How often do you go to church/synagogue?	*¿Cada cuánto va a la iglesia/la sinagoga?*	¿KAH-dah KWAHN-toh vah ah lah ee-GLEH-syah/lah seen-ah-GOH-gah?
How important is your faith to you?	*¿Qué importancia tiene su fe para usted?*	¿Keh eem-pohr-TAHN-syah TYEH-neh soo feh PAH-rah oos-TEHD?
PATIENT	*PACIENTE*	
It is (not) very important.	*(No) es muy importante.*	(Noh) ehs MOO-ee eem-pohr-TAHN-teh.
DOCTOR	*DOCTOR*	
Would you like to contact your…	*¿Le gustaría comunicarse con su…*	¿Leh goos-tah-REE-ah koh-moo-nee-KAHR-seh kohn soo…
• church/synagogue?	• *iglesia/sinagoga?*	• ee-GLEH-syah/ seen-ah-GOH-gah.
• priest/minister/rabbi?	• *sacerdote/ministro/ rabino?*	• sah-sehr-DOH-teh/ mee-NEES-troh/rah-BEE-noh?
What is his/her…	*¿Cuál es su…*	¿Kwahl ehs soo…

• name?	• *nombre?*	• NOHM-breh?
• address?	• *dirección?*	• dee-rehk-SYOHN?
• phone number?	• *número de teléfono.*	• NOO-meh-roh deh teh-LEH-fohn-oh?
PATIENT	***PACIENTE***	
His/her…is ____.	*Su…es ____.*	Soo…ehs ____.
• name	• *nombre*	• NOHM-breh
• address	• *dirección*	• dee-rehk-SYOHN
• phone number	• *número de teléfono*	• NOO-meh-roh deh teh-LEH-foh-noh
DOCTOR	***DOCTOR***	
Do you have plans for the future?	*¿Tiene usted planes para el futuro?*	¿TYEH-neh oos-TEHD PLAH-nehs PAH-rah ehl foo-TOO-roh?
PATIENT	***PACIENTE***	
I would like…	*Me gustaría…*	Meh goos-tah-REE-ah…
• to get married.	• *casarme.*	• kah-SAHR-meh.
• to have a son/daughter.	• *tener un hijo/una hija.*	• teh-NEHR oon EE-hoh/OO-nah EE-hah.
• to go to college.	• *ir a la universidad.*	• eer ah lah oon-ee-vehr-see-DAHD.
• to retire.	• *jubilarme.*	• hoo-bee-LAHR-meh.
• to return to the place where I was born.	• *regresar al lugar donde nací.*	• reh-greh-SAHR ahl loo-GAHR DOHN-deh nah-SEE.
DOCTOR	***DOCTOR***	
Has your life changed a lot recently?	*¿Ha cambiado mucho su vida recientemente?*	¿Ah kahm-BYAH-doh MOO-choh soo VEE-dah reh-syehn-teh-MEHN-teh?
How?	*¿Cómo?*	¿KOH-moh?
PATIENT	***PACIENTE***	
I had to start working.	*Tuve que empezar a trabajar.*	TOO-veh keh ehm-peh-SAHR ah trah-bah-HAHR.

I got married.	*Me casé.*	Meh kah-SEH.
My first child was born.	*Nació mi primer(a) hijo(a).*	Nah-SYOH mee pree-MEHR(MEH-rah) EE-hoh(hah).
My son/daughter got married.	*Se casó mi hijo/hija.*	Seh kah-SOH mee EE-hoh/EE-hah.
I lost my job of many years.	*Perdí mi trabajo de muchos años.*	Pehr-DEE mee trah-BAH-hoh deh MOO-chohs AH-nyohs.
I retired.	*Me jubilé.*	Meh hoo-bee-LEH.
I got divorced.	*Me divorcié.*	Meh dee-vohr-see-EH.
My spouse died.	*Murió mi esposo(a).*	Moo-RYOH mee ehs-POH-soh(sah).
DOCTOR	***DOCTOR***	
Do you have health insurance?	*¿Tiene usted seguro médico?*	¿TYEH-neh oos-TEHD seh-GOO-roh MEH-dee-koh?
How will you pay for this visit?	*¿Cómo va usted a pagar esta visita?*	¿KOH-moh vah oos-TEHD ah pah-GAHR EHS-tah vee-SEE-tah?
How will you recover your salary if you have to go to the hospital?	*¿Cómo va usted a reponer su sueldo si tiene que ir al hospital?*	¿KOH-moh vah oos-TEHD a reh-poh-NEHR soo SWEHL-doh see TYEH-neh keh eer ahl ohs-pee-TAHL?
PATIENT	***PACIENTE***	
I don't know.	*No sé.*	Noh seh.
I have health insurance.	*Tengo seguro de salud.*	TEHN-goh seh-GOO-roh deh sah-LOOD.
• My son/daughter...	• *Mi hijo/hija.*	• Mee EE-hoh/EE-hah...
• Welfare...	• *El "Welfare."*	• Ehl WEHL-fehr...
• My children...	• *Mis hijos...*	• Mees EE-hohs...
• My parents...	• *Mis padres...*	• Mees PAH-drehs...
• My church...	• *Mi iglesia...*	• Mee ee-GLEH-syah...
...will help me.	*...me va(n) a ayudar.*	...meh vah(n) ah ah-yoo-DAHR.

6. The Most Common Questions for Children and Their Parents

GRAMMAR NOTE ••••

THE FAMILIAR COMMAND To give an order to a friend, family member, child, or anyone else you are on familiar terms with, use the informal command form.

All three verb groups (*-ar, -er,* and *-ir* verbs) use the third person singular present to form the affirmative command. *-ar* verbs use the second person singular forms of *-er* verbs to form the negative command, and *-er* and *-ir* verbs use the second person singular forms of *-ar* verbs to form the negative command.

TO CALL *LLAM- AR*

you, don't call!	*¡no llam- es!*
you, call!	*¡llam- a!*

TO RUN *CORR- ER*

you, don't run!	*¡no corr- as!*
you, run!	*¡corr- e!*

TO WRITE *ESCRIB- IR*

you, don't write!	*¡no escrib- as!*
you, write!	*¡escrib- e!*

There are a few irregular informal commands:

put!	*¡pon!*
leave!	*¡sal!*
have!	*¡ten!*
come!	*¡ven!*
say!	*¡di!*
do!	*¡haz!*
go!	*¡ve!*
be!	*¡sé!*

A. QUESTIONS TO THE CHILD

CULTURE NOTE ••••

THE FAMILIAR *TÚ* As mentioned before, when speaking to children or young teenagers, use the familiar form of address *tú* and the first name. Remember that the verb form changes as well.

DOCTOR	*DOCTOR*	
Hi, what is your name?	*Hola, ¿cómo te llamas?*	OH-lah, ¿KOH-moh teh YAH-mahs?
How are you?	*¿Cómo estás?*	¿KOH-moh ehs-TAHS?
How old are you?	*¿Cuántos años tienes?*	¿KWAHN-tohs AH-nyohs TYEH-nehs?
Don't be afraid.	*No tengas miedo.*	Noh TEHN-gahs MYEH-doh.
I'm here to make you you feel better.	*Estoy aqui para hacerte sentir mejor.*	Ehs-TOY ah-KEE PAH-rah ah-SEHR-teh sehn-TEER meh-HOHR.

B. CHIEF COMPLAINT AND HISTORY OF THE PRESENT ILLNESS

GRAMMAR NOTE ••••

TENER (TO HAVE) AND _TENER QUE_ (TO HAVE TO)

The verb *tener* indicates possession, while *tener que* + infinitive indicates obligation.

TO HAVE *TENER*

SINGULAR	PLURAL
tengo	*tenemos*
tienes	*tenéis*

I have no money.	*Yo no tengo dinero.*
You have to come to the clinic.	*Ustedes tienen que venir a la clínica.*

DOCTOR	***DOCTOR***	
Do you feel sick?	*¿Te sientes enferma(o)?*	¿Teh SYEHN-tehs ehn-FEHR-mah(moh)?
Since when have you been sick?	*¿Desde cuándo estás enferma(o)?*	¿DEHS-deh KWAHN-doh ehs-TAHS ehn-FEHR-mah(moh)?
Tell me why you think your mother/father/brother/sister brought you here.	*Díme por qué crees que tu mamá/papá/hermano/hermana te trajo.*	DEE-meh pohr keh kreh-EHS keh too mah-MAH/pah-PAH/ehr-MAH-no/ehr-MAH-nah teh TRAH-hoh.
PATIENT	***PACIENTE***	
I don't know.	*No sé.*	Noh SEH.
Because…	*Porque…*	POHR-keh…
• I feel bad.	• *me siento mal.*	• meh SYEHN-toh mahl.
• I am sick.	• *estoy enferma(o).*	• ehs-TOY ehn-FEHR-mah(moh).
• I have a fever.	• *tengo fiebre.*	• TEHN-goh FYEH-breh.
• I fell.	• *me caí.*	• meh kah-EE.

• I had an accident.	• *tuve un accidente.*	• TOO-veh oon ahks-ee-DEHN-teh.
• I needed to come back.	• *necesitaba volver.*	• neh-seh-see-TAH-bah vohl-VEHR.
• I hurt.	• *tengo un dolor.*	• TEHN-goh oon doh-LOHR.
DOCTOR	***DOCTOR***	
Does it hurt in…	*¿Te duele…*	¿Teh DWEH-leh…
• your head?	• *la cabeza?*	• lah kah-BEH-sah?
• your chest?	• *el pecho?*	• ehl PEH-choh?
• your tummy?	• *la pancita?*	• lah pahn-SEE-tah?
• your arms?	• *los brazos?*	• lohs BRAH-sohs?
• your legs?	• *las piernas?*	• lahs PYEHR-nahs?
• your hands?	• *las manos?*	• lahs MAH-nohs?
• your feet?	• *las piernas?*	• lahs PYEHR-nahs?

VOCABULARY ••••

COMMON CHILDREN'S TERMS

tummy	*pancita*	pahn-SEE-tah
pinky	*dedito/dedo chiquito*	deh-DEE-toh/DEH-doh chee-KEE-toh
pee-pee	*pipí*	PEE-pee
stomach	*pancita*	pahn-SEE-tah
head	*cabecita*	Kah-beh-SEE-tah
foot	*patita/piecito*	pah-TEE-tah/pyeh-SEE-toh
penis	*pilinga*	pee-LEEN-gah
breasts	*piquitos*	pee-KEE-tohs
vagina	*cosita*	koh-SEE-tah
back	*espalda*	ehs-PAHL-dah

C. QUESTIONS TO THE ACCOMPANYING ADULT*

GRAMMAR NOTE ••••

THE IMPERFECT TENSE The imperfect tense is one of the three past tenses in Spanish (the others are the preterite and the perfect tenses). It emphasizes the duration or reception of an event in the past, rather than its completion, beginning, or end. It's also used to describe the background or scenario of an action that took place at a specific time in the past. There are two sets of endings for the imperfect tense. One for *-ar* verbs, and another for *-er,* and *-ir* verbs.

TO WORK *TRABAJAR*

trabaj- aba
trabaj- abas
trabaj- aba
trabaj- ábamos
trabaj- ábais
trabaj- aban

TO HAVE *TENER*	TO LIVE *VIVIR*
ten- ía	*viv-ía*
ten- ías	*viv-ías*
ten- ía	*viv-ía*
ten- íamos	*viv-íamos*
ten- íais	*viv-íais*
ten- ían	*viv-ían*

DOCTOR	**DOCTOR**	
What does the child have?	*¿Qué tiene el (la) niño(a)?*	¿Keh TYEH-neh ehl (lah) NEEN-yoh(yah)?

* Please refer to *The History of the Present Illness* for more questions and answers.

MOTHER/FATHER	*MADRE/PADRE*	
He has...	*Tiene...*	TYEH-neh...
• a headache.	• *un dolor de cabeza.*	• Oon doh-LOHR deh kah-BEH-sah.
• an earache.	• *un dolor de oído.*	• oon doh-LOHR deh oh-EE-doh.
• diarrhea.	• *diarrea.*	• DYAH-rreh-ah.
• a fever.	• *fiebre.*	• FYEH-breh.
He has been so quiet.	*Ha estado muy quieto.*	Ah ehs-TAH-doh moo-ee KYEH-toh.
He has difficulty waking up.	*Tiene dificultad para despertar.*	TYEH-neh dee-fee-kool-TAHD PAH-rah dehs-pehr-TAHR.
He cries so much.	*Llora mucho.*	YOH-rah MOO-choh.

D. BIRTH HISTORY

DOCTOR	*DOCTOR*	
Did you receive prenatal care?	*¿Recibió usted atención antes del parto?*	¿Reh-see-BYOH oos-TEHD ah-tehn-SYOHN AHN-tehs dehl PAHR-toh?
Why not?	*¿Por qué no?*	¿Pohr keh noh?
MOTHER	***MADRE***	
Because...	*Porque...*	POHR-keh...
• I lived far from a clinic.	• *vivía lejos de la clínica.*	• vee-VEE-ah LEH-hohs deh lah KLEE-nee-kah.
• I could not stop working.	• *no podía dejar de trabajar.*	• noh poh-DEE-ah deh-HAHR deh trah-bah-HAHR.
• I did not have the money to pay the doctor.	• *no tenía con que pagarle al doctor.*	• noh teh-NEE-ah kohn keh pah-GAHR-leh ahl dohk-TOHR.

DOCTOR	***DOCTOR***	
In what month of the pregnancy did you begin prenatal care?	*¿En qué mes del embarazo empezó a recibir cuidados prenatales?*	¿Ehn keh mehs dehl ehm-bah-RAH-soh ehm-peh-SOH ah reh-see-BEER kwee-DAH-dohs preh-nah-TAHL-ehs?
MOTHER	***MADRE***	
When I was...pregnant.	*Cuándo tenía...de embarazo.*	KWAHN-doh teh-NEE-ah...deh ehm-bah-RAH-soh.
• a month and a half	• *mes y medio*	• mehs ee MEH-dyoh
• three months	• *tres meses*	• trehs MEH-sehs
• four months	• *cuatro meses*	• KWAH-troh MEH-sehs
• six months	• *seis meses*	• sehs MEH-sehs
DOCTOR	***DOCTOR***	
How frequently did you see the doctor while you were pregnant?	*¿Con qué frecuencia vio al doctor cuando estaba embarazada?*	¿Kohn KEH freh-KWEHN-syah vyoh ahl dohk-TOHR KWAHN-doh ehs-TAH-bah ehm-bah-rah-SAH-dah?
MOTHER	***MADRE***	
Every month.	*Cada mes.*	KAH-dah mehs.
At the beginning, every month.	*Al principio, cada mes.*	Ahl preen-SEE-pyoh, KAH-dah mehs.
Later, every two weeks.	*Después, cada quince días.*	Dehs-PWEHS, KAH-dah KEEN-seh DEE-ahs.
At the end, every week.	*Al final, cada semana.*	Ahl fee-NAHL, KAH-dah seh-MAH-nah.
DOCTOR	***DOCTOR***	
Was the labor normal?	*¿Fue normal el trabajo de parto?*	¿Fweh nohr-MAHL ehl trah-BAH-hoh deh PAHR-toh?
What was not normal?	*¿Qué es lo que no fue normal?*	¿Keh ehs loh keh noh fweh NOHR-mahl?

MOTHER	*MADRE*	
I was past my due date.	*Se me pasó la fecha.*	Seh meh pah-SOH lah FEH-chah.
My water broke very early.	*Se me rompió la fuente muy temprano.*	Seh meh rehm-PYOH lah FWEHN-teh moo-ee tehm-PRAH-noh.
They had to induce labor.	*Me indujeron el trabajo de parto.*	Meh een-doo-HEH-rohn ehl trah-BAH-hoh deh PAHR-toh.
DOCTOR	*DOCTOR*	
Was the delivery normal?	*¿Fue normal el nacimiento?*	¿Fweh nohr-MAHL ehl nah-see-MYEHN-toh?
What was not normal?	*¿Qué es lo que no fue normal?*	¿Keh ehs loh keh noh fweh nohr-MAHL?
MOTHER	*MADRE*	
The contractions stopped.	*Las contracciones se detuvieron.*	Lahs kohn-trahk-SYOH-nehs seh deh-too-VYEH-rohn.
The child was lying sideways.	*El niño venía atravesado.*	Ehl NEEN-yoh veh-NEE-ah ah-trah-veh-SAH-doh.
The child was very big.	*El niño estaba muy grande.*	Ehl NEEN-yoh ehs-TAH-bah moo-ee GRAHN-deh.
The child came butt first.	*El niño venía de nalgas.*	Ehl NEEN-yoh veh-NEE-ah deh NAHL-gahs.
DOCTOR	*DOCTOR*	
Did they place forceps?	*¿Le pusieron fórceps?*	¿Leh poo-SYEH-rohn FOHR-sehps?
Did they do a cesarean section?	*¿Le hicieron una cesárea?*	¿Leh ee-SYEH-rohn OO-nah seh-SAH-reh-ah?
How much did she/he weigh at birth?	*¿Cuánto pesó al nacer?*	¿KWAHN-toh peh-SOH ahl nah-SEHR?

MOTHER	***MADRE***	
He/she weighed _____ lbs.	*Pesó _____ libras.*	Peh-SOH _____ LEE-brahs.
DOCTOR	**DOCTOR**	
Did he/she cry when he/she was born?	*¿Lloró al nacer?*	¿Yoh-ROH ahl nah-SEHR?
How long...	*¿Qué tiempo...*	¿Keh TYEHM-poh...
• did the baby stay in the hospital?	• *pasó el bebé en el hospital?*	• pah-SOH ehl beh-BEH ehn ehl ohs-pee-TAHL?
• did you stay in the hospital after you delivered?	• *pasó usted en el hospital después del parto?*	• pah-SOH oos-TEHD ehn ehl hos-pee-TAHL dehs-PWEHS dehl PAHR-toh?

E. NEONATAL HISTORY

DOCTOR	**DOCTOR**	
Did you notice anything abnormal during the first month of life?	*¿Notó algo anormal durante el primer mes de vida?*	¿Noh-TOH AHL-goh ah-nohr-MAHL doo-RAHN-teh ehl pree-MEHR mehs deh VEE-dah?
What did you notice?	*¿Qué fue lo que notó?*	¿Keh fweh loh keh noh-TOH?
MOTHER	***MADRE***	
I noticed that she/he...	*Noté que...*	Noh-TEH keh...
• cried too much.	• *lloraba mucho.*	• yoh-RAH-bah MOO-choh.
• cried softly.	• *lloraba muy quedito.*	• YOH-rah-bah MOO-ee keh-DEE-toh.
• slept too much.	• *dormía mucho.*	• dohr-MEE-ah MOO-choh.
• woke up with difficulty.	• *me costaba trabajo despertarla(lo).*	• meh koh-TAH-bah trah-BAH-hoh dehs-pehr-TAHR-lah(loh).

• did not take my breast well.	• *no tomaba bien el pecho.*	• noh toh-MAH-bah byehn ehl PEH-choh.
The stool had a strange color.	*Las defecaciones no hacía de color normal.*	Lahs deh-feh-kah-SYOH-nehs noh ah-SEE-ah deh koh-LOHR nohr-MAHL.
The stool had a foul smell.	*Las defecaciones lo que hacía olían muy feo.*	Lahs deh-feh-kah-SYOH-nehs loh keh ah-SEE-ah oh-LEE-ahn moo-ee FEH-oh.
The urine had a very strong odor.	*La orina tenía un olor muy fuerte.*	Lah oh-REE-nah teh NEE-ah oon oh-LOHR MOO-ee FWEHR-teh.
DOCTOR	*DOCTOR*	
Did you take her/him to the doctor?	*¿La (lo) llevó al doctor?*	¿Lah (loh) yeh-VOH ahl dohk-TOHR?
What did the doctor say?	*¿Qué le dijo el doctor?*	¿Keh leh DEE-hoh ehl dohk-TOHR?
MOTHER	*MADRE*	
He/she said that she/he had…	*Me dijo que tenía…*	Meh DEE-hoh keh teh-NEE-ah…
• a fever.	• *fiebre.*	• FYEH-breh.
• a urinary infection.	• *una infección en la orina.*	• OO-nah een-fehk-SYOHN ehn lah oh-REE-nah.
• diarrhea.	• *diarrea.*	• dyah-RREH-ah.
• a developmental problem.	• *un problema del desarrollo.*	• oon proh-BLEH-mah dehl deh-sah-RROH-yoh.
DOCTOR	*DOCTOR*	
Did the doctor prescribe treatment?	*¿Le dio tratamiento el doctor?*	¿Leh dyoh trah-tah-MYEHN-toh ehl dohk-TOHR?
Did she/he get better with the treatment?	*¿Se curó con el tratamiento?*	¿Seh koo-ROH kohn ehl trah-tah-MYEHN-toh?

F. GROWTH AND DEVELOPMENT

GRAMMAR NOTE ••••

NEGATION In Spanish, negation is indicated with the word *no,* which precedes the verb:

Did you call the doctor?	*¿Llamó usted a la doctora?*
I didn't (call her).	*No la llamé.*

There are other words to express the negative.

never	*nunca*
nothing	*nada*
nobody	*nadie*
none	*ningún/o/a*
neither	*tampoco*
neither...nor	*ni...ni*

Except for *nada* (nothing) and *ningún* (nobody), these words can either stand before or after the verb. *Nada* and *ningún* always come after the verb. Note the double negative if the negative stands after the verb.

I never drink.	*Yo nunca bebo.*
I never drink.	*Yo no bebo nunca.*

DOCTOR	*DOCTOR*	
Did you breastfeed?	*¿Le dio el pecho?*	¿Leh dyoh ehl PEH-choh?
How long?	*¿Cuánto tiempo?*	¿KWAHN-toh TYEHM-poh?
Why did you not breastfeed?	*¿Por qué no le dio el pecho?*	¿Pohr keh noh leh dyoh ehl PEH-choh?

MOTHER	*MADRE*	
Because...	*Porque...*	POHR-keh...
• I did not have (enough) milk.	• *no tenía (suficiente) leche.*	• noh teh-NEE-ah (soo-fee-SYEHN-teh) LEH-cheh.
• I had to work.	• *tenía que trabajar.*	• teh-NEE-ah keh trah-bah-HAHR.
• I did not want to.	• *no tenía ganas.*	• noh teh-NEE-ah GAH-nahs.
DOCTOR	*DOCTOR*	
What did you give her/him instead?	*¿Qué le dio en lugar del pecho?*	¿Keh leh dyoh ehn loo-GAHR dehl PEH-choh?
MOTHER	*MADRE*	
I gave him/her...	*Le di...*	Leh dee...
• powdered milk.	• *leche en polvo.*	• LEH-cheh ehn POHL-voh.
• a formula.	• *una fórmula.*	• OO-nah FOHR-moo-lah.
DOCTOR	*DOCTOR*	
When did you begin to give her/him other foods?	*¿Cuándo le empezó a dar otras comidas?*	¿KWAHN-doh leh ehm-peh-SOH ah dahr OH-trahs koh-MEE-dahs?
MOTHER	*MADRE*	
When he/she was _____ months old.	*Cuando tenía _____ meses.*	KWAHN-doh teh-NEE-ah _____ MEH-sehs.
DOCTOR	*DOCTOR*	
When did he/she...	*¿Cuándo...*	¿KWAHN-doh...
• begin to teeth?	• *le salieron los dientes?*	• leh sah-LYEH-rohn lohs DYEHN-tehs?
• begin to speak?	• *empezó a hablar?*	• ehm-peh-SOH ah ah-BLAHR?
• begin to walk?	• *empezó a caminar?*	• ehm-peh-SOH ah kah-mee-NAHR?

G. IMMUNIZATIONS

DOCTOR	*DOCTOR*	
What has she/he been vaccinated against?	*¿Contra qué enfermedades está vacunada(o)?*	¿KOHN-trah keh ehn-fehr-meh-DAH-dehs ehs-TAH vah-koon-AH-dah(doh)?
MOTHER	***MADRE***	
Against...	*Contra...*	KOHN-trah...
• diphtheria.	• *difteria.*	• deef-TEH-ryah.
• pertussis.	• *tos ferina.*	• tohs-feh-REE-nah.
• tetanus.	• *tétano.*	• TEH-tah-noh.
• measles.	• *sarampión.*	• sah-rahm-PYOHN.
• polio.	• *polio.*	• POH-lyoh.

H. PAST MEDICAL HISTORY

DOCTOR	*DOCTOR*	
What diseases has she/he had?	*¿Qué enfermedades ha tenido?*	¿Keh ehn-fehr-meh-DAH-dehs ah teh-NEE-doh?
MOTHER	***MADRE***	
She/he has had...	*Ha tenido...*	Ah teh-NEE-doh...
• coughs.	• *tos.*	• tohs.
• colds.	• *resfriados.*	• rehs-free-AH-dohs.
• fever.	• *fiebres.*	• FYEH-brehs.
• diarrhea.	• *diarrea.*	• dyah-RREH-ah.
• earaches.	• *dolor de oídos.*	• doh-LOHR deh oh-EE-dohs.
• measles.	• *sarampión.*	• sah-rahm-PYOHN.
• strep throat.	• *anginas.*	• ahn-HEE-nahs.
• chicken pox.	• *varicela.*	• vah-ree-SEH-lah.
• scarlet fever.	• *escarlatina.*	• ehs-kahr-lah-TEE-nah.
• German measles.	• *rubeola.*	• roo-beh-OH-lah.

DOCTOR	***DOCTOR***	
Has she/he had any accidents?	*¿Ha tenido algún accidente?*	¿Ah teh-NEE-doh ahl-GOON ahk-see-DEHN-teh?
MOTHER	***MADRE***	
None.	*Ninguno.*	Neen-goo-noh.
She/he fell…	*Se cayó de…*	Seh kah-YOH deh…
• out of bed.	• *la cama.*	• lah KAH-mah.
• from a chair.	• *una silla.*	• OO-nah SEE-yah.
• down the stairs.	• *de la escalera.*	• deh lah ehs-kah-LEH-rah.
• from a tree.	• *de un árbol.*	• deh oon AHR-bohl.
She/he broke…	*Se quebró…*	Seh keh-BROH…
• an arm.	• *un brazo.*	• oon BRAH-soh.
• a leg.	• *una pierna.*	• OO-nah PYEHR-nah.
• a finger.	• *un dedo.*	• oon DEH-doh.
• an ankle.	• *un tobillo.*	• oon toh-BEE-yoh.
• a wrist.	• *una muñeca.*	• OO-nah moo-NYEH-kah.
• his/her nose.	• *su nariz.*	• soo nah-REES.
DOCTOR	***DOCTOR***	
Has she/he started school?	*¿Empezó a ir a la escuela?*	¿Ehm-peh-SOH ah eer ah lah ehs-KWEH-lah?
What grade is she/he in?	*¿En qué año está?*	¿Ehn keh ah-NYOH ehs-TAH?
MOTHER	***MADRE***	
In…	*En…*	Ehn…
• kindergarten.	• *parvulario.*	• PAHR-voo-lah-ree-oh.
• first grade.	• *primer año.*	• pree-MEHR ah-NYOH.
• second grade.	• *segundo año.*	• seh-GOON-doh ah-NYOH.

DOCTOR	DOCTOR	
Has she/he had any problems in school?	*¿Ha tenido problemas en la escuela?*	¿Ah teh-NEE-doh proh-BLEH-mahs ehn lah ehs-KWEH-lah?
What problems?	*¿Qué problemas?*	¿Keh proh-BLEH-mahs?
MOTHER	**MADRE**	
She/he is always fighting.	*Es muy peleonero(a).*	Ehs MOO-ee peh-LEH-oh-NEH-rah(roh).
She/he does not…	*No…*	Noh…
• learn to read and write.	• *aprende a leer y escribir.*	• ah-PREHN-deh ah leh-EHR ee ehs-kree-BEER.
• like to do homework.	• *le gusta hacer su tarea.*	• leh GOOS-tah ah-SEHR soo tah-REH-ah.

VOCABULARY ••••

COMMON CHILDREN'S DISEASES

cold	*resfriado*	rehs-free-AH-doh
scarlet fever	*escarlatina*	ehs-kahr-lah-TEE-nah
diarrhea	*diarrea*	dyah-RREH-ah
allergy	*alergia*	ah-lehr-HEE-ah
measles	*sarampion*	sah-rahm-PYOHN
whooping cough	*tosferina*	tohs-feh-REE-nah
tetanus	*tetano*	teh-TAH-noh
polio	*polio*	POH-lyoh
chicken pox	*varicela*	vah-ree-SEH-lah
German measles	*rubeola*	roo-beh-OH-lah
strep throat	*anginas*	ahn-HEE-nahs
earache	*dolores de oído*	doh-LOHR-ehs deh oh-EE-doh

I. THE CHIEF COMPLAINTS OF CHILDREN

GRAMMAR NOTE ••••

THE PERFECT TENSE The perfect tense is formed with a conjugated form of the auxiliary verb *haber* (to have) and the past participle of the main verb. Participle endings are:

-ado for verbs in *-ar:*	*toc-ado*	robbed
-ido for verbs in *-er* and *-ir:*	*beb-ido*	drank

I have played.	*Yo he tocado.*
We have played.	*Nosotros hemos tocado.*

Irregular past participles are:

broken	*roto*
said	*dicho*
made/done	*hecho*
put	*puesto*
seen	*visto*
returned	*vuelto*
written	*escrito*

DOCTOR	***DOCTOR***	
How long has the child been complaining?	*¿Desde cuándo se está quejando la (el) niña(o)?*	¿Dehs-deh KWAHN-doh seh ehs-TAH keh-HAHN-doh lah (ehl) NEEN-yah(yoh)?
MOTHER	***MADRE***	
She/he began…	*Empezó…*	Ehm-peh-SOH…
• a while ago.	• *hace un rato.*	• AH-seh oon-RAH-toh.
• this morning/ afternoon.	• *en la mañana/tarde.*	• ehn lah mah-NYAH-nah/TAHR-deh.
• last night.	• *anoche.*	• ah-NOH-cheh.
• several days ago.	• *hace varios días.*	• AH-seh VAH-ryohs DEE-ahs.

DOCTOR	DOCTOR	
What do you think is wrong with her/him?	*¿Qué cree usted que tiene?*	¿Keh KREH-eh oos-TEHD keh TYEH-neh?
MOTHER	***MADRE***	
I don't know.	*No sé.*	Noh SEH.
She/he has…	*Tiene…*	TYEH-neh…
• a fever.	• *fiebre.*	• FYEH-breh.
• mumps.	• *paperas.*	• pah-PEH-rahs.
• measles.	• *sarampión.*	• sah-rahm-PYOHN.
• scarlet fever.	• *escarlatina.*	• ehs-kahr-lah-TEE-nah.
• pneumonia.	• *pulmonía.*	• pool-moh-NEE-ah.
• a cold.	• *un resfriado.*	• oon rehs-free-AH-doh.
DOCTOR	***DOCTOR***	
How do you know she/he has fever?	*¿Cómo sabe que tiene fiebre?*	¿KOH-moh SAH-beh keh TYEH-neh FYEH-breh?
MOTHER	***MADRE***	
She/he feels hot to the touch.	*Se siente muy caliente.*	Seh SYEHN-teh moo-ee kah-LYEHN-teh.
I took his/her temperature.	*Le tomé la temperatura.*	Leh toh-MEH lah tehm-peh-rah-TOO-rah.
DOCTOR	***DOCTOR***	
Has he/she been eating and drinking water as usual?	*¿Ha estado comiendo y bebiendo agua como lo usual?*	¿Ah ehs-TAH-doh koh-MYEHN-doh ee beh-BYEHN-doh AH-gwah KOH-moh loh oo-SOO-AHL?
MOTHER	***MADRE***	
No…	*No…*	Noh…
• she/he is eating/drinking more/less than usual.	• *está comiendo/bebiendo más/menos que lo usual.*	• ehs-TAH koh-MYEHN-doh/beh-BYEHN-doh mahs/MEH-nohs keh loh oo-SWAHL.

• she/he is eating/ drinking a lot/ very little.	• *está comiendo/ bebiendo mucho/ muy poco.*	• ehs-TAH koh-MYEHN-doh/beh-BYEHN-doh MOO-choh/moo-ee POH-koh.
DOCTOR	***DOCTOR***	
Has she/he been…	*¿Ha estado…*	¿Ah ehs-TAH-doh…
• sleeping more than usual?	• *durmiendo más de lo usual?*	• door-MYEHN-doh MAHS deh loh oo-SWAHL?
• crying more than usual?	• *llorando más de lo usual?*	• yoh-RAHN-doh mahs deh loh oo-SWAHL?
• less/more active than usual?	• *menos/más activa(o) que lo usual?*	• MEH-nohs/mahs ahk-TEE-vah(voh) keh loh oo-SWAHL?
• playing as usual?	• *jugando como es usual?*	• hoo-GAHN-doh KOH-moh ehs oo-SWAHL?
• smiling as usual?	• *sonriendo como es usual?*	• sohn-RYEHN-doh KOH-moh ehs oo-SWAHL?
Is the crying strong?	*¿Es fuerte el llanto?*	¿Ehs FWEHR-teh ehl YAHN-toh?
Does the child stop crying when you pick her/him up?	*¿Deja de llorar la (el) niña(o) cuando la (lo) carga?*	¿DEH-hah de yoh-RAHR lah (ehl) NEEN-yah(yoh) KWAHN-doh lah (loh) KAHR-gah?
Have you had difficulty waking the child up?	*¿Ha tenido dificultad para despertarla(lo)?*	¿Ah teh-NEE-doh dee-fee-kool-TAHD PAH-rah dehs-pehr-TAHR-lah(loh)?
Does the child have diarrhea?	*¿Tiene diarrea?*	¿TYEH-neh dyah-RREH-ah?
How many times does she/he go a day?	*¿Cuántas veces hace del baño al día?*	¿KWAHN-tahs VEH-sehs AH-seh dehl BAH-nyoh ahl DEE-ah?
What color are her/ his bowel movements?	*¿De qué color hace del baño?*	¿Deh KEH koh-LOHR AH-seh dehl BAH-nyoh?

MOTHER	***MADRE***	
Normal.	*Normal.*	Nohr-MAHL.
(Bright) yellow.	*(Muy) amarillas.*	(Moo-ee) ah-mah-REE-ahs.
Colorless.	*Sin color.*	Seen koh-LOHR.
DOCTOR	***DOCTOR***	
Are the bowel movements liquid or paste-like	*¿Las evacuaciones son líquidas o pastosas?*	¿Lahs eh-vah-KWAH-YOH-nehs sohn LEE-kee-dahs o pahs-TOH-sahs?
Do the bowel movements have a bad odor?	*¿Huelen mal las evacuaciones?*	¿WEH-lehn mahl lahs eh-vah-KWAH-SYOH-nehs?
Does the child complain of anything when he urinates?	*¿Se queja de algo el niño cuando orina?*	¿Seh KEH-hah deh AHL-goh ehl NEEN-yoh KWAHN-doh oh-REE-nah?
What does she/he complain about?	*¿De qué se queja la/el niña/niño?*	¿Deh keh seh KEH-hah lah/ehl NEEN-yah/NEEN-yoh?
MOTHER	***MADRE***	
That…	*De que…*	Deh keh…
• it hurts her/him a lot.	• *le duele mucho.*	• leh DWEH-leh MOO-choh.
• it burns a lot.	• *le arde mucho.*	• leh AHR-deh MOO-choh.
DOCTOR	***DOCTOR***	
Is she/he urinating more often than usual?	*¿Está orinando más veces de lo usual?*	¿Ehs-TAH oh-ree-NAHN-doh MAHS VEH-sehs deh loh oo-SWAHL?
Does her/his urine have a bad smell?	*¿Huele mal la orina?*	¿WEH-leh mahl lah oh-REE-nah?
Does she/he…	*¿Tiene…*	¿TYEH-neh…
• have a cough?	• *tos?*	• tohs?
• a sore throat?	• *dolor de garganta?*	• doh-LOHR deh gahr-GAHN-tah?

Have you taken the child to another doctor?	*¿Ha llevado a la (al) niña(o) a otro(a) doctor(a)?*	¿Ah yeh-VAH-doh ah lah (ahl) NEEN-yah(yoh) ah OH-troh (trah) dohk-TOHR (TOH-rah)?
What did the doctor prescribe?	*¿Qué le recetó el (la) doctor(a)?*	¿Keh leh reh-seh-TOH ehl (lah) dohk-TOHR(TOH-rah)?
Did you…	*¿Usted…*	¿Oos-TEHD…
• fill the prescription at the drugstore?	• *compró la medicina en la farmacia?*	• kohm-PROH lah meh-dee-SEE-nah ehn lah fahr-MAH-syah?
• give the child the medications?	• *le dió las medicinas a la (al) niña(o)?*	• leh dyoh lahs meh-dee-SEE-nahs ah lah (ahl) NEEN-yah (yoh)?
What have you given her/him?	*¿Qué le ha dado usted?*	¿Keh leh ah DAH-doh oos-TEHD?
Did the child improve with the medications?	*¿Mejoró la (el) niña(o) con las medicinas?*	¿Meh-hoh-ROH lah (ehl) NEEN-yah(yoh) kohn lahs meh-dee-SEE-nahs?

7. Questions for Adults About Their Daily Activities

DOCTOR	*DOCTOR*	
In general, how is your health?	*En general, ¿cómo está su salud?*	Ehn heh-neh-RAHL, ¿KOH-moh ehs-TAH soo sah-LOOD?
PATIENT	*PACIENTE*	
Very well.	*Muy bien.*	MOO-ee byehn.
Well.	*Bien.*	Byehn.
So, so.	*Más o menos.*	Mahs oh MEH-nohs.
Okay.	*Regular.*	Reh-GOO-lahr.
Bad.	*Mal.*	Mahl.
Very bad.	*Muy mal.*	MOO-ee mahl.

VOCABULARY ••••

DOSAGE

pills	*pastillas/píldoras*	pahs-TEE-yahs/ peel-DOH-rahs
tablets	*tabletas*	tah-BLEH-tahs
capsules	*cápsulas*	KAHP-soo-lahs
suppositories	*supositorios*	soo-poh-see-TOH-ryohs
liquid	*líquido*	LEE-kee-doh
injection	*inyección*	een-yehk-SYOHN
patches	*parchos*	PAHR-chohs
once a day	*una vez por día*	OO-nah vehs pohr DEE-ah
twice a week	*dos veces por semana*	dohs VEH-sehs pohr seh-MAH-nah
three times a month	*tres veces al mes*	trehs VEH-sehs ahl mehs
with food	*con comida*	kohn koh-MEE-dah
with water	*con agua*	kohn AH-gwah

DOCTOR	*DOCTOR*	
Do you have enough energy to do what you want to do?	*¿Tiene suficiente ánimo para hacer lo que quiere hacer?*	¿TYEH-neh soo-fee-SYEHN-teh AH-nee-moh PAH-rah ah-SEHR loh keh KYEH-reh ah-SEHR?
Do you…	*¿Usted…*	¿Oos-TEHD…
• sleep enough?	• *duerme lo suficiente?*	• DWEHR-meh loh soo-fee-SYEHN-teh?
• sleep well?	• *duerme bien?*	• DWEHR-meh byehn?

• feel refreshed when you wake up?	• *se siente descansado cuando despierta?*	• seh SYEHN-teh dehs-kahn-SAH-doh KWAHN-doh dehs-PYEHR-tah?
• wake up during the night?	• *se despierta durante la noche?*	• seh dehs-PYEHR-tah doo-RAHN-teh lah NOH-cheh?
How often?	*¿Con qué frecuencia?*	¿Kohn keh freh-KWEHN-syah?
PATIENT	***PACIENTE***	
I have trouble falling asleep.	*Es difícil quedarme dormido.*	Ehs dee-FEE-seel keh-DAHR-meh dohr-MEE-doh.
It takes me a long time to fall asleep.	*Tardo mucho para dormirme.*	TAHR-doh MOO-choh PAH-rah dohr-MEER-meh.
I wake up…	*Me despierto…*	Meh dehs-PYEHR-toh…
• many times.	• *muchas veces.*	• MOO-chahs VEH-sehs.
• every once in a while.	• *de vez en cuando.*	• deh vehs ehn KWAHN-doh.
• only a few times.	• *sólo pocas veces.*	• SOH-loh POH-kahs VEH-sehs.
DOCTOR	***DOCTOR***	
What do you do when you wake up?	*¿Qué hace cuando se despierta?*	¿Keh AH-seh KWAHN-doh seh dehs-PYEHR-tah?
PATIENT	***PACIENTE***	
I…	*Me…*	Meh…
• go back to sleep.	• *vuelvo a dormir.*	• VWEHL-voh ah dohr-MEER.
• remain in bed.	• *quedo acostado.*	• KEH-doh ah-kohs-TAH-doh.
• begin to think.	• *pongo a pensar.*	• POHN-goh ah pehn-SAHR.
• start to pray.	• *pongo a rezar.*	• POHN-goh ah reh-SAHR.

• go urinate.	• *me levanto a orinar.*	• meh leh-VAHN-toh ah oh-ree-NAHR.
• get up and work.	• *me levanto a trabajar.*	• meh leh-VAHN-toh ah trah-bah-HAHR.
DOCTOR	***DOCTOR***	
Do you sometimes get hungry?	*¿A veces le dan ganas de comer?*	¿Ah VEH-sehs leh dahn GAH-nahs deh koh-MEHR?
PATIENT	***PACIENTE***	
I am always hungry.	*Siempre tengo hambre.*	SYEHM-preh TEHN-goh AHM-breh.
Very frequently.	*Con mucha frecuencia.*	Kohn MOO-chah freh-KWEHN-syah.
Once in a while.	*De vez en cuando.*	Deh vehs ehn KWAHN-doh.
Almost never.	*Casi nunca.*	KAH-see NOON-kah.
Never.	*Nunca.*	NOON-kah.
DOCTOR	***DOCTOR***	
Do you eat enough?	*¿Come suficiente?*	¿KOH-meh soo-fee-SYEHN-teh?
How much do you weigh?	*¿Cuánto pesa?*	¿KWAHN-toh PEH-sah?
Have you gained or lost weight lately?	*¿Ha aumentado o bajado de peso últimamente?*	¿Ah ow-mehn-TAH-doh oh bah-HAH-doh deh PEH-soh OOL-tee-mah-MEHN-teh?
How much weight have you gained or lost?	*¿Cuánto ha aumentado o bajado de peso?*	KWAHN-toh ah ow-mehn-TAH-doh oh bah-HAH-doh deh PEH-soh?
PATIENT	***PACIENTE***	
No. Not really.	*No. Realmente, no.*	Noh. Reh-ahl-MEHN-teh, noh.
A lot.	*Mucho.*	MOO-choh.
Just a little.	*Un poquito.*	Oon poh-KEE-toh.
Very little.	*Muy poquito.*	MOO-ee-poh-KEE-toh.

Some ____ kilos.	*Unos ____ kilos.*	Oo-nohs ____ KEE-lohs.
DOCTOR	**DOCTOR**	
How long did it take for you to gain/lose that weight?	*¿En cuánto tiempo ganó/perdió ese peso?*	¿Ehn KWAHN-toh TYEHM-poh gah-NOH/pehr-DYOH EH-seh PEH-soh?
PATIENT	**PACIENTE**	
One year.	*Un año.*	Oon ah-NYOH.
Six months.	*Seis meses.*	Sehs MEH-sehs.
Three months.	*Tres meses.*	Trehs MEH-sehs.
Just a few weeks.	*Unas cuantas semanas.*	OO-nahs KWAHN-tahs seh-MAH-nahs.
A short time.	*Poco tiempo.*	POH-koh TYEHM-poh.
DOCTOR	**DOCTOR**	
How do you know you have gained/lost that much weight?	*¿Cómo sabe que ése es el peso que aumentó/perdió?*	¿KOH-moh SAH-beh keh EH-seh ehs ehl PEH-soh keh ow-mehn-TOH/pehr-DYOH?
PATIENT	**PACIENTE**	
My clothes…	*La ropa…*	Lah ROH-pah…
• are too small/big for me.	• *me queda muy chica/grande.*	• meh KEH-dah moo-ee CHEE-kah/GRAHN-deh.
• don't fit me.	• *ya no me queda bien.*	• yah noh meh KEH-dah byehn.
I can see it when I look in the mirror.	*Lo veo cuando me miro en el espejo.*	Loh veh-oh KWAHN-doh meh MEE-roh ehn ehl ehs-PEH-hoh.
I weighed myself on a scale.	*Me pesé en una báscula.*	Meh peh-SEH ehn OO-nah BAHS-koo-lah.

GRAMMAR NOTE ••••

REFLEXIVES Reflexive pronouns are used with reflexive verbs. Verbs are reflexive when the subject and the object of the verb are the same. Reflexive pronouns stand between the subject pronoun and the verb, or are attached to an affirmative command.

myself	*me*
yourself (inf. singular)	*te*
himself/herself/yourself (form.)/itself/yourselves/ themselves	*se*
ourselves	*nos*
yourselves (inf. plural)	*os*

I'm bathing myself.	*Yo me baño.*
How are you feeling yourself?	*¿Cómo se siente usted?*
Sit yourself down!	*¡Siéntese!*

VOCABULARY ••••

DIET AND NUTRITION

to eat breakfast/ breakfast	*desayunar/ desayuno*	dehs-ah-yoo-NAHR/ dehs-ah-YOO-noh
to eat/lunch	*comer/almuerzo*	koh-MEHR/ahl-MWEHR-soh
to dine/dinner	*cenar/cena*	seh-NAHR/SEH-nah
to snack/snack	*merendar/merienda*	meh-rehn-DAHR/ meh-REE-EHN-dah
cereal(s)	*cereal(es)*	seh-reh-AHL(ehs)
grain(s)	*grano(s)*	GRAH-noh(s)
sugar(s)	*azucar(es)*	ah-soo-KAHR(KAH-rehs)
protein(s)	*proteina(s)*	pro-TEH-EE-nah(s)
fat(s)	*grasa(s)*	GRAH-sah(s)
salt(s)	*sal(es)*	SAH-l(ehs)
mineral(s)	*mineral(es)*	mee-neh-RAHL(ehs)
water	*agua*	ah-GWAH
diet	*dieta*	DYEH-tah
meat	*carne*	KAHR-neh
vegetable	*verdura*	vehr-DOO-rah
carbohydrate	*carbohidratos*	kahr-boh-ee-DRAH-tohs
liquid	*líquido*	LEE-kee-doh
rice	*arroz*	ah-RROHS
fruit	*fruta*	FROO-tah
vitamin	*vitamina*	vee-tah-MEH-nah

DOCTOR	*DOCTOR*	
Are you on a diet?	*¿Está usted siguiendo alguna dieta?*	¿Ehs-TAH oos-TEHD see-GYEHN-doh ahl-GOO-nah DYEH-tah?
What diet?	*¿Qué dieta?*	¿Keh DYEH-tah?
Who prescribed your diet?	*¿Quién le recetó la dieta?*	¿Kyehn leh reh-seh-TOH lah DYEH-tah?
PATIENT	***PACIENTE***	
A doctor.	*Un(a) doctor(a).*	Oon (OO-nah) dohk-TOHR(TOH-rah).
A nutritionist.	*Un(a) nutricionista.*	Oon (OO-nah) noo-tree-syoh-nees-tah.
A natural healer.	*Un(a) curandero(a).*	Oon (OO-nah) koo-rahn-DEH-roh(rah).
A friend of mine.	*Un(a) amigo(a).*	Oon (OO-nah) ah-MEE-goh(gah).
I read about it in a newspaper/book.	*La leí en un periódico/libro.*	Lah leh-EE ehn oon peh-ree-OH-dee-koh/LEE-broh.

8. Review of Systems

VOCABULARY ••••

BODY PARTS 2

ankle	*tobillo*	toh-BEE-yoh
anus	*ano*	AH-noh
armpits	*sobacos*	soh-BAH-kohs
body hair	*vello*	VEH-yoh
breasts	*pechos*	PEH-chohs
chest	*pecho*	PEH-choh
finger	*dedo*	DEH-doh
hair	*pelo*	PEH-loh
heart	*corazón*	koh-rah-SOHN
hip	*cadera*	kah-DEH-rah
knee	*rodilla*	roh-DEE-yah
nails	*uñas*	OO-nyahs
nipples	*pezones*	peh-SOH-nehs
penis	*pene/miembro*	PEH-neh/mee-EHM-broh
scalp	*cuero cabelludo*	kweh-roh kah-beh-YOO-doh
scrotum	*escroto*	ehs-KROH-toh
shoulder	*hombro*	OHM-broh
skin	*piel*	pyehl
skull	*cráneo*	KRAH-neh-oh
stomach	*estómago*	ehs-TOH-mah-goh
temples	*sienes*	SYEH-nehs
testicle	*testículo*	tehs-TEE-koo-loh
toe	*dedo del pié*	DEH-doh dehl pyeh
vagina	*vagina*	VAH-hee-nah
wrist	*muñeca*	moo-NYEH-kah

A. THE SKIN

DOCTOR	*DOCTOR*	
Do you have a problem with your skin?	*¿Tiene algún problema en la piel?*	TYEH-neh ahl-GOON proh-BLEH-mah ehn lah pyehl?
Where?	*¿Dónde?*	¿DOHN-deh?
Show me, please!	*¡Me lo enseña, por favor!*	¡Meh loh ehn-seh-NYAH, pohr fah-VOHR!
Does it itch anywhere?	*¿Tiene comezón en alguna parte?*	¿TYEH-neh koh-meh-SOHN ehn ahl-GOO-nah PAHR-teh?
Where?	*¿Dónde?*	¿DOHN-deh?
PATIENT	***PACIENTE***	
My _____ itch(es).	*Tengo comezón en…*	TEHN-goh koh-meh SOHN ehn…
• nose	• *la nariz.*	• lah nah-REES.
• ears	• *los oídos.*	• lohs oh-EE-dohs.
• scalp	• *el cuero cabelludo.*	• ehl KWEH-roh kah-beh-YOO-doh.
• back	• *la espalda.*	• lah ehs-PAHL-dah.
• armpits	• *los sobacos/axilas.*	• lohs soh-BAH-kohs/ ahk-SEE-lahs.
• scrotum	• *el escroto.*	• ehl ehs-KROH-toh.
• anus	• *el ano.*	• ehl AH-noh.
• feet	• *los pies.*	• lohs pyehs.
DOCTOR	***DOCTOR***	
Do you have any ulcers or scabs that do not heal?	*¿Tiene úlceras o granos que no cicatrizan?*	TYEH-neh OOL-seh-rahs oh GRAH-nohs keh noh see-kah-TREE-sahn?
Do you bruise easily?	*¿A usted se le hacen moretones fácilmente?*	¿Ah oos-TEHD seh leh AH-sehn moh-reh-TOH-nehs FAH-seel-mehn-teh?

Do you…	*¿Usted…*	¿Oos-TEHD…
• bleed easily?	• *sangra con facilidad?*	• SAHN-grah kohn fah-see-lee-DAHD?
• have any problems with your hair?	• *tiene algún problema con el pelo?*	• TYEH-neh ahl-GOON proh-BLEH-mah kohn ehl PEH-loh?
What problem?	*¿Qué problema tiene?*	¿KEH proh-BLEH-mah TYEH-neh?
PATIENT	***PACIENTE***	
It…	*Se…*	Seh…
• does not shine.	• *quedó sin brillo.*	• keh-DOH seen BREE-yoh.
• is falling out.	• *me está cayendo.*	• meh ehs-TAH kah-YEHN-doh.
DOCTOR	***DOCTOR***	
Do you have any problems with your nails?	*¿Tiene algún problema con las uñas?*	¿TYEH-neh ahl-GOON proh-BLEH-mah kohn lahs oo-NYAHS?
What is the problem?	*¿Cuál es el problema?*	¿Kwahl ehs ehl proh-BLEH-mah?
PATIENT	***PACIENTE***	
They…		
• do not shine anymore.	• *ya no brillan.*	• yah noh-BREE-yahn.
• break easily.	• *se quiebran muy fácilmente.*	• seh kee-EH-bran moo-ee FAH-seel-mehn-teh.
• are stained.	• *se me mancharon.*	• seh meh mahn-CHAH-rohn.
DOCTOR	***DOCTOR***	
Has your body hair changed?	*¿Le ha cambiado el vello del cuerpo?*	¿Leh ah kahm-BYAH-doh ehl VEH-yoh dehl KWEHR-poh?
What changes did you notice?	*¿Qué cambios notó?*	¿Keh KAHM-byohs noh-TOH?

PATIENT	*PACIENTE*	
It is…	*Se me está…*	Seh meh ehs-TAH…
• becoming very thin.	• *poniendo muy delgado.*	• poh-NYEHN-doh moo-ee dehl-GAH-doh.
• becoming very thick.	• *poniendo muy grueso.*	• poh-NYEHN-doh moo-ee GROO-eh-soh.
• falling out.	• *cayendo.*	• kah-YEHN-doh.
It is growing all over.	*Me está saliendo por todos lados.*	Meh ehs-TAH sahl-YEHN-doh pohr TOH-dohs LAH-dohs.

B. THE HEAD

GRAMMAR NOTE ••••

IRREGULAR PRETERITES The most common irregular verbs in the preterite are listed below. While they have irregular stems, their endings follow the *-ir, -er* pattern.

to want	*querer*	*quise*	I wanted
to know	*saber*	*supe*	I knew
to do, to make	*hacer*	*hice*	I did/I made
to say	*decir*	*dije*	I said
to bring	*traer*	*traje*	I brought
to come	*venir*	*vine*	I came
to be able to	*poder*	*pude*	I was able to
to put	*poner*	*puse*	I put
to have	*tener*	*tuve*	I had
to be	*estar*	*estuve*	I was
to go	*ir*	*fui*	I went
to be	*ser*	*fui*	I was
to walk	*andar*	*anduve*	I walked
to give	*dar*	*di*	I gave

DOCTOR	*DOCTOR*	
Have you ever suffered an injury to the head?	*¿Alguna vez ha sufrido una herida en la cabeza?*	¿Ahl-GOO-nah vehs ah soo-FREE-doh OO-nah eh-REE-dah ehn lah kah-BEH-sah?
What kind of injury was it?	*¿Qué tipo de herida fue?*	¿Keh TEE-poh deh eh-RHEE-dah fweh?
PATIENT	*PACIENTE*	
A bruise.	*Una contusión/ un moretón.*	OO-nah kohn-too syohn/oon moh-reh-TOHN.
A skull fracture.	*Una fractura del cráneo.*	OO-nah frahk-TOO-rah dehl KRAH-neh-oh.
DOCTOR	*DOCTOR*	
How did you injure yourself?	*¿Cómo se hirió?*	¿KOH-moh se ee-RYOH?
PATIENT	*PACIENTE*	
I fell.	*Me caí.*	Meh kah-EE.
I was playing ____ (name of sport).	*Estaba jugando ____ (nombre de un deporte).*	Ehs-TAH-bah hoo-GAHN-doh ____.
Something fell on me.	*Me cayó algo encima.*	Meh kah-YOH AHL-goh ehn-SEE-mah.
I was in an accident.	*Tuve un accidente.*	TOO-veh oon ahk-see-DEHN-teh.
DOCTOR	*DOCTOR*	
Did you lose consciousness?	*¿Perdió el conocimiento?*	¿Pehr-DYOH ehl koh-noh-see-MYEHN-toh?
Did you have to be hospitalized?	*¿Tuvieron que hospitalizarlo?*	¿Too-VYEH-rohn keh ohs-pee-tah-lee-SAHR-loh?
What treatment did they give you?	*¿Qué tratamiento le dieron?*	¿Keh trah-tah-MYEHN-toh leh DYEH-rohn?
PATIENT	*PACIENTE*	
I was sutured.	*Me cosieron.*	Meh koh-SYEH-rohn.
I had an operation.	*Me operaron.*	Meh oh-peh-RAH-rohn.

I had to rest for several days.	*Tuve que descansar varios días.*	TOO-veh keh dehs-kahn-SAHR VAH-yohs DEE-ahs.
DOCTOR	***DOCTOR***	
Have you ever hit your head and fainted?	*¿Alguna vez se golpeó en la cabeza y se desmayó?*	¿Ahl-GOO-nah vehs seh gohl-peh-OH ehn lah kah-BEH-sah ee seh dehs-mah-YOH?
When?	*¿Cuándo?*	¿KWAHN-doh?
Do you have headaches frequently?	*¿Tiene dolores de cabeza frecuentes?*	¿TYEH-neh doh-LOHR-ehs deh kah-BEH-sah freh-KWEHN-tehs?
In what part of your head?	*¿En qué parte de la cabeza?*	¿Ehn keh PAHR-teh de lah kah-BEH-sah?
PATIENT	***PACIENTE***	
In the entire head.	*En toda la cabeza.*	Ehn TOH-dah lah kah-BEH-sah.
On the right/left side.	*En el lado derecho/izquierdo.*	Ehn ehl LAH-doh deh-REH-choh/ees-KYEHR-doh.
In the back.	*En la nuca.*	En lah NOO-kah.
Behind the eyes.	*Detrás de los ojos.*	Deh-TRAHS deh lohs OH-hohs.
Around my temples.	*En las sienes.*	Ehn las SYEH-nehs.
DOCTOR	***DOCTOR***	
Are there any signs before the headache starts?	*¿Hay alguna señal antes de que empiece el dolor?*	¿Ay ahl-GOO-nah seh-NYAHL AHN-tehs deh keh ehm-PYEH-seh ehl doh-LOHR?
PATIENT	***PACIENTE***	
My head feels hot.	*Siento la cabeza caliente.*	SYEHN-toh lah kah-BEH-sah kah-LEE-EHN-teh.
I see lights.	*Veo luces.*	VEH-oh LOO-sehs.
Light bothers me a lot.	*Me molesta mucho la luz.*	Meh moh-LEHS-tah MOO-choh lah loos.

DOCTOR	*DOCTOR*	
How often do you have headaches?	*¿Cada cuánto le dan los dolores?*	¿KAH-dah KWAHN-toh leh dahn lohs ehl doh-LOHR-ehs?
PATIENT	*PACIENTE*	
Every day.	*Todos los días.*	TOH-dohs lohs DEE-ahs.
Almost everyday.	*Casi a diario.*	KAH-see ah DYAH-ryoh.
Once a week/month.	*Una vez por semana/mes.*	OO-nah vehs pohr seh-MAH-nah/mehs.
Once in a while.	*De vez en cuando.*	Deh vehs ehn KWAHN-doh.
DOCTOR	*DOCTOR*	
How long do the headaches last?	*¿Cuánto tiempo le duran los dolores?*	¿KWAHN-toh TYEHM-poh leh DOO-rahn lohs doh-LOHR-ehs?
PATIENT	*PACIENTE*	
They last...	*Me dura...*	Meh DOO-rah...
• a while.	• *un rato.*	• oon RAH-toh.
• several hours.	• *varias horas.*	• VAH-rhyahs OH-rahs.
• one day.	• *un día.*	• oon DEE-ah.
• several days.	• *varios días.*	• VAH-ryohs DEE-ahs.
That depends.	*Eso depende.*	EH-soh deh-PEHN-deh.
DOCTOR	*DOCTOR*	
What do you do to stop them?	*¿Qué hace para que se le quite el dolor?*	¿Keh AH-seh PAH-rah keh seh leh KEE-teh ehl doh-LOHR?
PATIENT	*PACIENTE*	
They go away by themselves.	*Se me quita solo.*	Seh meh KEE-tah SOH-loh.
I take aspirin/tylenol.	*Tomo aspirina/tylenol.*	TOH-moh ahs-pee-RHEE-nah/tee-leh-NOHL.

I lie down and try to sleep.	*Me acuesto y trato de dormir.*	Meh ah-KWEHS-toh ee TRAH-toh deh dohr-MEER.
I use oxygen.	*Uso oxígeno.*	OO-soh oh-HEE-heh-noh.
DOCTOR	*DOCTOR*	
At this moment, do you feel as if things were going round and round?	*¿Siente en este momento que las cosas dan vueltas?*	¿SYEHN-teh ehn EHS-teh moh-MEHN-toh keh lahs KOH-sahs dahn VWEHL-tahs?
Do you feel as if you were going to faint?	*¿Siente como que se vaya a desmayar?*	¿SYEHN-teh KOH-moh keh seh vah-yah ah dehs-mah-YAHR?
Have you ever fainted?	*¿Se ha desmayado alguna vez?*	Seh ah dehs-mah-YAH-doh ahl-GOO-nah vehs?
DOCTOR	*DOCTOR*	
Why did you faint?	*¿Por qué se desmayó?*	¿Pohr keh seh dehs-mah-YOH?
PATIENT	*PACIENTE*	
I was…	*Me sentía…*	Meh sehn-TEE-ah…
• very hungry.	• *con mucha hambre.*	• kohn MOO-chah AHM-breh.
• very weak.	• *muy débil.*	• MOO-ee DEH-beel.
• very nervous.	• *muy nerviosa(o).*	• MOO-ee nehr-VYOH-sah(soh).
DOCTOR	*DOCTOR*	
How long did you remain unconscious?	*¿Cuánto tiempo estuvo inconsciente?*	¿KWAHN-toh TYEHM-poh ehs-TOO-voh een-kohn-SYEHN-teh?
When you fainted did you…	*Al desmayarse,…*	Ahl dehs-mah-YAHR-seh,…
• fall to the ground?	• *¿se cayó al suelo?*	• ¿seh kah-YOH ahl SWEH-loh?
• hurt yourself?	• *¿se hirió de alguna manera?*	• ¿seh ee-RYOH deh ahl-GOO-nah mah-NEH-rah?

C. THE EYES

GRAMMAR NOTE ••••

DEMONSTRATIVE PRONOUNS AND ADJECTIVES

The demonstrative adjectives and pronouns point out people and things. Demonstrative adjectives accompany a noun, demonstrative pronouns stand by themselves. The pronouns show an accent mark when they are not followed by a noun. *Este/esta/estos/estas* refer to people or things that are near the speaker. *Ese/esa/esos/esas* refer to people or things that are near the listener and away from the speaker.

Aquel/aquella/aquellos/aquellas are further away from the speaker and the listener.

	M.	F.
this	*este*	*esta*
that	*ese*	*esa*
that over there	*aquel*	*aquella*
	M.PL.	F.PL.
these	*estos*	*estas*
those	*esos*	*esas*
those over there	*aquellos*	*aquellas*

This man over there is a patient.	*Aquel hombre es un paciente.*
Who is this?	*¿Quién es éste?*
This man is sick.	*Este señor está enfermo.*

DOCTOR	*DOCTOR*	
Do you wear eyeglasses?	*¿Usa anteojos?*	¿OO-sah ahn-teh-OH-hohs?
When?	*¿Cuándo?*	¿KWAHN-doh?

PATIENT	***PACIENTE***	
I have 20/20 vision.	*Tengo visión 20/20.*	¿TEHN-goh vee-SYOHN veh-EEN-teh/veh-EEN-teh.
I am nearsighted/ farsighted.	*Soy miope/ hipermétrope.*	Soy MYOH-peh/ee-pehr-MEH-troh-peh.
I have to wear my glasses…	*Tengo que usar anteojos…*	TEHN-goh keh oo-SAHR ahn-teh-OH-hohs…
• all the time.	• *todo el tiempo.*	• TOH-doh ehl TYEHM-poh.
• when I read.	• *cuando leo.*	• KWAHN-doh LEH-oh.
• to see things…	• *para ver…*	• PAH-rah vehr…
• nearby.	• *de cerca.*	• deh SEHR-kah.
• far away.	• *de lejos.*	• deh LEH-hohs.
DOCTOR	***DOCTOR***	
Who prescribed your glasses?	*¿Quién le recetó sus anteojos?*	¿Kyehn leh reh-seh-TOH soos ahn-teh-OH-hohs?
PATIENT	***PACIENTE***	
A doctor.	*Un(a) doctor(a).*	Oon (OO-nah) dohk-TOHR(TOH-rah).
An optometrist.	*Un optometrista.*	Oon ohp-toh-meh-TREES-tah.
I bought them at a store.	*Los compré en una tienda.*	Lohs kohm-PREH ehn OO-nah TYEHN-dah.
DOCTOR	***DOCTOR***	
Do you have any problems with your eyes?	*¿Tiene algún problema con los ojos?*	¿TYEH-neh ahl-GOON proh-BLEH-mah kohn lohs OH-hohs?
What is not okay?	*¿Qué es lo que no está bien?*	¿KEH ehs loh keh noh ehs-TAH byehn?
PATIENT	***PACIENTE***	
My eyes…	*Tengo los ojos…*	TEHN-goh lohs OH-hohs…

• are irritated.	• *irritados.*	• ee-rree-TAH-dohs.
• are swollen.	• *hinchados.*	• een-CHAH-dohs.
• are red all the time.	• *rojos todo el tiempo.*	• ROH-hohs TOH-doh ehl TYEHM-poh.
My eyes feel as if they were full of sand.	*Los ojos están como si estuvieran llenos de arena.*	Lohs OH-hohs ehs-tahn KOH-moh see ehs-too-VYEH-rahn YEH-nohs deh ah-REH-nah.
My eyes burn all the time.	*Los ojos me arden todo el tiempo.*	Lohs OH-hohs meh AHR-dehn TOH-doh ehl TYEHM-poh.
I don't see well.	*No veo bien.*	Noh VEH-oh byehn.
DOCTOR	*DOCTOR*	
When was the last time your eyes were examined?	*¿Cuándo fue la última vez que le examinaron los ojos?*	¿KWAHN-doh fweh lah OOL-tee-mah vehs keh leh ehks-ah-mee-NAH-rohn lohs OH-hohs?
PATIENT	*PACIENTE*	
I don't remember.	*No me acuerdo.*	Noh meh ah-KWEHR-doh.
A long time ago.	*Hace mucho tiempo.*	AH-seh MOO-choh TYEHM-poh.
_____ months ago.	*Hace _____ meses.*	AH-seh _____ MEH-sehs.
DOCTOR	*DOCTOR*	
Has your eyesight gotten worse lately?	*¿Ha estado empeorando su vista últimamente?*	¿Ah ehs-TAH-doh ehm-peh-oh-RAHN-doh soo VEES-tah OOL-tee-mah-mehn-teh?
Do you see…	*¿Ve usted las cosas…*	¿Veh oos-TEHD lahs KOH-sahs…
• things blurred?	• *borrosas?*	• boh-RROH-sahs?
• double?	• *como si fueran dobles?*	• KOH-moh see FWEH-rahn DOH-blehs?

Since when?	*¿Desde cuándo?*	¿DEHS-deh KWAHN-doh?
PATIENT	***PACIENTE***	
• A little while…	*Hace…*	AH-seh…
• A month…	*• poquito.*	• poh-KEE-toh.
• Several weeks…	*• un mes.*	• oon mehs.
…ago.	*• varias semanas.*	• VAH-ryahs seh-MAH-nahs.
DOCTOR	***DOCTOR***	
Do your eyes get…	*¿Se le ponen los ojos…*	¿Seh leh POH-nehn lohs OH-hohs…
• red?	*• rojos?*	• ROH-hohs?
• irritated?	*• irritados?*	• ee-ree-TAH-dohs?
When?	*¿Cuándo?*	¿KWAHN-doh?
PATIENT	***PACIENTE***	
When…	*¿Cuándo…*	¿KWAHN-doh…
• I stay in the sun.	*• tomo sol.*	• TOH-moh sohl.
• I go to the swimming pool.	*• voy a la alberca.*	• VOH-ee ah lah ahl-BEHR-kah.
• the weather changes.	*• cambia el tiempo.*	• KAHM-byah ehl TYEHM-poh.
DOCTOR	***DOCTOR***	
Do your eyes secrete anything?	*¿Le sale algo de los ojos?*	¿Leh SAH-leh AHL-goh deh lohs OH-hohs?
Do you…	*¿Usted…*	¿Oos-TEHD…
• have dry eyes?	*• tiene los ojos secos?*	• TYEH-neh lohs OH-hohs SEH-kohs?
• see bright lights?	*• ve luces brillantes?*	• veh LOO-sehs bree-YAHN-tehs?
• see lightning?	*• ve luces como relámpagos?*	• veh LOO-sehs KOH-moh reh-LAHM-pah-gohs?

• see a halo around objects?	• *ve una aureola alrededor de los objetos?*	• veh OO-nah ah-oo-reh-OH-lah ahl-reh-deh-DOHR deh lohs ohb-HEH-tohs?
Since when?	*¿Desde cuándo?*	¿DEHS-deh KWAHN-doh?

GRAMMAR NOTE ••••

THE VERB *HACER* (TO DO/TO MAKE) WITH EXPRESSIONS OF TIME The structure *hace* + period of time + *que* + verb in the preterite is equivalent to the simple English "ago" + past tense, and it indicates that an event happened some time ago.

The accident happened one hour ago.	*Hace una hora que ocurrió el accidente.*

If the word order is reversed, *que* is dropped.

The accident happened one hour ago.	*El accidente ocurrió hace una hora.*

The structure *hace* + period of time + *que* + the verb in the present is equivalent to the English "since" + present perfect continuous, and it indicates how long an action has been going on.

It has been a week since I haven't had a home.	*Hace una semana que no tengo casa.*

D. THE EARS

GRAMMAR NOTE ••••

VERBS WITH IRREGULAR *YO* FORMS The following verbs are irregular in the first person singular only: *poner* (to put), *salir* (to leave), *traer* (to bring), *caer* (to fall), *hacer* (to do), *venir* (to come), *oír* (to hear), *decir* (to say). Please note that the other forms of the verb are regular.

I put	*pongo*	we put	*ponemos*
I leave	*salgo*	we leave	*salimos*
I bring	*traigo*	we bring	*traemos*
I fall	*caigo*	we fall	*caemos*
I do	*hago*	we do	*hacemos*
I come	*vengo*	we come	*venimos*
I hear	*oigo*	we hear	*oímos*
I say	*digo*	we say	*decimos*

DOCTOR	***DOCTOR***	
Do you have any problem with your ears?	*¿Tiene algún problema en los oídos?*	¿TYEH-neh ahl-GOON proh-BLEH-mah ehn lohs oh-EE-dohs?
What problem?	*¿Qué problema?*	¿KEH proh-BLEH-mah?
Since when?	*¿Desde cuándo?*	¿DEHS-deh KWAHN-doh?
PATIENT	***PACIENTE***	
They hurt.	*Me duelen.*	Meh DWEH-lehn.
I don't hear well.	*No oigo bien.*	Noh OY-goh byehn.
Something comes out.	*Me sale algo.*	Meh SAH-leh AHL-goh.
I hear buzzing.	*Tengo un zumbido.*	TEHN-goh oon soom-BEE-doh.

DOCTOR	*DOCTOR*	
Do you hear well?	*¿Puede oír bien?*	¿PWEH-deh oh-EER byehn?
Do you hear worse with one ear?	*¿Oye peor con un oído?*	¿OH-yeh peh-OHR kohn oon oh-EE-doh?
PATIENT	*PACIENTE*	
I hear…	*Oigo…*	OY-goh…
• worse with the right/left ear.	• *peor con el derecho/izquierdo.*	• peh-OHR kohn ehl deh-REH-choh/ees-KYEHR-doh.
• better with the right/left ear.	• *mejor con el derecho/izquierdo.*	• meh-HOHR kohn ehl deh-REH-choh/is-KYEHR-doh.
• equally badly with both.	• *igual de mal con los dos.*	• ee-GWAHL deh mahl kohn lohs dohs.
DOCTOR	*DOCTOR*	
Do you have an earache?	*¿Tiene dolor de oídos?*	¿TYEH-neh doh-LOHR deh oh-EE-dohs?
In which ear?	*¿En qué oído?*	¿Ehn keh oh-EE-doh?
PATIENT	*PACIENTE*	
In the right/left ear.	*En el oído derecho/izquierdo.*	Ehn ehl oh-EE-doh deh-REH-choh/ees-KYEHR-doh.
In both ears.	*En los dos oídos.*	Ehn lohs dohs oh-EE-dohs.
DOCTOR	*DOCTOR*	
Do your ears secrete anything?	*¿Le sale algo de los oídos?*	¿Leh SAH-leh AHL-goh deh lohs oh-EE-dohs?
What?	*¿Qué?*	¿Keh?
From which ear?	*¿De qué oído?*	¿Deh keh oh-EE-doh?
PATIENT	*PACIENTE*	
A clear liquid.	*Un líquido cristalino.*	Oon LEE-kee-doh Krees-tah-LEE-noh.
Pus.	*Pus.*	Poos.
Wax.	*Cera.*	Seh-RAH.

DOCTOR	*DOCTOR*	
Do your ears itch?	*¿Tiene comezón en los oídos?*	¿TYEH-neh koh-meh-SOHN ehn lohs oh-EE-dohs?
Do your ears buzz or tingle?	*¿Le zumban los oídos o hacen ruidos como campanitas?*	¿Leh SOOM-bahn lohs oh-EE-dohs oh ah-SEHN RWEE-dohs KOH-moh kahm-pah-NEE-tahs?
Which one?	*¿En cuál?*	¿Ehn KWAHL?

E. THE NOSE

DOCTOR	*DOCTOR*	
Do you have any problems with your nose?	*¿Tiene algún problema en la nariz?*	¿TYEH-neh ahl-GOON proh-BLEH-mah ehn lah nah-REES?
What is wrong?	*¿Qué problema?*	¿Keh proh-BLEH-mah?
PATIENT	***PACIENTE***	
It itches.	*Tengo mucha comezón.*	TEHN-goh MOO-chah koh-meh-SOHN.
It burns a lot.	*Me arde mucho.*	Meh AHR-deh MOO-choh.
It bleeds.	*Me sangra.*	Meh SAHN-grah.
It is stopped up.	*La siento tapada.*	Lah SYEHN-toh tah-PAH-dah.
DOCTOR	***DOCTOR***	
Does your nose secrete anything?	*¿Le sale algo de la nariz?*	¿Leh SAH-leh AHL-goh deh lah nah-REES?
What?	*¿Qué?*	¿Keh?
PATIENT	***PACIENTE***	
Mucus.	*Moco.*	MOH-koh.
A clear liquid.	*Un líquido cristalino.*	Oon LEE-kee-doh krees-tah-LEE-noh.
Blood.	*Sangre.*	SAHN-greh.

Pus.	*Pus.*	Poos.
DOCTOR	***DOCTOR***	
Does your nose bleed?	*¿Le sangra la nariz?*	¿Leh SAHN-grah lah nah-REES?
How often?	*¿Cada cuánto?*	¿KAH-dah KWAHN-toh?
PATIENT	***PACIENTE***	
Every day.	*Todos los días.*	TOH-dohs lohs DEE-ahs.
Several times a day.	*Varias veces al día.*	VAH-ryahs VEH-sehs ahl DEE-ah.
Once a week.	*Una vez por semana.*	OO-nah vehs pohr seh-MAH-nah.
Once in a while.	*De vez en cuando.*	Deh vehs ehn KWAHN-doh.
DOCTOR	***DOCTOR***	
Why does it bleed?	*¿Por qué le sangra?*	¿Pohr keh leh sahn-GRAH?
PATIENT	***PACIENTE***	
I don't know.	*No sé.*	Noh SEH.
Because…	*Porque…*	POHR-keh…
• I hit myself.	• *me di un golpe.*	• meh dee oon GOHL-peh.
• it is very dry.	• *la tengo muy seca.*	• lah TEHN-goh moo-ee SEH-kah.
• I blow my nose.	• *me la sueno.*	• meh lah SWEH-noh.
For no reason at all.	*Sin ninguna razón.*	Seen neen-GOO-nah rah-SOHN.
DOCTOR	***DOCTOR***	
Can you smell things?	*¿Puede oler las cosas?*	¿PWEH-deh oh-LEHR lahs KOH-sahs?
When did you stop smelling things?	*¿Desde cuándo dejó de oler las cosas?*	¿DEHS-deh KWAHN-doh deh-HOH deh oh-LEHR lahs KOH-sahs?

F. THE MOUTH AND THROAT

GRAMMAR NOTE ••••

COMMANDS WITH PRONOUNS When the verb indicates that the action is performed by oneself or directed to somebody else, a pronoun is attached to the command form in the affirmative. If the command is negative, the pronoun is placed before the verb.

to take something off	*quitar*
to look at	*mirar*
Take your clothes off!	*¡Quítese la ropa!*
Don't take your clothes off!	*¡No se quite la ropa!*
Look at me!	*¡Míreme!*
Don't look at me!	*¡No me mire!*

DOCTOR	***DOCTOR***	
Do you have a problem with your mouth?	*¿Tiene algún problema en la boca?*	¿TYEHN-eh ahl-GOON proh-BLEH-mah ehn lah BOH-kah?
PATIENT	***PACIENTE***	
• My tongue…	• *La lengua…*	• Lah LEHN-gwah…
• The inside of my mouth…	• *El interior de la boca…*	• Ehl in-teh-ree-OHR deh lah BOH-kah…
…burns.	*…me arde.*	…meh AHR-deh.
I have…	*Tengo…*	TEHN-goh…
• a bad taste.	• *mal sabor.*	• mahl sah-BOHR.
• bad breath.	• *mal olor.*	• mahl oh-LOHR.
DOCTOR	***DOCTOR***	
Do you have any problems with your teeth?	*¿Tiene alguna molestia en los dientes o muelas?*	¿TYEH-neh ahl-GOO-nah moh-LEHS-tee-ah ehn lohs DYEHN-tehs oh MWEH-lahs?

PATIENT	*PACIENTE*	
They hurt.	*Me duelen.*	Meh DWEH-lehn.
They are falling out.	*Se me están cayendo.*	Seh meh ehs-TAHN kah-YEHN-doh.
I have cavities.	*Tengo unos picados cariados.*	TEHN-goh OO-nohs pee-KAH-dohs kah-ree-AH-dohs.
DOCTOR	***DOCTOR***	
Do you have any cavities?	*¿Tiene alguna picadura?*	¿TYEH-neh ahl-GOO-nah pee-kah-DOO-rah?
Can you…	*¿Puede…*	¿PWEH-deh…
• chew your food?	• *masticar bien sus alimentos?*	• mahs-tee-KAHR byehn soos ah-lee-MEHN-tohs?
• taste the food you chew?	• *saborear los alimentos?*	• sah-bohr-eh-AHR ah lohs ah-lee-MEHN-tohs?
• swallow without difficulty?	• *tragar sin dificultad?*	• trah-GAHR seen dee-fee-kool-TAHD?
PATIENT	***PACIENTE***	
It hurts when I swallow.	*Me duele al tragar.*	Meh DWEH-leh ahl trah-GAHR.
I feel…	*Siento como que…*	SYEHN-toh KOH-moh keh…
• as if I could not pass the food.	• *no me pasa la comida.*	• noh meh PAH-sah lah koh-MEE-dah.
• as if the food comes back.	• *se me regresa la comida.*	• seh meh reh-GREH-sah lah koh-MEE-dah.
DOCTOR	***DOCTOR***	
Do you wear bridges or dentures?	*¿Usa usted puentes o dentaduras postizas?*	¿OO-sah oos-TEHD PWEHN-tehs oh dehn-tah-DOO-rahs pohs-TEE-sahs?
Do you feel comfortable with them?	*¿Está usted a gusto con ellos?*	¿Ehs-TAH oos-TEHD ah-GOOS-toh kohn EH-yohs?

Why not?	*¿Por qué no?*	¿Pohr keh noh?
PATIENT	***PACIENTE***	
Because…	*Porque…*	POHR-keh…
• they are loose.	• *me quedan flojas.*	• meh KEH-dahn FLOH-hahs.
• they are very tight.	• *me aprietan.*	• meh ah-PRYEH-tahn.
• they hurt when I bite.	• *me duelen al morder.*	• meh DWEH-lehn ahl mohr-DEHR.
DOCTOR	**DOCTOR**	
Do you have any ulcers in your mouth?	*¿Tiene alguna úlcera en la boca?*	¿TYEH-neh ahl-GOO-nah OOL-seh-rah ehn lah BOH-kah?
Show me.	*Enséñemela.*	Ehn-seh-NYEH-meh-lah.
Does your tongue bother you?	*¿Le molesta la lengua?*	¿Leh moh-LEHS-tah lah LEHN-gwah?
How?	*¿Cómo?*	¿KOH-moh?
PATIENT	***PACIENTE***	
It…		
• is swollen.	• *Está hinchada.*	• Ehs-TAH een-CHAH-dah.
• itches.	• *Me da comezón.*	• meh dah koh-meh-SOHN.
• it burns.	• *Me arde.*	• meh AHR-deh.
DOCTOR	**DOCTOR**	
Have you observed a change in your voice?	*¿Ha notado algún cambio en su voz?*	¿Ah noh-TAH-doh ahl-GOON KAHM-byoh ehn soo vohs?
What kind of change?	*¿Qué clase de cambio?*	¿Keh KLAH-seh deh KAHM-byoh?
PATIENT	***PACIENTE***	
• My voice is…	• *Mi voz está…*	• Mee vohs ehs-TAH…
• I am…	• *Estoy…*	• Ehs-TOY…
…hoarse.	*…ronca.*	…ROHN-kah.

I can't speak as loud as I used to.	*No puedo hablar tan fuerte como acostumbro.*	Noh PWEH-doh ah-BLAHR tahn FWEHR-teh KOH-moh ah-kohs-TOOM-broh.
It hurts to speak.	*Me duele al hablar.*	Meh DWEH-leh ahl ah-BLAHR.

G. THE NECK

DOCTOR	*DOCTOR*	
Do you have a problem in your neck?	*¿Tiene algún problema en el cuello?*	¿TYEH-neh ahl-GOON proh-BLEH-mah ehn ehl KWEH-yoh?
What problem?	*¿Qué problema?*	¿Keh proh-BLEH-mah?

PATIENT	*PACIENTE*	
It…		
• is stiff.	• *Lo siento tieso.*	• Loh SYEHN-toh TYEH-soh.
• hurts when I turn.	• *Me duele al voltear.*	• Meh DWEH-leh ahl vohl-teh-AHR.
• is swollen.	• *Está hinchado.*	• Ehs-TAH een-CHAH-doh.

H. THE LYMPH NODES

DOCTOR	*DOCTOR*	
Have you felt any swollen nodules or glands?	*¿Se ha palpado algún nódulo o glándula hinchada?*	¿Seh ah pahl-PAH-doh ahl-GOON NOH-doo-loh oh GLAHN-doo-lah een-CHAH-dah?
Where?	*¿Dónde?*	¿DOHN-deh?

PATIENT	*PACIENTE*	
In my/under my…	*En…*	Ehn…
• neck.	• *el cuello.*	• ehl KWEH-yoh.
• armpit.	• *el sobaco.*	• ehl soh-BAH-koh.

• groin.	• *la ingle.*	• lah EEN-gleh.
• breasts.	• *los senos.*	• lohs SEH-nohs.
DOCTOR	**DOCTOR**	
Have you had an infection nearby?	*¿Ha tenido alguna infección ahí cerca?*	¿Ah teh-NEE-doh ahl-GOO-nah in-fehk-SYOHN ah-EE SEHR-kah?
Does it hurt when you touch it?	*¿Le duele cuando se lo toca?*	¿Leh DWEH-leh KWAHN-doh seh loh TOH-kah?

GRAMMAR NOTE ••••

DOUBLE OBJECT PRONOUNS When the direct object pronouns *lo, la, los, las* (him, her, you, it, them) appear in the sentence with the indirect object pronouns *le, les* (to him, to her, to them, to you), *le* or *les* becomes *se:*

I told it to my mother. *Se lo dije a mi madre.*

I. THE BREASTS

DOCTOR	**DOCTOR**	
Do you have any problems with your breasts?	*¿Tiene algún problema en los senos?*	¿TYEH-neh ahl-GOON proh-BLEH-mah ehn lohs SEH-nohs?
What's wrong?	*¿Qué tiene?*	¿Keh TYEH-neh?
PATIENT	**PACIENTE**	
They…	*Se sienten…*	Seh SYEHN-tehn…
• feel tight.	• *apretados.*	• ah-preh-TAH-dohs.
• feel swollen.	• *hinchados.*	• een-CHAH-dohs.
• hurt.	• *doloridos.*	• doh-loh-REE-dohs.

I have a lump.	*Tengo una bolita.*	TEHN-goh OO-nah boh-LEE-tah.
I secrete...	*Me sale...*	Meh SAH-leh...
• milk.	• *leche.*	• LEH-cheh.
• something from the nipple.	• *algo del pezón.*	• AHL-goh dehl peh-SOHN.
DOCTOR	***DOCTOR***	
Do you examine your breasts regularly?	*¿Se examina los senos con frequencia?*	¿Seh ehks-ah-MEE-nah lohs SEH-nohs kohn freh-KWEHN-syah?
How often do you examine your breasts?	*¿Cada cuánto se examina los senos?*	¿KAH-dah KWAHN-toh seh ehks-ah-MEE-nah lohs SEH-nohs?
PATIENT	***PACIENTE***	
Every day.	*Todos los días.*	TOH-dohs lohs DEE-ahs.
Each time I take a bath.	*Cada vez que me baño.*	KAH-dah vehs keh meh bah-NYOH.
Once a month.	*Una vez al mes.*	OO-nah vehs ahl mehs.
DOCTOR	***DOCTOR***	
When was the last time you examined your breasts?	*¿Cuándo fue la ultima vez que se examinó los senos.*	¿KWAHN-doh foo-EH lah OOL-tee-mah vehs keh seh ehks-ah-mee-NOH lohs SEH-nohs?
PATIENT	***PACIENTE***	
Today.	*Hoy.*	Oh-ee.
Yesterday.	*Ayer.*	Ah-YEHR.
A few days ago.	*Hace unos días.*	AH-seh OO-nohs DEE-ahs.
Last week.	*La semana pasada.*	Lah seh-MAH-nah pah-SAH-dah.
Last month.	*El mes pasado.*	Ehl mehs pah-SAH-doh.
DOCTOR	***DOCTOR***	
Did you notice anything abnormal?	*¿Notó algo anormal?*	¿Noh-TOH AHL-goh ah-nohr-MAHL?

PATIENT	***PACIENTE***	
Nothing.	*Nada.*	NAH-dah.
Yes, a lump.	*Sí, una bolita.*	See, OO-nah boh-LEE-tah.
Yes, that it hurts when I touch them.	*Sí, que me duelen al tocarme.*	See, keh meh DWEHL-eh ahl toh-KAHR-meh.
DOCTOR	***DOCTOR***	
Do you feel any pain in your breasts?	*¿Siente algún dolor en los senos?*	¿SYEHN-teh ahl-GOON doh-LOHR ehn los SEH-nohs?
Since when?	*¿Desde cuándo?*	¿DEHS-deh KWAHN-doh?
Show me where you felt the lump.	*Muestreme donde sintió la bolita.*	MWEHS-treh-meh DOHN-deh SEEN-tyoh lah boh-LEE-tah.
Does anything come out of your nipples?	*¿Le sale algo por el pezón?*	¿Leh SAH-leh AHL-goh pohr ehl peh-SOHN?
PATIENT	***PACIENTE***	
Milk.	*Leche.*	LEH-cheh.
Pus.	*Pus.*	Poos.
Blood.	*Sangre.*	SAHN-greh.
DOCTOR	***DOCTOR***	
It would be a good idea for you to examine your breasts twice a month.	*Será bueno que se examine los senos dos veces al mes.*	Seh-RAH BWEH-noh keh seh ehks-AH-mee-neh lohs SEH-nohs dohs VEH-sehs ahl mehs.
Would you like to learn how to do it?	*Le gustaría aprender como hacerlo?*	Leh goos-tah-REE-ah ah-prehn-DEHR KOH-moh ah-SEHR-loh?

GRAMMAR NOTE ••••

STEM-CHANGING VERBS There are a few verbs in Spanish that don't follow the rules we established for the present tense. Some of them change the *e* in their stem to an *ie* in some forms:

TO WANT *QUERER*

quiero	*queremos*
quieres	*queréis*
quiere	*quieren*

Other verbs following this pattern are *pensar* (to think), *sentir* (to feel), *empezar* (to begin), *entender* (to understand), and *preferir* (to prefer).

Other verbs change their *o* to *ue:*

TO BE ABLE TO *PODER*

puedo	*podemos*
puedes	*podéis*
puede	*pueden*

Other verbs following these patterns are *encontrar* (to find), *morir* (to die), *volver* (to return), *jugar* (to play), and *dormir* (to sleep).

Pedir (to ask for) changes *e* to *i*

TO ASK FOR *PEDIR*

pido	*pedimos*
pides	*pedís*
pide	*piden*

DOCTOR	***DOCTOR***	
Do you have any complaints about your chest?	*¿Tiene algún problema en el pecho?*	¿TYEH-neh ahl-GOON proh-BLEH-mah ehn ehl PEH-choh?
What's wrong?	*¿Qué tiene?*	¿Keh TYEH-neh?
PATIENT	***PACIENTE***	
It hurts…	*Me duele…*	Meh DWEH-leh…
• constantly.	• *constantemente.*	• kohn-STAN-teh-MEHN-teh.
• when I breathe.	• *al respirar.*	• ahl rehs-pee-RAHR.
DOCTOR	***DOCTOR***	
Does your chest hurt when you breathe?	*¿Le duele el pecho al respirar?*	¿Leh DWEH-leh ehl PEH-choh ahl rehs-pee-RAHR?
Do you have difficulty breathing?	*¿Tiene alguna dificultad para respirar?*	¿TYEH-neh ahl-GOO-nah dee-fee-kool-TAHD PAH-rah rehs-pee-RAHR?
Do you run out of breath when…	*¿Se le acaba el aire cuando…*	¿Seh leh ah-KAH-bah ehl AY-reh KWAHN-doh…
• you walk normally?	• *camina normalmente?*	• kah-MEE-nah nohr-MAHL-mehn-teh?
• you climb stairs?	• *sube escaleras?*	• SOO-beh ehs-kah-LEH-rahs?
• you run?	• *corre?*	• KOH-rreh?
• you lie down without pillows?	• *se acuesta sin almohadas?*	• seh ah-KWEHS-tah seen ahl-MWAH-dahs?
How many pillows do you use to sleep?	*¿Cuántas almohadas usa para dormir?*	¿KWAHN-tahs ahl-MWAH-dahs OO-sah PAH-rah dohr-MEER?
Do you…	*¿Usted…*	¿Oos-TEHD…
• wake up having difficulty breathing?	• *se despierta con dificultad para respirar?*	• seh dehs-PYEHR-tah kohn dee-fee-kool-TAHD PAH-rah rehs-pee-RAHR?

• wheeze when you breathe?	• *hace algún ruido al respirar?*	• AH-seh ahl-GOON roo-EE-doh ahl rehs-pee-RAHR?
• have a cough?	• *tiene tos?*	• TYEH-neh tohs?
• cough up blood?	• *escupe con sangre?*	• ehs-KOO-peh kohn SAHN-greh?
How much?	*¿Cuánto?*	¿KWAHN-toh?
PATIENT	***PACIENTE***	
A little.	*Un poquito.*	Oon poh-KEE-toh.
A lot.	*Mucho.*	MOO-choh.
DOCTOR	***DOCTOR***	
Does your sputum have streaks of blood?	*¿Su espoto está rayado con sangre?*	¿Soo ehs-POO-toh ehs-TAH rah-YAH-doh kohn SAHN-greh?
What is the color of your sputum?	*¿De qué color es el esputo?*	¿Deh keh koh-LOHR ehs ehl ehs-POO-toh?
PATIENT	***PACIENTE***	
Red.	*Rojo.*	ROH-hoh.
Yellow/yellowish.	*Amarillo/amarillento.*	Ah-mah-REE-yoh/Ah-mah-ree-YEHN-toh.
Green/greenish.	*Verde/verdoso.*	VEHR-deh/vehr-DOH-soh.
It has streaks of blood.	*Está rayado con sangre.*	ehs-TAH rah-YAH-doh kohn SAHN-greh.
DOCTOR	***DOCTOR***	
What is the odor of your sputum?	*¿Qué olor tiene el esputo?*	¿Keh oh-LOHR TYEH-neh ehl ehs-POO-toh?
PATIENT	***PACIENTE***	
It does not smell.	*No huele a nada.*	Noh WEH-leh ah NAH-dah.
It smells foul.	*Huele feo.*	WEH-leh FEH-oh.
DOCTOR	***DOCTOR***	
How frequently does this happen?	*¿Con qué frecuencia le sucede esto?*	¿Kohn keh freh-KWEHN-syah leh soo-SEH-deh EHS-toh?

PATIENT	***PACIENTE***	
All day.	*Todo el día.*	TOH-doh ehl DEE-ah.
Once in a while.	*De vez en cuando.*	Deh vehs ehn KWAHN-doh.
Every time I cough.	*Cada vez que toso.*	KAH-dah vehs keh TOH-soh.
DOCTOR	***DOCTOR***	
Do you have a heart problem?	*¿Tiene algún problema en el corazón?*	¿TYEH-neh ahl-GOON proh-BLEH-mah ehn ehl koh-rah-SOHN?
PATIENT	***PACIENTE***	
It beats...	*Palpita...*	Pahl-PEE-tah...
• very fast.	• *muy rápido.*	• MOO-ee RAH-pee-doh.
• irregularly.	• *irregularmente.*	• ee-reh-goo-LAHR-mehn-teh.
DOCTOR	***DOCTOR***	
Do you feel...	*¿Siente...*	¿SYEHN-teh...
• that your heartbeat is too rapid/irregular?	• *que el corazón le late muy rápido/ irregularmente?*	• keh ehl koh-rah-SOHN leh LAH-teh MOO-ee-RAH-pee-doh/ee-reh-goo-LAHR-mehn-teh?
• a sensation of pressure over your chest?	• *una sensación de presión sobre el pecho?*	• OO-nah sehn-sah-SYOHN deh preh-SYOHN soh-breh ehl PEH-choh?
• as if someone were pressing against your chest?	• *como si alguien le estuviera apretando el pecho?*	• KOH-moh see AHL-gyehn leh ehs-too-VYEH-rah ah-preh-TAHN-doh ehl PEH-choh?
• as if someone were walking on your chest?	• *como si alguien le estuviera caminando en el pecho?*	• KOH-moh see AHL-gyehn leh ehs-too-VYEH-rah kah-mee-NAHN-doh ehn ehl PEH-choh?

• as if your chest were burning?	• *como si el pecho le estuviera ardiendo?*	• KOH-moh see ehl PEH-choh leh ehs-too-VYEH-rah ahr-DYEHN-doh?
Have you seen a doctor about these complaints?	*¿Ha visto al (a la) doctor(a) por estas molestias?*	¿Ah VEE-stoh ahl (ah lah) dohk-TOHR (TOH-rah) pohr EHS-tahs moh-LEHS-tyahs?
DOCTOR	***DOCTOR***	
What did the doctor say?	*¿Qué le dijo el (la) doctor(a)?*	¿Keh leh DEE-hoh ehl (lah) dohk-TOHR (TOH-rah)?
PATIENT	***PACIENTE***	
That I…	*Que…*	Keh…
• have heartburn.	• *tengo acidez.*	• TEHN-goh ah-see-DEHS.
• have a gastric hernia.	• *tengo hernia gástrica.*	• TEHN-goh EHR-nee-ah GAHS-tree-kah.
• have gastric reflux.	• *tengo reflujo gástrico.*	• TEHN-goh reh-FLOO-hoh GAHS-tree-koh.
• don't have enough blood.	• *me falta sangre.*	• meh FAHL-tah SAHN-greh.
DOCTOR	***DOCTOR***	
What treatment did she/he prescribe?	*¿Qué tratamiento le dió?*	¿Keh trah-tah-MYEHN-toh leh dee-OH?
PATIENT	***PACIENTE***	
Some medications.	*Unas medicinas.*	OO-nahs meh-dee-SEE-nahs.
A change in my diet.	*Que cambie la dieta.*	Keh KAHM-byeh lah DYEH-tah.
Exercise.	*Ejercicio.*	Eh-hehr-SEE-syoh.
I had an operation…	*Me operó…*	Meh oh-peh-ROH…
• on my heart.	• *del corazón.*	• dehl koh-rah-SOHN.
• on my stomach.	• *del estómago.*	• dehl ehs-TOH-mah-goh.

K. GASTROINTESTINAL

DOCTOR	*DOCTOR*	
Do you have any trouble digesting your food?	*¿Tiene alguna molestia para digerir las comidas?*	• TYEH-neh ahl-GOO-nah moh-LEHS-tee-ah PAH-rah dee-heh-REER lahs koh-MEE-dahs?
PATIENT	***PACIENTE***	
I burp too much.	*Erupto mucho.*	Eh-ROOP-toh MOO-choh.
I have...	*Tengo...*	TEHN-goh...
• heartburn.	• *acidez.*	• ah-see-DEHS.
• indigestion.	• *indigestión.*	• een-dee-hehs-TYOHN.
• gas.	• *gas.*	• gahs.
DOCTOR	***DOCTOR***	
Does your stomach ache?	*¿Le duele el estómago?*	¿Leh DWEH-leh ehl ehs-TOH-mah-goh?
When?	*¿Cuándo?*	¿KWAHN-doh?
PATIENT	***PACIENTE***	
Before/after meals.	*Antes de/después de las comidas.*	AHN-tehs deh/dehs-PWEHS lahs koh-MEE-dahs.
When I drink...	*Cuando tomo...*	KWAHN-doh TOH-moh...
• coffee.	• *café.*	• kah-FEH.
• alcohol.	• *alcohol.*	• ahl-koh-OHL.
• juice.	• *jugo.*	• HOO-goh.
DOCTOR	***DOCTOR***	
Do you...	*¿Usted...*	¿Oos-TEHD...
• feel bloated?	• *se siente hinchada(o)?*	• seh SYEHN-teh een-CHAH-dah(doh)?
• have indigestion?	• *siente indigestión?*	• SYEHN-teh een-dee-hehs-TYOHN?

• belch a lot?	• *erupta mucho?*	• eh-ROOP-tah MOO-choh?
• have heartburn.	• *tiene acidez.*	• TYEH-neh ah-see-DEHS?
• have acid regurgitations.	• *regurgitaciones ácidas?*	• reh-goor-hee-tah SYOH-nehs AH-see-dahs?
• feel nauseous?	• *se siente con náuseas?*	• seh SYEHN-teh kohn NAHW-seh-ahs?
• vomit?	• *vomita?*	• voh-MEE-tah?
What is the color of your vomit?	*¿De qué color es el vómito?*	¿Deh KEH koh-LOHR ehs ehl VOH-mee-toh?
When you vomit, is the food digested?	*¿Cuando vomita está la comida digerida?*	¿KWAHN-doh voh-MEE-tah ehs-TAH lah koh-MEE-dah dee-heh-REE-dah?
Do you vomit blood?	*¿Vomita con sangre?*	¿Voh-MEE-tah kohn SAHN-greh?
Is the blood red?	*¿La sangre es de color rojo?*	¿Lah SAHN-greh ehs deh koh-LOHR ROH-hoh?
Does your vomit look like coffee grounds?	*¿Parece asientos de café lo que vomita?*	¿Pah-REH-seh ah-SYEHN-tohs deh kah-FEH loh keh voh-MEE-tah?
Do you have diarrhea?	*¿Tiene diarrea?*	¿TYEH-neh dyah-RREH-ah?
Are you constipated?	*¿Está estreñido(a)?*	¿Ehs-TAH ehs-treh-NYEE-dah(doh)?
How many times a day do you go to the restroom?	*¿Cuántas veces al día va al baño?*	¿KWAHN-tahs VEH-sehs ahl DEE-ah vah ahl bah-NYOH?
Is your excrement…	*¿Su excremento es…*	¿Soo ehks-kreh-MEHN-toh ehs…
• soft/hard?	• *blando/duro?*	• BLAHN-doh/DOO-roh?
• thin/thick?	• *delgado/grueso?*	• dehl-GAH-doh/GROO-eh-soh?

• normal in color?	• *de color normal?*	• deh koh-LOHR nohr-MAHL?
• tarry?	• *como asfalto?*	• KOH-moh ahs-FAHL-toh?
Has your excrement changed lately?	*¿Ha cambiado últimamente su exremento?*	¿Ah kahm-BYAH-doh OOL-tee-mah-mehn-teh soo ehks-kreh-MEHN-toh?
How?	*¿Cómo?*	¿KOH-moh?
PATIENT	*PACIENTE*	
It has turned black/green in color.	*Se ha puesto de color negro/verde.*	Seh ah PWEHS-toh deh koh-LOHR NEH-groh/VEHR-deh.
It lost its color.	*Perdió el color.*	Pehr-DYOH ehl koh-LOHR.
It is stained with blood.	*Está manchado de sangre.*	Ehs-TAH mahn-CHAH-doh deh SAHN-greh.
DOCTOR	*DOCTOR*	
Do you suffer from hemorrhoids?	*¿Sufre usted de hemorroides?*	¿SOO-freh oos-TEHD deh heh-moh-RROY-dehs?
Do you have…	*¿Tiene…*	¿TYEH-neh…
• hemorrhoids?	• *hemorroides?*	• heh-moh-RROY-dehs?
• pain?	• *dolor?*	• doh-LOHR?
• gas?	• *gas?*	• gahs?
• itching?	• *comezón?*	• koh-meh-SOHN?
Do you bleed?	*¿Sangra?*	¿SAHN-grah?
Have your skin and the white of your eyes ever turned yellow?	*¿Alguna vez se le ha puesto la piel y lo blanco de los ojos de color amarillo?*	¿Ahl-GOO-nah vehs seh leh ah PWEHS-toh lah pyehl ee loh BLAHN-koh deh lohs OH-hohs deh koh-LOHR ah-mah-REE-oh?

L. URINARY

DOCTOR	*DOCTOR*	
Do you experience any difficulty urinating?	*¿Tiene alguna molestia al orinar?*	¿TYEH-neh ahl-GOO-nah moh-LEHS-tyah ahl oh-ree-NAHR?
PATIENT	***PACIENTE***	
I have lost strength.	*He perdido fuerza.*	Eh pehr-DEE-doh FWEHR-sah.
It burns.	*Me arde.*	Meh AHR-deh.
I urinate…	*Orino…*	Oh-REE-noh…
• a lot.	• *mucho.*	• MOO-choh.
• very often.	• *a cada rato.*	• ah KAH-dah RAH-toh.
• with blood.	• *con sangre.*	• kohn SAHN-greh.
DOCTOR	***DOCTOR***	
Do you…	*¿Tiene…*	¿TYEH-neh…
• experience pain/burning when you urinate?	• *dolor/ardor cuando orina?*	• doh-LOHR/ahr-DOHR KWAHN-doh oh-REE-nah?
• urinate more frequently than you used to?	• *que orinar más veces de lo que acostumbraba?*	• keh oh-ree-NAHR MAHS VEH-sehs deh loh keh ah-kohs-toom-BRAH-bah?
• urinate more in volume than you used to?	• *que orínar más volumen que lo que acostrumbraba?*	• keh oh-ree-NAHR MAHS voh-LOO-mehn keh loh keh ah-kohs-toom-BRAH-bah?
• get up at night to urinate?	• *que levantarse de noche a orinar?*	• keh leh-vahn-TAHR-seh deh NOH-cheh ah oh-ree-NAHR?
How often?	*¿Con qué frecuencia?*	¿Kohn KEH freh-KWEHN-syah?
Is there blood/pus in your urine?	*¿Tiene sangre/pus en la orina?*	¿TYEH-neh SAHN-greh/poos ehn soo oh-REE-nah?

Do you have difficulty…	*¿Tiene dificultad…*	¿TYEH-neh dee-fee-kool-TAHD…
• to begin urinating?	• *para empezar a orinar?*	• PAH-rah ehm-peh-SAHR ah oh-ree-NAHR?
• to finish urinating?	• *para terminar de orinar?*	• PAH-rah tehr-mee-NAHR deh oh-ree-NAHR?
Do you lose urine when you cough/sneeze?	*¿A usted le sale sola la orina cuando tose/estornuda?*	¿Ah oos-TEHD leh SAH-leh SOH-lah lah oh-REE-nah KWAHN-doh TOH-seh/ehs-tohr-NOO-dah?
Do you sometimes have an urgent need to urinate?	*¿Usted necesita a veces orinar urgentemente?*	¿Oos-TEHD neh-seh-SEE-tah ah VEHS-ehs ohr-EE-nahr oor-HEN-teh-mehn-teh?
Have you noticed any changes in the strength of the stream?	*¿Ha notado algún cambio en la fuerza del chorro de orina?*	¿Ah noh-TAH-doh ahl-GOON KAHM-byoh ehn lah FWEHR-sah dehl CHOH-rroh deh oh-REE-nah?
Do you feel that you emptied your bladder completely when you finish urinating?	*¿Siente que vació completamente la vejíga de orina al terminar?*	¿SYEHN-teh keh vah-SYOH kohm-PLEH-tah-mehn-teh lah veh-HEE-gah deh oh-REE-nah ahl tehr-mee-NAHR?

M. FEMALE GENITALIA

DOCTOR	*DOCTOR*	
Do you have any problems with your genitalia?	*¿Tiene algún problema con sus partes de mujer?*	¿TYEH-neh ahl-GOON proh-BLEH-mah kohn soos PAHR-tehs deh moo-HEHR?
PATIENT	***PACIENTE***	
	Tengo…	TEHN-goh…
I itch.	• *comezón.*	• koh-meh-SOHN.

I have a discharge.	• *descargas.*	• dehs-KAHR-gahs.
I bleed.	*Me sale sangre.*	Meh sah-leh SAHN-greh.
I missed my period.	*No me ha llegado la regla.*	Noh meh ah yeh-GAH-doh lah REH-glah.
I don't menstruate.	*No tengo la regla.*	Noh TEHN-goh lah REH-glah.
DOCTOR	***DOCTOR***	
Do you have…	*¿Tiene…*	¿TYEH-neh…
• any itching/ discharge?	• *comezón/descargas?*	• koh-meh-SOHN/ dehs-KAHR-gahs?
• an ulcer in your genitalia?	• *alguna úlcera en sus partes?*	• ahl-GOO-nah OOHL-seh-rah ehn soos PAHR-tehs?
• an infection in your feminine parts?	• *una infección en sus partes?*	• OO-nah een-fehk-SYOHN ehn soos PAHR-tehs?
At what age did you begin to menstruate?	*¿A qué edad tuvo su primer regla?*	¿Ah keh eh-DAHD too-VOH soo PREE-mehr REH-glah?
How many weeks/days are there between your menstruations?	*¿Cada cuántas semanas/días tiene la regla?*	¿KAH-dah KWAHN-tahs seh-MAH-nahs/DEE-ahs TYEH-neh lah REH-glah?
Do you always menstruate regularly?	*¿Siempre tiene la regla regularmente?*	¿SYEHM-preh TYEH-neh lah REH-glah reh-goo-LAHR-mehn-teh?
How long do you bleed?	*¿Cuántos días le dura la regla?*	¿KWAHN-tohs DEE-ahs leh DOO-rah lah REH-glah?
Do you…	*¿Usted…*	¿Oos-TEHD…
• feel bloated/colicky when you menstruate?	• *se siente hinchada con cólicos cuando tiene la regla?*	• seh SYEHN-teh een-CHAH-dah kohn KOH-lee-kohs KWAHN-doh TYEH-neh lah REH-glah?
• sometimes bleed between your menstruations?	• *sangra a veces entre sus reglas?*	• SAHN-grah ah VEH-sehs EHN-treh soos REH-glahs?

• have headaches before/during your menstruation?	• *le duele la cabeza antes de tener la regla/cuando tiene la regla?*	• leh DWEH-leh lah kah-BEH-sah AHN-tehs deh teh-NEHR lah reh-glah/ KWAHN-doh TYEH-neh lah REH-glah?
• have mood swings before/when you are menstruating?	• *tiene cambios en su estado de ánimo días antes de tener la regla/ cuando tiene la regla?*	• TYEH-neh KAHM-byohs deh soo ehs-TAH-doh deh AH-nee-moh DEE-ahs AHN-tehs deh teh-NEHR lah REH-glah/ KWAHN-doh TYEH-neh lah REH-glah.
• still menstruate?	• *todavía tiene la regla?*	• toh-dah-VEE-ah TYEH-neh lah REH-glah?
What is the date of your last menstruation?	*¿Cuándo fue su última regla?*	¿KWAHN-doh FWEH soo OOL-tee-mah REH-glah?
Have you had hot flashes?	*¿Ha sentido bochornos?*	¿Ah sehn-TEE-doh boh-CHOHR-nohs?
Do you have sexual relations?	*¿Tiene usted relaciones sexuales?*	¿TYEH-neh reh-lah-SYOHN-ehs sehk-SWAH-lehs?
Do you have relations…	*¿Tiene relaciones…*	¿TYEH-neh reh-lah-SYOHN-ehs…
• with men?	• *con hombres?*	• kohn OHM-brehs?
• with women?	• *con mujeres?*	• kohn moo-HEHR-ehs?
• with men and women?	• *con hombres y mujeres?*	• kohn OHM-brehs ee moo-HEHR-ehs?
Have you lost interest in sex?	*¿Ha perdido interés en las relaciones sexuales?*	¿Ah pehr-DEE-doh een-teh-REHS ehn lahs reh-lah-SYOH-nehs sehk-SWAHL-ehs?

Do you…	*¿Usted…*	¿Oos-TEHD…
• have difficulty achieving an orgasm?	• *tiene dificultad para venirse/terminar/ tener un orgasmo?*	• TYEH-neh dee-fee-kool-TAHD PAH-rah veh-NEER-seh tehr-mee-NAHR/teh-NEHR oon ohr-GAHS-moh?
• have pain during sex?	• *tiene dolor durante la relación sexual?*	• TYEH-neh doh doh-LOHR doo-RAHN-teh lah reh-lah-SYOHN sehk-SWAHL?
Do you protect yourself from infections?	*¿Se protege para no infectarse?*	¿Seh proh-TEH-heh PAH-rah noh een-fehk-TAHR-seh?
How?	*¿Cómo?*	¿KOH-moh?
PATIENT	***PACIENTE***	
We use a condom.	*Usamos condón.*	Oo-SAH-mohs kohn-DOHN.
I wash after intercourse.	*Me lavo después del acto.*	Meh LAH-voh dehs-PWEHS dehl AHK-toh.
I never complete the intercourse.	*Nunca completo el acto.*	NOON-kah kohm-PLEH-toh ehl AHK-toh.
DOCTOR	**DOCTOR**	
Are you satisfied with your sexual relations?	*¿Está satisfecha con sus relaciones sexuales?*	¿Ehs-TAH sah-tees-FEH-chah kohn soos reh-lah-SYOH-nehs sehks-SWAHL-ehs?
Why not?	*¿Por qué no?*	¿Pohr keh noh?
PATIENT	***PACIENTE***	
Because…	*Porque…*	POHR-keh…
• I almost never have them.	• *casi nunca tengo.*	• KAH-see NOON-kah TEHN-goh.
• because my spouse does not like to have them.	• *a mi esposo no le gusta tenerlas.*	• ah mee ehs-POH-soh noh leh GOOS-tah teh-NEHR-lahs.
• I get very nervous.	• *me pongo muy nerviosa.*	• meh POHN-goh moo-ee nehr-VYOH-sah.

My spouse does not do what I like.	*A mi esposo no le gusta hacer lo que me gusta.*	Ah mee-ehs-POH-soh noh leh GOOS-tah ah-SEHR loh keh meh GOOS-tah.
DOCTOR	***DOCTOR***	
Have you lost interest in having sex?	*¿Ha perdido interés en las relaciones sexuales?*	¿Ah pehr-DEE-doh een-teh-REHS ehn lahs reh-lah-SYOH-nehs sehk-SWAH-lehs?
Why?	*¿Por qué?*	¿Pohr keh?
PATIENT	***PACIENTE***	
Because…	*Porque…*	POHR-keh…
• I don't want to be infected.	• *no quiero infectarme.*	• noh KYEH-roh een-fehc-TAHR-meh.
• I am too old.	• *ya estoy muy vieja.*	• yah ehs-TOY MOO-ee VYEH-hah.
• I do not want the responsibility.	• *no quiero la responsabilidad.*	• noh KYEH-roh lah rehs-pohn-sah-bee-lee-DAHD.

N. MALE GENITALIA

DOCTOR	***DOCTOR***	
Do you have…	*¿Tiene…*	¿TYEH-neh…
• problems with your penis?	• *molestias en el miembro?*	• moh-LEHS-tyahs ehn ehl MYEHM-broh?
PATIENT	***PACIENTE***	
• It hurts…	• *Me duele…*	• Meh DWEH-leh…
• It burns…	• *Me arde…*	• Meh AHR-deh…
…during intercourse.	*…durante el acto sexual.*	…doo-RAHN-teh ehl AHK-toh sehk-SWAHL.
…when I urinate.	*…cuando orino.*	…KWAHN-doh oh-REE-noh.
I discharge pus.	*Me sale pus.*	Meh SAH-leh poos.
I have an ulcer.	*Tengo una úlcera.*	TEHN-goh OO-nah OOHL-seh-rah.

DOCTOR	*DOCTOR*	
Do you have/have you had…	*¿Tiene/ha tenido…*	¿TYEH-neh/ah teh-NEE-doh…
• ulcers in your penis?	• *úlceras en el miembro?*	• OOHL-seh-rahs ehn soo MYEHM-broh?
• a discharge from your penis?	• *algún supuración en el miembro?*	• ahl-GOON soo-poo-rah-SYOHN ehn ehl MYEHM-broh?
• pain or swollen testicles?	• *dolor o hinchazón en los testículos?*	• doh-LOHR oh een-chah-SOHN ehn lohs tehs-TEE-koo-lohs?
• a hernia in your testicles?	• *una hernia en los testículos?*	• OO-nah EHR-nyah ehn lohs tehs-TEE-koo-lohs?
• sexual relations with someone?	• *relaciones sexuales con alguien?*	• reh-lah-SYOH-nehs sehk-SWAH-lehs kohn AHL-gyehn?
• sexual relations with…	• *relaciones sexuales con…*	• reh-lah-SYOH-nehs sehk-SWAH-lehs kohn…
• women?	• *mujeres?*	• moo-HEHR-ehs?
• men?	• *hombres?*	• OHM-brehs?
• men and women?	• *hombres y mujeres?*	• OHM-brehs ee moo-HEHR-ehs?
Do you protect yourself from infections?	*¿Se protege para no infectarse?*	¿Seh proh-TEH-heh PAH-rah noh een-fehk-TAHR-seh?
How? *	*¿Cómo?*	¿KOH-moh?

O. MUSCULOSKELETAL

DOCTOR	*DOCTOR*	
Do you have any problems with your joints?	*¿Tiene algun molestia en las coyunturas?*	¿TYEH-neh ahl-GOON mohl-EHS-tyah ehn lahs koh-yoon-TOO-rahs?

* For further questions and answers, please refer to section C.8.M. on female genitalia.

Which ones?	*¿Cuáles?*	¿KWAH-lehs?
PATIENT	***PACIENTE***	
• My neck…	• *…el cuello.*	• …mee KWEH-yoh.
• My shoulder(s)…	• *…el (los) hombro(s).*	• …ehl (lohs) OHM-broh(s).
• My elbow(s)…	• *…el (los) codo(s).*	• …ehl (lohs) KOH-doh(s).
• My wrist(s)…	• *…la(s) muñecas.*	• …lah(s) moo-NYEH-kah(s).
• My hip(s)…	• *…la(s) cadera(s).*	• …lah(s) kah-DEH-rah(s).
• My knee(s)…	• *…la(s) rodilla(s).*	• …lah(s) roh-DEE-yah(s).
• My ankle(s)…	• *…el (los) tobillo(s).*	• …ehl (lohs) toh-BEE-yoh(s).
…hurt(s).	*Me duele(n)…*	Meh DWEH-leh(n)…
…swell(s).	*Se me hincha(n)…*	Seh meh EEN-cha(n)…
…is (are) stiff.	*Está(n) tiesa(s)…*	Ehs-TAH(N) TYEH-sah(s)…
DOCTOR	***DOCTOR***	
Do you…	*¿Usted…*	¿Oos-TEHD…
• have cramps/pain in your legs?	• *tiene calambres/dolores en las piernas?*	• TYEH-neh kah-LAHM-brehs/doh-LOH-rehs ehn lahs PYEHR-nahs?
• have these cramps/pain when…	• *tiene los dolores/calambres cuando…*	• TYEH-neh lohs doh-LOH-rehs/kah-LAHM-brehs KWAHN-doh…
• you walk?	• *camina?*	• kah-MEE-nah?
• you are resting?	• *descansa?*	• dehs-KAHN-sah?
Are the veins of your legs swollen?	*¿Tiene las venas de las piernas hinchadas?*	¿TYEH-neh lahs VEH-nahs deh lahs PYEHR-nahs een-CHAH-dahs?
Do your ankles swell?	*¿Se le hinchan los tobillos?*	¿Seh leh EEN-chan lohs toh-BEE-yohs?

Do your joints ache?	*¿Le duelen las coyunturas?*	¿Leh DWEH-lehn lahs koh-yoon-TOO-rahs?
Do your joints swell or redden?	*¿Se le hinchan o enrojecen las conyunturas?*	¿Seh leh EEN-chan oh ehn-roh-HEH-sehn lahs koh-yoon-TOO-rahs?
Do your joints get stiff?	*¿Se le ponen tiesas las conyunturas?*	¿Seh leh POH-nehn TYEH-sahs lahs koh-yoon-TOO-rahs?
Does your back hurt?	*¿Le duele la espalda?*	¿Leh DWEH-leh lah ehs-PAHL-dah?
When?	*¿Cuándo?*	¿KWAHN-doh?
PATIENT	***PACIENTE***	
When…	*Cuando…*	KWAHN-doh…
• I work.	• *trabajo.*	• trah-BAH-hoh.
• I bend over.	• *me agacho.*	• meh ah-GAH-choh.
• I carry something.	• *cargo algo.*	• KAHR-goh AHL-goh.
• I walk.	• *camino.*	• kah-MEE-noh.

P. ENDOCRINE

DOCTOR	***DOCTOR***	
Are you cold/warm when most other people are comfortable?	*¿Siente usted frío/calor cuando la mayoría de la gente está a gusto?*	¿Syehn-teh oos-TEHD FREE-oh/kah-lohr KWAHN-doh lah mah-yoh-REE-ah deh lah HEHN-teh ehs-TAH ah GOOS-toh?
Have you…	*¿Usted…*	¿Oos-TEHD…
• been drinking a lot of water lately?	• *ha estado tomando mucha agua últimamente?*	• ah ehs-TAH-doh toh-MAHN-doh MOO-chah AH-gwah OOL-tee-mah-mehn-teh?
• been eating a lot lately?	• *ha estado comiendo mucho últimamente?*	• ah ehs-TAH-doh koh-MYEHN-doh MOO-choh OOL-tee-mah-mehn-teh?

• lost weight rapidly?	• *ha bajado de peso muy rápido?*	• ah bah-HAH-doh deh PEH-soh moo-ee RAH-pee-doh?
Do you...	*¿Usted...*	¿Oos-TEHD...
• sweat a lot?	• *suda mucho?*	• SOO-dah MOO-choh?
• feel that your hands shake?	• *siente que le tiemblan las manos?*	• SYEHN-teh keh leh TYEHM-blahn lahs MAH-nohs?
Have your eyelids changed?	*¿Le han cambiado los párpados?*	¿Leh ahn kahm-BYAH-doh lohs PAHR-pah-dohs?
Has the color of your skin changed?	*¿Le ha cambiado el color de la piel?*	¿Leh ah kahm-BYAH-doh ehl koh-LOHR deh lah pyehl?
How?	*¿Cómo?*	¿KOH-moh?
PATIENT	***PACIENTE***	
My skin is...	*Mi piel está...*	Mee pyehl ehs-TAH...
• darker.	• *más oscura.*	• mahs ohs-KOO-rah.
• warmer/colder.	• *más caliente/fría.*	• MAHS kah-LYEHN-teh/FREE-ah.
• more humid/dry.	• *más húmeda/seca.*	• mahs OO-meh-dah/SEH-kah.
• stained.	• *manchada.*	• mahn-CHAH-dah.
DOCTOR	***DOCTOR***	
Has your body hair changed?	*¿Le ha cambiado el vello del cuerpo?*	¿Leh ah kahm-BYAH-doh ehl VEH-yoh dehl KWEHR-poh?
How?	*¿Cómo?*	¿KOH-moh?
PATIENT	***PACIENTE***	
The hair of my genitals is thinner/thicker.	*El vello de mis partes está más delgado/grueso.*	Ehl VEH-yoh deh mees PAHR-tehs ehs-TAH mahs dehl-GAH-doh/GROO-EH-soh.

Q. NERVOUS SYSTEM

DOCTOR	***DOCTOR***	
Do you feel a weakness in any part of your body?	*¿Siente debilidad en alguna parte del cuerpo?*	¿SYEHN-teh deh-bee-lee-DAHD ehn ahl-GOO-nah PAHR-teh dehl KWEHR-poh?
Where?	*¿Dónde?*	¿DOHN-deh?
PATIENT	***PACIENTE***	
In my…	*En el (la/los/las)…*	Ehn ehl/lah/lohs/ lahs…
• neck.	• *cuello.*	• KWEH-yoh.
• shoulder(s).	• *hombro(s).*	• OHM-broh(s).
• arm(s).	• *brazo(s).*	• BRAH-soh(s).
• hand(s).	• *mano(s).*	• MAH-noh(s).
• finger(s).	• *dedo(s).*	• DEH-doh(s).
• leg(s).	• *pierna(s).*	• PYEHR-nah(s).
• knee(s).	• *rodilla(s).*	• roh-DEE-yah(s).
• foot (feet).	• *pie(s).*	• pyeh(s).
• toe(s).	• *dedo(s) del pie.*	• DEH-doh(s) dehl pyeh.
DOCTOR	***DOCTOR***	
Do you have difficulty getting up from a chair?	*¿Tiene dificultad para levantarse de una silla?*	¿TYEH-neh dee-fee-kool-TAHD PAH-rah leh-vahn-TAHR-seh deh OO-nah SEE-yah?
Is there a part of your body that you cannot move?	*¿Hay alguna parte del cuerpo que no puede mover?*	¿Ah-ee ahl-GOO-nah PAHR-teh dehl KWEHR-poh keh noh PWEH-deh moh-VEHR?
What part?	*¿Qué parte?*	¿Keh PAHR-teh?
Is there a side of your face that pulls?	*¿Hay algún lado de la cara que siente que le jala?*	¿Ay ahl-GOON LAH-doh deh lah KAH-rah keh SYEHN-teh keh leh HAH-lah?
Which one?	*¿Cuál?*	¿Kwahl?

Is there a part of your body that you do not feel?	*¿Hay alguna parte del cuerpo que no siente?*	¿Ay ahl-GOO-nah PAHR-teh dehl KWEHR-poh keh noh SYEHN-teh?
Do you feel as if you were being pierced by needles?	*¿Siente como si le estuvieran clavando alfileres?*	¿SYEHN-teh KOH-moh see leh ehs-too-VYEH-rahn klah-VAHN-doh ahl-fee-LEHR-ehs?
Where?	*¿Dónde?*	¿DOHN-deh?
Do you feel…	*¿Siente…*	¿SYEHN-teh…
• as if your feet were burning?	• *que le queman los pies?*	• keh leh KEH-mahn lohs pyehs?
• sluggish with things that you used to do easily?	• *torpeza para hacer cosas que hacía fácilmente?*	• tohr-PEH-sah PAH-rah ah-SEHR KOH-sahs keh ah-SEE-ah FAH-seel-mehn-teh?
Have you lost your balance?	*¿Ha perdido el equilibrio?*	¿Ah pehr-DEE-doh ehl eh-kee-LEE-bryoh?
Do you have difficulty walking?	*¿Usted tiene dificultad para caminar?*	¿Oos-TEHD TYEH-neh dee-fee-kool-TAHD PAH-rah kah-mee-NAHR?
Does (do) your… shake?	*¿Le tiembla(n) el (la/los las)…*	¿Leh tyehm-blah(n) ehl (lah/lohs/lahs)…
• head.	• *cabeza?*	• kah-BEH-sah?
• neck.	• *cuello?*	• KWEH-yoh?
• arms.	• *brazos?*	• BRAH-sohs?
• hands.	• *manos?*	• MAH-nohs?
• fingers.	• *dedos?*	• DEH-dohs?
• legs.	• *piernas?*	• PYEHR-nahs?
• knees.	• *rodillas?*	• roh-DEE-yahs?
• feet.	• *pies?*	• pyehs?
Do you feel as if any part of your body were moving by itself?	*¿Siente como si alguna parte del cuerpo se le mueve sola?*	¿SYEHN-teh keh KOH-moh see ahl-GOO-nah PAHR-teh dehl KWEHR-poh seh leh MWEH-veh SOH-lah?

Have you had seizures?	*¿Ha tenido ataques?*	¿Ah teh-NEE-doh ah-TAH-kehs?
How often?	*¿Cada cuanto?*	¿KAH-dah KWAHN-doh?
How long have you had them?	*¿Cuanto tiempo las ha tenido?*	¿KWAHN-toh TYEHM-poh lahs ah teh-NEE-doh?
PATIENT	***PACIENTE***	
All my life.	*Toda mi vida.*	TOH-dah mee VEE-dah.
Since my accident.	*Desde mi accidente.*	DEHS-deh mee ahk-see-DEHN-teh.
For only a short while.	*Poco tiempo.*	POH-koh TYEHM-poh.
Several times a day.	*Varias veces al día.*	VAH-ryahs VEH-sehs ahl DEE-ah.
Every day.	*Todos los días.*	TOH-dohs lohs DEE-ahs.
Every few days.	*De vez en cuando.*	Deh vehs ehn KWAHN-doh.
Every other day.	*Cada otro día.*	KAH-dah OH-troh DEE-ah.
Once in a while.	*De vez en cuando.*	Deh vehs ehn KWAHN-doh.
DOCTOR	***DOCTOR***	
Do you…	*¿Usted…*	¿Oos-TEHD…
• have difficulty remembering what happens?	• *tiene dificultad para recordar lo que pasa?*	• TYEH-neh dee-fee-kool-TAHD PAH-rah reh-kor-DAHR loh keh PAH-sah?
• remember well what happened a long time ago?	• *se acuerda bien de lo que pasó hace mucho tiempo?*	• seh ah-KWEHR-dah byehn deh loh keh pah-SOH AH-seh MOO-choh TYEHM-poh?
Have you been getting lost lately?	*¿Se ha estado perdiendo últimamente?*	¿Seh ah ehs-TAH-doh pehr-DYEHN-doh OOL-tee-mah-mehn-teh?

Are you able to concentrate as well as you always have?	*¿Puede concentrarse como siempre lo ha hecho?*	¿PWEH-deh kohn-sehn-TRAHR-seh KOH-moh SYEHM-preh loh ah EH choh?
Have you had thoughts…	*¿Ha tenido pensamientos…*	¿Ah teh-NEE-doh pehn-sah-MYEHN-tohs…
• that scare you?	• *que la(o) asustan?*	• keh lah(oh) ah-SOOS-tahn?
• that you do not like?	• *que no le gustan?*	• keh noh leh GOOS-tahn?
What thoughts?	*¿Qué pensamientos?*	¿Keh pehn-sah-MYEHN-tohs?
PATIENT	***PACIENTE***	
That I was dead.	*Que estaba muerta(o).*	Keh ehs-TAH-bah MWEHR-tah(oh).
That I wanted to kill someone.	*Que quería matar a alguien.*	Keh keh-REE-ah mah-TAHR ah AHL-gyehn.
That something bad happened.	*Que había pasado algo malo.*	Keh ah-BEE-ah pah-SAH-doh AHL-goh MAH-loh.
DOCTOR	***DOCTOR***	
Have you…	*¿Usted…*	¿Oos-TEHD…
• had difficulty speaking, as if you were drunk?	• *tiene dificultad para hablar, como si estuviera borracho?*	• TYEH-neh dee-fee-kool-TAHD PAH-rah ah-BLAHR, KOH-moh see ehs-too-VYEH-rah boh-RRAH-choh?
• felt nervous, unable to relax?	• *se ha sentido nerviosa(o), sin poder descansar?*	• seh ah sehn-TEE-doh nehr-VYOH-sah (soh), seen poh-DEHR dehs-KAHN-sahr?
Why?	*¿Por qué?*	¿Pohr keh?

PATIENT	*PACIENTE*	
Because...	*Porque...*	POHR-keh...
• I don't have work.	• *no tengo trabajo.*	• noh TEHN-goh trah-BAH-hoh.
• I don't have enough money.	• *no me alcanza el dinero.*	• noh meh ahl-KAHN-sah ehl dee-NEH-roh.
• my spouse/child is sick/is using drugs.	• *mi esposo(a)/mi hijo(a) está enfermo(usando drogas).*	• mee ehs-POH-soh (sah)/EE-hoh(hah) ehs-TAH ehn-FEHR-moh(oo-SAHN-doh DROH-gahs).
I don't know why.	*No sé por qué.*	Noh seh pohr keh.
DOCTOR	***DOCTOR***	
Have you felt sad?	*¿Se ha sentido triste?*	¿Seh ah sehn-TEE-doh TREES-teh?
Why?	*¿Por qué?*	¿Pohr keh?
PATIENT	***PACIENTE***	
Because...	*Porque...*	POHR-keh...
• I am alone.	• *estoy sola(o) ahora.*	• ehs-TOY SOH-lah(loh) ah-OH-rah.
• I am very far from my family.	• *estoy muy lejos de mi familia.*	• ehs-TOY moo-ee LEH-hohs deh mee fah-MEE-lyah.
• I am very far from my country.	• *estoy muy lejos de mi tierra.*	• ehs-TOY moo-ee LEH-hohs deh mee TYEH-rrah.
I don't know why.	*No sé por qué.*	Noh SEH pohr KEH.
DOCTOR	***DOCTOR***	
Have you lost interest in life?	*¿Ha perdido el interés en la vida?*	¿Ah pehr-DEE-doh ehl een-teh-REHS ehn lah VEE-dah?
Why?	*¿Por qué?*	¿Pohr keh?
PATIENT	***PACIENTE***	
I don't know.	*No sé.*	Noh seh.
I cannot do anything anymore.	*Ya no puedo hacer nada.*	Yah noh PWEH-doh ah-SEHR NAH-dah.

I am not good for anything.	*No sirvo para nada.*	Noh SEER-voh PAH-rah NAH-dah.
DOCTOR	**DOCTOR**	
Have you had the wish to kill yourself?	*¿Ha sentido ganas de matarse?*	¿Ah teh-NEE-doh GAH-nahs deh mah-TAHR-seh?
Why?	*¿Por qué?*	¿Pohr keh?
PATIENT	**PACIENTE**	
Because …	*Porque…*	POHR-keh…
• I am lonely.	• *estoy solo(a).*	• ehs-TOY SOH-loh (lah).
• I am depressed.	• *estoy deprimido(a).*	• ehs-TOY deh-pree-MEE-doh(dah).
• I am in a lot of pain.	• *tengo mucho dolor.*	• TEHN-goh MOO-choh doh-LOHR.
• I am a failure.	• *soy un(a) fracaso(a).*	• soh-ee oon(OO-nah) frah-KAH-soh(sah).
I don't know.	*No sé.*	Noh seh.
DOCTOR	**DOCTOR**	
How would you kill yourself?	*¿Cómo se mataría?*	¿KOH-moh seh mah-tah-REE-ah?
PATIENT	**PACIENTE**	
I would kill myself…	*Me mataría…*	Meh mah-tah-REE-ah…
• with a bullet.	• *de un balazo.*	• deh oon bah-LAH-soh.
• by taking poison.	• *con veneno.*	• kohn veh-NEH-noh.
• by overdosing with my medications.	• *tomándome una sobredosis de mis medicinas.*	• toh-MAHN-doh-meh OO-nah soh-breh-DOH-sees deh mees meh-dee-SEE-nahs.
• by hanging myself.	• *colgándome.*	• kohl-GAHN-doh-meh.
• by jumping from a high place.	• *saltando de un lugar alto.*	• sahl-TAHN-doh deh oon loo-GAHR AHL-toh.

DOCTOR	*DOCTOR*	
Have you done anything?	*¿Ha hecho algo?*	¿Ah EH-choh AHL-goh?
PATIENT	*PACIENTE*	
I bought…	*Compré…*	Kohm-PREH…
• a pistol.	• *una pistola.*	• OO-nah pees-TOH-lah.
• poison.	• *veneno.*	• veh-NEH-noh.
• a rope.	• *una cuerda.*	• OO-nah KWEHR-dah.
I am saving my medications.	*Estoy juntando mis medicinas.*	Ehs-TOY hoon-TAHN-doh mees meh-dee-SEE-nahs.
I have chosen the place from which I will jump.	*He escogido el lugar de dónde saltare.*	Eh ehs-koh-HEE-doh ehl loo-GAHR deh DOHN-deh sahl-TAH-reh.
DOCTOR	*DOCTOR*	
Have you seen a doctor?	*¿Ha visto al médico?*	¿Ah VEES-toh ahl MEH-dee-koh?
What did she/he prescribe?	*¿Qué le recetó?*	¿Keh leh reh-seh-TOH?
PATIENT	*PACIENTE*	
Tranquilizers.	*Tranquilizantes.*	Trahn-kee-lee-SAHN-tehs.
Antidepressants.	*Antidepresivos.*	Ahn-tee-deh-preh-SEE-vohs.
Counseling.	*Consejería.*	Kohn-seh-heh-REE-ah.
Psychotherapy.	*Psicoterapia.*	See-koh-teh-RAH-pee-ah.
DOCTOR	*DOCTOR*	
Did you improve with the treatment?	*¿Mejoró con el tratamiento?*	¿Meh-hoh-ROH kohn ehl trah-tah-MYEHN-toh?

9. The Most Common Questions for the Elderly

CULTURE NOTE ••••

ADDRESSING THE ELDERLY Latino culture bestowes a lot of respect upon the elderly. Always address elderly patients with the formal *usted,* and use *señor* or *señora. Don* or *Doña* can be used as well. Elderly patients are usually accompanied to doctor's appointments by a relative, most often by the daughter. If during the interview the person accompanying your patient is present, be careful with questions regarding sexual activities, as Latinos find it inappropriate to discuss sexuality in front of their children.

DOCTOR	*DOCTOR*	
Where do you live?	*¿Dónde vive usted?*	¿DOHN-deh VEE-veh oos-TEHD?
With whom do you live?	*¿Con quién vive?*	¿Kohn kyehn VEE-veh?
PATIENT	*PACIENTE*	
I live...	*Vivo...*	VEE-voh...
• alone.	• *sola(o).*	• SOH-lah(loh).
• with my spouse.	• *con mi esposo(a).*	• kohn mee ehs-POH-soh(sah).
• with my children.	• *con mis hijos.*	• kohn mees EE-hos.
• with (a) friend(s).	• *con un(a/os/as) amigo(a/os/as).*	• kohn/oon (OO-nah/nohs/nahs) ah-MEE-goh(gah/gohs/gahs).

DOCTOR	*DOCTOR*	
Do you live in a safe…	*¿Vive en un(a) …seguro(a)?*	¿VEE-veh ehn oon (OO-nah)…seh-GOO-roh(rah)?
• apartment?	• *apartamento?*	• ah-pahr-tah-MEHN-toh?
• house?	• *casa?*	• KAH-sah?
• neighborhood?	• *barrio?*	• BAH-ryoh?
Why do you feel unsafe?	*¿Por qué se siente insegura(o)?*	¿Pohr KEH seh SYEHN-teh een-seh-GOO-rah(roh)?
PATIENT	*PACIENTE*	
Because…	*Porque…*	POHR-keh…
• it is a dangerous street.	• *es una calle peligrosa.*	• ehs OO-nah KAH-yeh peh-lee-GROH-sah.
• it is an ugly neighborhood.	• *es un barrio feo.*	• ehs oon BAH-roh FEH-oh.
• there are many gangs.	• *hay muchas pandillas.*	• ay MOO-chahs pahn-DEE-yahs.
• there are many burglaries.	• *hay muchos robos.*	• ay MOO-chohs ROH-bohs.
• there are many drive-by shootings.	• *hay muchas balaceras.*	• ay MOO-chahs bah-lah-SEH-rahs.
DOCTOR	*DOCTOR*	
What is your monthly income?	*¿Cuáles son sus ingresos mensuales?*	¿KWAH-lehs sohn soos een-GREH-sohs mehn-SWAH-lehs?
Do you have enough money…	*¿Tiene suficiente dinero para…*	¿TYEH-neh soo-fee-SYEHN-teh dee-NEH-roh PAH-rah…
• to make all your payments?	• *pagar todas sus cuentas?*	• pah-GAHR TOH-dohs soos KWEHN-tahs?
• to buy food?	• *comprar comida?*	• kohm-PRAHR koh-MEE-dah?

How much money are you short a month?	*¿Cuánto dinero le falta al mes?*	¿KWAHN-toh dee-NEH-roh leh FAHL-tah ahl mehs?
Is your spouse...	*¿Su esposo(a) está...*	¿Soo ehs-POH-soh(sah) ehs-TAH...
• alive?	• *vivo(a)?*	• VEE-voh(vah)?
• healthy?	• *sano(a)?*	• SAH-noh(nah)?
What is wrong with him/her?	*¿De qué está enfermo(a)?*	¿Deh KEH ehs-TAH ehn-FEHR-moh(mah)?
PATIENT	***PACIENTE***	
She/he has...	*Está enfermo(a)...*	Ehs-TAH ehn-FEHR-moh(mah)...
• heart problems.	• *del corazón.*	• dehl koh-rah-SOHN.
• kidney problems.	• *de los riñones.*	• deh lohs ree-NYOHN-ehs.
• liver problems.	• *del hígado.*	• dehl EE-gah-doh.
• memory problems.	• *de la memoria.*	• deh la meh-MOH-ryah.
• cancer.	• *de cáncer.*	• deh KAHN-sehr.
• Alzheimer's disease.	• *de Alzheimer.*	• deh Ahlz-HEH-ee-mehr.
• Parkinson's disease.	• *de Parkinson.*	• deh PAHR-keen-sohn.
• diabetes.	• *de diabetes.*	• deh dyah-BEH-tehs.
She/he cannot walk anymore.	*Ya no puede caminar.*	Yah noh PWEH-deh kah-mee-NAHR.
DOCTOR	***DOCTOR***	
How long has your spouse been sick?	*¿Desde cuándo está enfermo(a) su esposo(a)?*	¿DEHS-deh KWAHN-doh ehs-TAH ehn-FEHR-moh(mah) soo ehs-POH-soh(sah)?
PATIENT	***PACIENTE***	
A long/short time.	*Hace mucho/poco tiempo.*	Ah-seh MOO-choh/POH-koh TYEHM-poh.
A few weeks/months/years.	*Hace unas semanas/meses/años.*	AH-seh OO-nahs seh-MAH-nahs/MEH-sehs/ah-NYOHS.

DOCTOR	*DOCTOR*	
Where is your spouse now?	*¿Dónde está su esposo(a) ahora?*	¿DOHN-deh ehs-TAH soo ehs-POH-soh(sah) ah-OH-rah?
How long has she/he been there?	*¿Cuánto hace que está ahí?*	¿KWAHN-toh AH-seh keh ehs-TAH ah-EE?
PATIENT	*PACIENTE*	
At home.	*En casa.*	Ehn KAH-sah.
In...	*En...*	Ehn...
• a hospital.	• *un hospital.*	• oon ohs-PEE-tahl.
• a home for the elderly.	• *una casa para viejitos.*	• OO-nah KAH-sah PAH-rah vyeh-HEE-tohs.
• a rehabilitation center.	• *un centro de rehabilitación.*	• oon SEHN-troh deh reh-ah-bee-lee-tah-SYOHN.
DOCTOR	*DOCTOR*	
How long ago did you lose your spouse?	*¿Cuánto tiempo hace que perdió a su esposo(a)?*	¿KWAHN-toh TYEHM-poh AH-seh keh pehr-DYOH ah soo ehs-POH-soh(sah)?
What did your spouse die from?	*¿De qué murió su esposo(a)?*	¿Deh keh moo-RYOH soo ehs-POH-soh(sah)?
PATIENT	*PACIENTE*	
Of...	*De...*	Deh...
• heart disease.	• *una enfermedad del corazón.*	• OO-nah ehn-fehr-meh-DAHD dehl koh-rah-SOHN.
• kidney disease.	• *una enfermedad de los riñones.*	• OO-nah ehn-fehr-meh-DAHD deh lohs ree-NYOHN-ehs.
• liver disease.	• *una enfermedad del hígado.*	• OO-nah ehn-fehr-meh-DAHD dehl EE-gah-doh.
• lung disease.	• *una enfermedad pulmonar.*	• OO-nah ehn-fehr-meh-DAHD pool-moh-NAHR.

• diabetes.	• *diabetes.*	• dyah-BEH-tehs.
• Alzheimer's disease.	• *Alzheimer.*	• Ahls-HE-EE-mehr.
• a stroke.	• *un embolio.*	• oon ehm-BOH-lyoh.
• cancer.	• *cáncer.*	• KAHN-sehr.
DOCTOR	*DOCTOR*	
Do your sons and daughters live near you?	*¿Sus hijos e hijas viven cerca de usted?*	¿Soos EE-hohs eh EE-hahs VEE-vehn SEHR-kah deh oos-TEHD?
Do you have any grandsons or granddaughters?	*¿Tiene usted nietos y nietas?*	¿TYEH-neh oos-TEHD NYEH-tohs ee NYEH-tahs?
How many?	*¿Cuántos?*	¿KWAHN-tohs?
Do you have any friends?	*¿Tiene usted amistades?*	¿TYEH-neh oos-TEHD ah-mees-TAH-dehs?
What are their ages?	*¿De qué edad son?*	¿Deh KEH eh-DAHD sohn?
PATIENT	*PACIENTE*	
They are as old as I am.	*Están viejas como yo.*	Ehs-TAHN VYEH-hahs KOH-moh yoh.
Of all ages.	*De todas edades.*	Deh TOH-dahs lahs eh-DAH-dehs.
DOCTOR	*DOCTOR*	
Do you see these friends…	*¿Ve usted a estas amistades…*	¿Veh oos-TEHD ah EHS-tahs ah-mees-TAH-dehs…
• at church?	• *en la iglesia?*	• ehn lah ee-GLEH-syah.
• in the synagogue?	• *en la sinagoga?*	• ehn lah seen ah-GOH-gah?
• at a social center?	• *en un centro social?*	• ehn oon SEHN-troh soh-SYAHL?
How often do you see them?	*¿Cada cuánto se los ve?*	¿KAH-dah KWAHN-toh seh lohs veh?
What do you do with them when you see them?	*¿Qué hace con ellos (ellas) cuando los (las) ve?*	¿Keh AH-seh kohn EH-yohs (EH-yahs) KWAHN-doh lohs (lahs) veh?

PATIENT	*PACIENTE*	
We…	*Nosotros…*	Noh-SOH-trohs…
• talk.	• *platicamos.*	• plah-tee-KAH-mohs.
• go out.	• *salimos a pasear.*	• sah-LEE-mohs ah pah-seh-AHR.
• play.	• *jugamos.*	• hoo-GAH-mohs.
DOCTOR	*DOCTOR*	
Can you get dressed by yourself?	*¿Se puede vestir sola(o)?*	¿Seh PWEH-deh vehs-TEER SOH-lah(loh)?
Do you need help to get dressed?	*¿Necesita ayuda para vestirse?*	¿Neh-seh-SEE-tah ah-YOO-dah PAH-rah vehs-TEER-seh?
Please put on this gown by yourself.	*Por favor, póngase sola(o) esta bata.*	Pohr fah-VOHR, POHN-gah-seh SOH-lah (loh) EHS-tah BAH-tah.
Can you bathe yourself?	*¿Puede bañarse sola(o)?*	¿PWEH-deh bah-NYAHR-seh SOH-lah(loh)?
Do you need help to take a bath?	*¿Necesita ayuda para bañarse?*	¿Neh-seh-SEE-tah ah-YOO-dah PAH-rah bah-NYAHR-seh?
Can you sit on the commode by yourself?	*¿Se sienta sola(o) en el inodoro?*	¿Seh SYEHN-tah lah(loh) ehn ehl een-oh-DOH-roh?
Do you need help to sit on the commode?	*¿Necesita ayuda para sentarse en el inodoro?*	¿Neh-seh-SEE-tah ah-YOO-dah PAH-rah sehn-TAHR-seh ehn ehl een-oh-DOH-roh?
Do you prepare your own meals?	*¿Se prepara usted sus comidas?*	¿Seh preh-PAH-rah oos-TEHD soos koh-MEE-dahs?
Do you need help to prepare your meals?	*¿Necesita ayuda para preparar sus comidas?*	¿Neh-seh-SEE-tah ah-YOO-dah PAH-rah preh-pah-RAHR soos koh-MEE-dahs?
Who helps you?	*¿Quién le ayuda?*	¿Kyehn leh ah-YOO-dah?

PATIENT	*PACIENTE*	
My...	*Mi...*	Mee...
• spouse.	• *esposo(a).*	• ehs-POH-soh(sah).
• son/daughter.	• *hijo/hija.*	• EE-hoh/EE-hah.
The nurse.	*La enfermera.*	Lah ehn-fehr-MEH-rah.
DOCTOR	***DOCTOR***	
Tell me what you had for breakfast/lunch/ dinner the last three days.	*Dígame qué desayunó/comió/cenó los últimos tres días.*	DEE-gah-meh KEH dehs-ah-yoo-NOH/ koh-MYOH/seh-NOH lohs OOL-tee-mohs trehs DEE-ahs.
Can you walk without help?	*¿Puede caminar sin ayuda?*	¿PWEH-deh kah-mee-NAHR seen ah-YOO-dah?
What do you use to help yourself to walk?	*¿Con qué se ayuda para caminar?*	¿Kohn keh seh ah-YOO-dah PAH-rah kah-mee-NAHR?
Do you need...to help you walk?	*¿Necesita...para ayudarse a caminar?*	¿Neh-seh-SEE-tah ...pah-rah ah-yoo-DAHR-seh ah kah-mee-NAHR?
• a person	• *una persona*	• OO-nah pehr-SOHN-ah
• a cane	• *un bastón*	• oon bahs-TOON
• a walker	• *una andadera*	• OO-nah ahn-dah-DEH-rah
• a wheelchair	• *una silla de ruedas.*	• OO-nah SEE-yah deh roo-EH-dahs.
PATIENT	***PACIENTE***	
Yes, I use...	*Sí, uso...*	See, OO-soh...
• a cane.	• *un bastón.*	• oon bahs-TOHN.
• a walker.	• *una andadera.*	• OO-nah ahn-dah-DEH-rah.
• an electric wheelchair.	• *una silla eléctrica de ruedas.*	• OO-nah SEE-yah eh-LEHK-tree-kah deh roo-EH-dahs.

DOCTOR	*DOCTOR*	
Do you take walks regularly?	*¿Camina regularmente?*	¿Kah-MEE-nah reh-goo-LAHR-mehn-teh?
How often?	*¿Con qué frecuencia?*	¿Kohn keh freh-KWEHN-syah?
Where?	*¿Dónde?*	¿DOHN-deh?
PATIENT	*PACIENTE*	
Several times a day.	*Varias veces al día.*	VAH-ryahs VEH-sehs ahl DEE-ah.
Once a day.	*Una vez al día.*	OO-nah vehs ahl DEE-ah.
Several times a week.	*Varias veces a la semana.*	VAH-ryahs VEH-sehs ah lah seh-MAH-nah.
Once a week.	*Una vez por semana.*	OO-nah vehs pohr seh-MAH-nah.
Once in a while.	*De vez en cuando.*	Deh vehs ehn KWAHN-doh.
Around the house.	*Alrededor de la casa.*	Ahl-reh-deh-DOHR deh lah KAH-sah.
In the street where I live.	*En la calle donde vivo.*	Ehn lah KAH-yeh DOHN-deh VEE-voh.
In a park nearby.	*En un parque cercano.*	Ehn oon PAHR-keh sehr-KAH-noh.
DOCTOR	*DOCTOR*	
Do you have sexual relations?	*¿Tiene relaciones sexuales?*	¿TYEH-neh reh-lah-SYOH-nehs sehk-SWAH-lehs?
How often?	*¿Con qué frecuencia?*	¿Kohn keh freh-KWEHN-syah?
With whom?	*¿Con quién?*	¿Kohn kyehn?
PATIENT	*PACIENTE*	
With…	*Con…*	Kohn…
• my spouse.	• *mi esposo(a).*	• mee ehs-POH-soh (sah).
• someone I know.	• *un(a) conocido(a).*	• oon (OO-nah) koh-noh-SEE-doh(dah).

• another man/woman.	• *otro(a) hombre/mujer.*	• OH-troh(trah) OHM-breh/MOO-hehr.
DOCTOR	***DOCTOR***	
Tell me the names of all the medications that you have in your house.	*Dígame los nombres de todas las medicinas que tiene en su casa.*	DEE-gah-meh lohs NOHM-brehs deh TOH-dahs lahs meh-dee-SEE-nahs keh TYEH-neh ehn soo KAH-sah.
PATIENT	***PACIENTE***	
I have many.	*Tengo muchas.*	TEHN-goh MOO-chahs.
I do not remember all of them.	*No me acuerdo de todas.*	Noh meh ah-KWEHR-doh deh TOH-dahs.
I have medicines for…	*Tengo medicinas para…*	TEHN-goh meh-dee-SEE-nahs PAH-rah…
• the heart.	• *el corazón.*	• ehl koh-rah-SOHN.
• blood pressure.	• *la presión.*	• lah preh-SYOHN.
• sadness.	• *la tristeza.*	• lah trees-TEH-sah.
• nervousness.	• *los nervios.*	• lohs NEHR-vyohs.
• diabetes.	• *la diabetes.*	• lah dyah-BEH-tehs.
DOCTOR	***DOCTOR***	
Which of those medications are you taking?	*¿Cuáles está tomando?*	¿KWAH-lehs ehs-TAH toh-MAHN-doh?
PATIENT	***PACIENTE***	
None of them.	*Ninguna.*	Neen-GOO-nah.
All of them.	*Todas.*	TOH-dahs.
The medications for ____.	*Las medicinas para ____.*	Lahs meh-dee-SEE-nahs PAH-rah ____.
DOCTOR	***DOCTOR***	
Who prescribed these medications for you?	*¿Quién se las recetó?*	¿Kyehn seh lahs reh-seh-TOH?
PATIENT	***PACIENTE***	
A physician.	*Un(a) doctor(a).*	Oon (OO-nah) dohk-TOHR(TOH-rah).

They were recommended by...	*Me las recomendó...*	Meh lahs reh-koh-mehn-DOH...
• my spouse.	• *mi esposo(a)*	• mee ehs-POH-soh (sah).
• a (lady) friend of mine.	• *un(a) señor(a) amiga mía.*	• oon (OO-nah) seh-NYOHR(NYOH-rah) ah-MEE-gah MEE-ah.
• a natural healer.	• *un(a) naturista.*	• Oon (OO-nah) nah-too-REHS-tah.
DOCTOR	***DOCTOR***	
Did you improve with the medications?	*¿Mejoró con las medicinas?*	¿Meh-hoh-ROH kohn lahs meh-dee-SEE-nahs?

10. The Patient's Mental Status

CULTURE NOTE ••••

THE IMAGE OF MENTAL ILLNESS Mental problems are less of a stigma in Latino cultures than in the U.S., so you may find it much easier to discuss questions of mental illness with your Latino patients than with patients of other cultural backgrounds. Please note, however, that many Latinos may not be able to distinguish between sadness and depression, and may not consider depression an illness. It is important that you explain and clarify the difference. When you do, please remember that the word "blue" is just a color and is not considered a reference to sadness.

DOCTOR	***DOCTOR***	
How have you been feeling lately?	*¿Cómo se ha sentido últimamente?*	¿KOH-moh seh ah sehn-TEE-doh OOL-tee-mah-mehn-teh?
PATIENT	***PACIENTE***	
Very well.	*Muy bien.*	MOO-ee byehn.
Well.	*Bien.*	Byehn.
Not very well.	*No muy bien.*	Noh MOO-ee byehn.
So, so.	*Más o menos.*	Mahs oh MEH-nohs.
Anxious.	*Ansioso(a).*	Ahn-SYOH-soh(sah).
Angry.	*Enojado(a).*	Eh-noh-HAH-doh(dah).
Nervous.	*Nervioso(a).*	Nehr-VYOH-soh(sah).
Sad.	*Triste.*	TREES-teh.
Depressed.	*Deprimido(a).*	Deh-pree-MEE-doh (dah).
DOCTOR	***DOCTOR***	
How are you feeling now?	*¿Cómo se siente en este momento?*	¿KOH-moh seh SYEHN-teh ehn EHS-teh moh-MEHN-toh?
PATIENT	***PACIENTE***	
The same.	*Igual.*	Ee-GWAHL.
A little better.	*Un poco mejor.*	Oon POH-koh meh-HOHR.
Worse.	*Peor.*	Peh-OHR.
I don't know.	*No sé.*	Noh SEH.
DOCTOR	***DOCTOR***	
Are you…	*¿Está usted…*	¿Esh-TAH oos-TEHD…
• anxious?	• *ansiosa(o)?*	• ahn-SYOH-sah(soh)?
• angry?	• *enojada(o)?*	• eh-noh-HAH dah(doh)?
• nervous?	• *nerviosa(o)?*	• nehr-VYOH-sah(soh)?
• sad?	• *triste?*	• TREES-teh?

• depressed?	• *deprimida(o)?*	• deh-pree-MEE-dah(doh)?
Why?	*¿Por qué?*	¿Pohr keh?
PATIENT	***PACIENTE***	
Because…	*Porque…*	POHR-keh…
• I don't know what is going to happen.	• *no sé qué va a pasar.*	• noh SEH KEH vah ah pah-SAHR.
• they are going to have to operate on me.	• *me van a tener que operar.*	• meh vahn ah teh-NEHR keh oh-peh-RAHR.
• my daughter/son has not called.	• *mi hija/hijo no me ha hablado.*	• mee EE-hah/EE-hoh noh meh ah ah-BLAH-doh.
• I feel impotent.	• *me siento impotente.*	• me SYEHN-toh eem-poh-TEHN-teh.
• I have an incurable disease.	• *tengo una enfermedad incurable.*	• TEHN-goh OO-nah ehn-fehr-meh-DAHD een-koo-RAH-bleh.
• I have lost all hope about my…	• *he perdido toda esperanza de curarme de mi…*	• eh pehr-DEE-doh TOH-dah chs-peh-RAHN-sah de koo-RAHR-meh deh mee…
• alcoholism.	• *alcoholismo.*	• ahl-koh-ohl-EES-moh.
• smoking.	• *hábito a fumar.*	• AH-bee-toh ah FOO-mahr.
• drug addiction.	• *adicción a las drogas.*	• ah-deek-SYOHN ah lahs DROH-gahs.
• I have lost everything I had.	• *he perdido todo lo que tenía.*	• eh pehr-DEE-doh TOH-doh loh keh teh-NEE-ah.

DOCTOR	*DOCTOR*	
Is there a situation that makes you feel especially anxious?	*¿Hay alguna situación que la/lo haga sentirse especialmente ansiosa(o)?*	¿Ay ahl-GOO-nah see-too-ah-SYOHN keh lah AH-gah sehn-TEER-seh ehs-peh-SYAHL-mehn-teh ahn-SYOH-sah(soh)?
PATIENT	*PACIENTE*	
Being alone.	*Quedarme sola(o).*	Keh-DAHR-meh SOH-lah(loh).
Going to the market.	*Ir al mercado.*	Eer ahl mehr-KAH-doh.
Dealing with people I don't know.	*Tratar con desconocidos.*	Trah-TAHR kohn dehs-koh-noh-SEE-dohs.
DOCTOR	*DOCTOR*	
Are you angry?	*¿Se siente enojada(o)?*	¿Se SYEHN-teh eh-noh-HAH-dah(doh)?
Why?	*¿Por qué?*	¿Pohr keh?
PATIENT	*PACIENTE*	
My spouse…	*Mi esposo(a)…*	Mee ehs-POH-soh(sah)…
• left me.	• *me dejó.*	• meh deh-HOH.
• does not pay attention to me.	• *no me hace caso.*	• noh meh AH-seh KAH-soh.
I just got divorced.	*Me acabo de divorciar.*	Meh ah-KAH-boh de dee-vohr-SEE-AHR.
DOCTOR	*DOCTOR*	
Do you feel as if you can't control your anger?	*¿Siente que no puede controlar su enojo?*	¿SYEHN-teh keh noh PWEH-deh kohn-troh-LAHR soo eh-NOH-hoh?
What do you want to do?	*¿Qué quiere hacer?*	¿Keh KYEH-reh ah-SEHR?
PATIENT	*PACIENTE*	
I want to…	*Quiero…*	KYEH-roh…
• break something.	• *romper algo.*	• rohm-PEHR AHL-goh.

• hit something/ someone.	• *pegarle a algo/ alguien.*	• Peh-GAHR-leh ah AHL-goh/AHL-gyehn.
• go far away.	• *irme muy lejos.*	• EER-meh moo-ee LEH-hohs.
• kill someone.	• *matar a alguien.*	• mah-TAHR ah AHL-gyehn.
• send everything to hell.	• *mandar todo al diablo.*	• mahn-DAHR TOH-doh ahl DYAH-bloh.
DOCTOR	**DOCTOR**	
Are you sad?	*¿Está usted triste?*	¿Ehs-TAH oos-TEHD TREES-teh?
When you are sad, you can relate your feeling to an undesirable event.	*Cuando está triste, su sentimiento esta relacionado con un evento indeseado.*	KWAHN-doh ehs-TAH TREES-teh, soo sehn-tee-MYEHN-toh ehs-TAH reh-lah-SYOH-nah-doh kohn oon eh-VEHN-toh een-deh-seh-AH-doh.
Are you depressed?	*¿Está usted deprimido(a)?*	¿Ehs-TAH oos-TEHD deh-pree-MEE-doh(dah)?
When you are depressed, everything seems inadequate, independent of what is happening.	*Cuando esta deprimido(a), todo parece inadequado independientemente de lo que este pasando.*	KWAHN-doh EHS-tah deh-pree-MEE-doh(dah) TOH-doh pah-REH-seh een-ah-deh-KWAH-doh een-deh-pehn-DYEHN-teh-mehn-teh deh loh keh EHS-teh pah-SAHN-doh.
It is important to treat depression properly.	*Es importante tratar la depresión bien.*	Ehs eem-pohr-TAHN-teh TRAH-tahr lah deh-preh-SYOHN byehn.
Do you feel you have no energy?	*¿Siente que no tiene energia?*	¿SYEHN-teh keh noh TYEH-neh eh-nehr-HEE-ah?
Why?	*¿Por qué?*	¿Pohr keh?

PATIENT	*PACIENTE*	
Because...	*Porque...*	POHR-keh...
• I don't know what to do.	• *no sé qué hacer.*	• noh seh keh ah-SEHR.
• I feel very alone.	• *me siento muy sola(o).*	• meh SYEHN-toh moo-ee SOH-lah(loh).
• I just lost my job.	• *acabo de perder mi trabajo.*	• ah-KAH-boh deh pehr-DEHR mee trah-BAH-hoh.
• I never finished school.	• *nunca acabé la escuela.*	• NOON-kah ah-kah-BEH lah ehs-KWEH-lah.
• I don't make enough to support my family.	• *no gano suficiente para mantener a mi familia.*	• noh GAH-noh soo-fee-SYEHN-teh PAH-rah mahn-teh-NEHR ah mee fah-MEE-lyah.
• I will never amount to anything.	• *nunca voy a ser nada.*	• NOON-kah voh-ee ah sehr NAH-dah.
• I am not good for anything.	• *no sirvo para nada.*	• noh SEER-voh PAH-rah NAH-dah.
• I am not healthy.	• *no estoy sano.*	• noh ehs-TOY SAH-noh.
• I cannot be cured.	• *no me puedo curar.*	• noh meh PWEH-doh koo-RAHR.
• I suffer from a lot of pain.	• *sufro de mucho dolor.*	• SOO-froh deh MOO-choh doh-LOHR.
• I am going to die.	• *me voy a morir.*	• meh VOH-ee a moh-REER.

GRAMMAR NOTE ••••

TELLING TIME To ask for the time, use:

What time is it?	*¿Qué hora es?*
It is one o'clock.	*Es la una.*

Only for one o'clock, the singular of *ser—es*—is used. For all other times, use the plural *son.*

It is 11:00.	*Son las once.*
It is 3:00.	*Son las tres.*

Use *y* to add minutes past the hour.

It's 11:25.	*Son las once y veinticinco.*
It's 1:15.	*Es la una y cuarto.*
It's 2:30.	*Son las dos y treinta.*
	Son las dos y media.

DOCTOR	***DOCTOR***	
Do you feel confused sometimes?	*¿A veces se siente confundido(a)?*	¿Ah VEH-sehs seh SYEHN-teh kohn-FOON-dee-doh (dah)?
What year are we in?	*¿En qué año estamos?*	¿Ehn keh ah-NYOH ehs-TAH-mohs?
What time is it?	*¿Qué hora es?*	¿Keh OH-rah ehs?
Where are we?	*¿Dónde estamos?*	¿DOHN-deh ehs-TAH-mohs?
Who am I?	*¿Quién soy yo?*	¿Kyehn soy yoh?
PATIENT	***PACIENTE***	
We're in the year _____.	*Estamos en _____.*	Ehs-TAH-mohs en _____.
It is _____ o'clock.	*Es la/son las _____.*	Ehs lah/sohn lahs _____.
We are in _____.	*Estamos en _____.*	Ehs-TAH-mohs en _____.

You are Dr. _____.	*Usted es el/la Doctor(a) _____.*	Oos-TEHD ehs ehl/lah Dohk-TOHR(TOH-rah) _____.
I don't know.	*No sé.*	Noh seh.
DOCTOR	***DOCTOR***	
Do you know why I am asking you these questions?	*¿Sabe por qué le estoy haciendo estas preguntas?*	¿SAH-beh pohr KEH leh ehs-TOY ah-SYEHN-doh ehs-TAHS preh-GOON-tahs?
PATIENT	***PACIENTE***	
I don't know.	*No sé.*	Noh seh.
To find out what is wrong with me, because you are a doctor.	*Para saber lo que tengo porque usted es doctor(a).*	PAH-rah sah-BEHR loh keh TEHN-goh, POHR-keh oos-TEHD ehs dohk-TOHR (TOH-rah).
DOCTOR	***DOCTOR***	
Tell me some of the important things that have happened in the world in the last few years.	*Dígame algunas cosas importantes que han pasado en el mundo en los últimos años.*	DEE-gah-meh ahl-GOO-nahs KOH-sahs eem-pohr-TAHN-tehs keh ahn pah-SAH-doh ehn ehl MOON-doh ehn lohs OOL-tee-mohs ah-NYOHS.
How did you get here?	*¿Cómo llegó hasta aquí?*	¿KOH-moh yeh-GOH AHS-tah ah-KEE?
PATIENT	***PACIENTE***	
I came by car/bus/subway.	*Vine en carro/autobús/metro.*	VEE-neh ehn KAH-roh/ah-oo-toh-BOOS/MEH-troh.
My spouse/daughter/son/the police brought me here.	*Me trajo mi esposo(a)/hijo(a)/la policía.*	Meh TRAH-hoh mee ehs-POH-soh(sah)/EE-hoh(hah)/lah poh-lee-SEE-ah.
I don't know.	*No sé.*	Noh seh.
DOCTOR	***DOCTOR***	
How long have you been here?	*¿Cuánto tiempo ha estado aquí?*	¿KWAHN-toh TYEHM-poh ah ehs-TAH-doh ah-KEE?

PATIENT	***PACIENTE***	
A while.	*Un rato.*	Oon RAH-toh.
All morning/ afternoon/day.	*Toda la mañana/ tarde/el día.*	TOH-dah lah mah-NYAH-nah/TAHR-deh/ehl DEE-ah.
A long time.	*Mucho tiempo.*	MOO-choh TYEHM-poh.
I don't know.	*No sé.*	Noh seh.
DOCTOR	***DOCTOR***	
Do you feel that people pay too much attention to you?	*¿Siente usted que la gente se fija demasiado en usted?*	¿SYEHN-teh oos-TEHD keh lah HEN-teh seh FEE-hah deh-mah-SYAH doh ehn oos-TEHD?
Why?	*¿Por qué?*	¿Pohr keh?
PATIENT	***PACIENTE***	
Because...	*Porque...*	POHR-keh...
• they are persecuting me.	• *me andan persiguiendo.*	• meh AHN-dahn pehr-see-GYEHN-doh.
• they think I'm crazy.	• *creen que estoy loco(a).*	• KREH-ehn keh ehs-TOY LOH-koh(kah).
• they want to hurt me.	• *me quieren herir.*	• meh KYEH-rehn eh-REER.
• they want to kidnap me.	• *me quieren secuestrar.*	• meh KYEH-rehn seh-kwehs-TRAHR.
• they want to kill me.	• *me quieren matar.*	• Meh KYEH-rehn mah-TAHR.
DOCTOR	***DOCTOR***	
Do you hear voices?	*¿Oye voces?*	¿Oh-yeh VOH-sehs?
Whose?	*¿De quién?*	¿Deh kyehn?
PATIENT	***PACIENTE***	
The voices of...	*Las voces de...*	Lahs VOH-sehs deh...
• the people who...	• *los que me...*	• lohs keh meh...
• are persecuting me.	• *están persiguiendo.*	• ehs-TAHN pehr-see-GHYEHN-doh.

• want to hurt me.	• *quieren herirme.*	• KYEH-rehn eh-REER-meh.
• want to kill me.	• *quieren matarme.*	• KYEH-rehn mah-TAHR-meh.
• kidnap me.	• *quieren secuestrarme.*	• KYEH-rehn seh-kwehs-TRAHR-meh.
• God.	• *Dios.*	• Dyohs.
• the devil.	• *el diablo.*	• ehl DYAH-bloh.
DOCTOR	***DOCTOR***	
Are there thoughts that you cannot get out of your head?	*¿Tiene usted pensamientos que no se puede quitar de la cabeza?*	¿TYEH-neh oos-TEHD pehn-sah-MYEHN-tohs keh noh seh PWEH-deh kee-TAHR deh lah kah-BEH-sah?
PATIENT	***PACIENTE***	
That I…	*Que yo…*	Keh yoh…
• am guilty.	• *soy culpable.*	• soy kool-PAH-bleh.
• need to wash my hands.	• *tengo que lavarme las manos.*	• TEHN-goh keh lah-VAHR-meh lahs MAH-nohs.
• do not smell well.	• *no huelo bien.*	• noh WEH-loh byehn.
• am ugly.	• *soy feo.*	• soy FEH-oh.
• have to get out of here.	• *me tengo que ir de aquí.*	• meh TEHN-goh keh eer deh ah-KEE.
DOCTOR	***DOCTOR***	
Have you felt the desire to hurt or kill someone?	*¿Ha sentido ganas de herir o matar a alguien?*	¿Ah sehn-TEE-doh GAH-nahs deh heh-REER oh mah-TAHR ah AHL-gyehn?
Whom?	*¿A quién?*	¿Ah kyehn?

PATIENT	*PACIENTE*	
The people… • persecuting me.	*Los que me andan persiguiendo.*	Lohs keh meh AHN-dahn pehr-see-GYEHN-doh.
• who want to kill me.	*Los que me quieren matar.*	Lohs keh meh KYEH-rehn mah-TAHR.
My…	*Mi(s)…*	Mee(s)…
• spouse.	• *esposo(a).*	• ehs-POH-soh(sah).
• neighbor.	• *vecino(a).*	• veh-SEE-noh(nah).
• children.	• *niños.*	• nee-NYOHS.
DOCTOR	***DOCTOR***	
We will…	*Le…*	Leh…
• get you the help you need.	• *conseguieremos la ayuda que necesita.*	• kohn-seh-GYEH-REH-mohs lah ah-YOO-dah keh neh-seh-SEE-tah.
• take care of you.	• *cuidaremos.*	• KWEE-dah-REH-mohs.
• bring you to a place where you will be safe and well cared for.	• *internaremos en un lugar donde será seguro(a) y bien cuidado(a).*	• een-tehr-nah-REH-mohs ehn oon LOO-gahr DOHN-deh seh-RAH seh-GOO-roh (rah) ee byehn kwee-DAH-doh(dah).
It's okay.	*Está bien.*	Ehs-TAH byehn.
You will be fine.	*Va a estar bien.*	Vah ah ehs-TAHR byehn.
I will not let anyone hurt you.	*No permitiré que nadie la (lo) hiera.*	Noh pehr-mee-tee-REH keh NAH-dyeh lah (loh) YEH-rah.
Calm down.	*Cálmese.*	KAHL-meh-seh.
Lie down.	*Acuéstese.*	Ah-KWEHS-teh-seh.
Sit down.	*Siéntese.*	SYEHN-teh-seh.
No need to cry.	*No necesita llorar.*	Noh neh-seh-SEE-tah yoh-RAHR.

It's okay to cry.	*Está bien que llore.*	Ehs-TAH byehn keh YOH-reh.
You can cry if you want.	*Puede llorar si quiere.*	PWEH-deh yoh-RAHR see KYEH-reh.
Do you want to have...here with you?	*¿Quiere tener a... aquí con usted?*	¿KYEH-reh teh-NEHR ah...ah-KEE kohn oos-TEHD?
• a friend	• *un(a) amigo(a)*	• oon (OO-nah) ah-MEE-goh(gah)
• your family	• *su familia*	• soo fah-MEE-lyah
Would you like me to call him/her/them?	*¿Quiere que lo/la/los/las llame?*	¿KYEH-reh keh loh/lah/lohs/lahs YAH-meh?
Does he/she/do they speak English?	*¿Habla/hablan inglés?*	AH-blah/AH-blahn een-GLEHS?
PATIENT	***PACIENTE***	
Yes. I need my...	*Sí. Necesito...*	See. Neh-seh-SEE-toh...
• family.	• *a mi familia.*	• ah mee fah-MEE-lyah.
• friends.	• *a mis amigos(as).*	• ah mees ah-MEE-gohs(gahs).
I don't have family/friends here.	*No tengo familia/amigos(as) aquí.*	Noh TEHN-goh fah-MEE-lyah/ah-MEE-gohs(gahs) ah-KEE.
Please call ____.	*Por favor, llame a ____.*	Pohr fah-VOHR, YAH-meh ah ____.
He/she/they don't speak English.	*No habla/hablan inglés.*	Noh AH-blah/AH-blahn een-GLEHS.
He/she/they speak only Spanish.	*Solamente habla/hablan español.*	Soh-lah-MEHN-teh AH-blah/AH-blahn ehs-pah-NYOHL.
I don't need anybody, thank you.	*No necesito a nadie, gracias.*	Noh neh-seh-SEE-toh ah NAH-dyeh, GRAH-syahs.

VOCABULARY ••••

ADJECTIVES OF EMOTION

sad	*triste*	TREES-teh
happy	*contento(a)*	kohn-TEHN-toh(tah)
depressed	*deprimido(a)*	deh-pree-MEE-doh(dah)
tired	*cansado(a)*	kahn-SAH-doh(dah)
drunk	*borracho(a)*	boh-RRAH-choh(chah)
crazy	*loco(a)*	LOH-koh(kah)
nervous	*nervioso(a)*	nehr-vee-OH-soh(sah)
busy	*ocupado(a)*	oh-koo-PAH-doh(dah)
relaxed	*relajado(a)*	reh-lah-HAH-doh(dah)
tranquil	*tranquilo(a)*	trahn-KEE-loh(lah)
agitated	*agitado(a)*	ah-hee-TAH-doh(dah)
sick	*enfermo(a)*	ehn-FEHR-moh(mah)
angry	*enojado(a)*	ehn-noh-HAH-doh(dah)
dead	*muerto(a)*	MWEHR-toh(tah)

11. Special Interview Situations

A. FAMILY VIOLENCE

CULTURE NOTE ····

DOMESTIC VIOLENCE Some Latino families, but by no means all, may tolerate violence to a degree without considering it a problem, especially if the perpetrator is the father. Latino culture tends to prescribe more traditional male and female roles, and thus, the father is often considered the unquestioned authority in the family hierarchy, even if he uses violence towards his spouse or children. Family problems are considered a private matter, and so it may be very difficult to discuss domestic abuse with your patients. The female victim of physical abuse may not consider it appropriate to disclose such information to her physician. Of course, family violence is not more common among Latino families than among other ethnic groups. Physical abuse is a problematic issue in all ethnic, cultural and socio-economic environments, and should be treated with delicacy and sensitivity. If you suspect abuse to be the cause for physical injuries or psychological problems, it might be best to call in an interpreter to discuss the issue with your patient to make sure that language problems will not stand in the way.

DOCTOR	*DOCTOR*	
Whom do you live with?	*¿Con quiénes vive?*	¿Kohn KYEH-nehs VEE-veh?
PATIENT	***PACIENTE***	
I live with...	*Vivo con...*	VEE-voh kohn...
• my family.	• *mi familia.*	• mee fah-MEE-lyah.

• my parents and brothers and sisters.	• *mis padres y hermanos.*	• mees PAH-drehs ee ehr-MAH-nohs.
• my spouse/fiancee.	• *mi esposo(a)/novio(a).*	• mee ehs-POH-soh (sah)/NOH-vyoh (vyah).
• my children.	• *mis hijos.*	• mees EE-hohs.
• a group of people.	• *un grupo de gente.*	• oon GROO-poh deh HEN-teh.
DOCTOR	***DOCTOR***	
Do you all get along well?	*¿Se llevan bien todos?*	¿Seh YEH-vahn byehn TOH-dohs?
How do you resolve your disagreements?	*¿Cómo resuelvan sus desacuerdos?*	¿KOH-moh reh-SWEHL-vehn soos dehs-ah-KWEHR-dohs?
PATIENT	***PACIENTE***	
We discuss them.	*Los discutimos.*	Lohs dees-koo-TEE-mohs.
We fight about them.	*Nos peleamos.*	Nohs peh-leh-AH-mohs.
DOCTOR	***DOCTOR***	
I will ask you some important questions.	*Le voy a hacer unas preguntas importantes.*	Leh voy ah ah-SEHR OO-nahs preh-GOON-tahs eem-pohr-TAHN-tehs.
Would you be more comfortable speaking to an interpreter in Spanish?	*¿Se sentiría más a gusto hablando con un intérprete en español?*	¿Seh sehn-tee-REE-ah MAHS ah GOOS-toh ah-BLAHN-doh kohn oon een-TEHR-preh-teh ehn ehs-pah-NYOHL?
I'll call in an interpreter.	*Llamaré al intérprete.*	Yah-mah-REH ahl een-TEHR-preh-teh.
She/he will understand you better.	*Ella/él lo(la) entenderá mejor.*	EH-yah/EHL loh (lah) ehn-tehn-deh-RAH meh-HOHR.
Just a moment.	*Un momento.*	Oon moh-MEHN-toh.
Has anyone ever hit you during a discussion?	*¿Alguna vez la (lo) ha golpeado alguien durante una discusión?*	¿Ahl-GOO-nah vehs lah (loh) ah gohl-peh-AH-doh AHL-gyehn doo-RAHN-teh OO-nah dees-koo-SYOHN?

Who?	*¿Quién?*	¿Kyehn?
You can tell me.	*Me lo puede decir.*	Meh loh PWEH-deh deh-SEER.
I will not tell anyone.	*No se le diré a nadie.*	Noh seh leh dee-REH ah NAH-dyeh.
Everything you tell me will remain confidential.	*Cualquier cosa que me diga será confidencial.*	KWAHL-kyehr KOH-sah keh meh DEE-gah seh-RAH kohn-fee-dehn-SYAHL.
PATIENT	***PACIENTE***	
My spouse.	*Mi esposo(a).*	Mee ehs-POH-soh(sah).
My mother/father.	*Mi madre/padre.*	Mee MAH-dreh/PAH-dreh.
My son/daughter.	*Mi hijo/hija.*	Mee EE-hoh/EE-hah.
My boyfriend/ girlfriend.	*Mi novio/novia.*	Mee NOH-vyoh/NOH-vyah.
DOCTOR	***DOCTOR***	
How frequently does this happen?	*¿Con qué frecuencia pasa esto?*	¿Kohn KEH freh-KWEHN-syah PAH-sah EHS-toh?
PATIENT	***PACIENTE***	
Not often.	*Raramente.*	RAH-rah-mehn-teh.
Every day.	*Todos los días.*	TOH-dohs lohs DEE-ahs.
Once in a while.	*De vez en cuando.*	Deh vehs ehn KWAHN-doh.
When he/she is angry.	*Cuando está enojado(a).*	KWAHN-doh ehs-TAH eh-noh-HAH-doh(dah).
When I was bad.	*Cuando me portaba mal.*	KWAHN-doh meh pohr-TAH-bah mahl.
DOCTOR	***DOCTOR***	
Has a beating been so bad that…	*¿Alguna vez fue tan dura la golpiza que…*	Ahl-GOO-nah vehs FWEH tahn-DOO-rah lah gohl-PEE-sah keh…
• you suffered a broken bone?	• *le fracturó un hueso?*	• leh frahk-too-ROH oon WEH-soh?

• you had to be hospitalized?	• *tuvo que ser hospitalizada(o)?*	• TOO-voh keh sehr ohs-pee-tah-LEE-sah-dah(doh)?
When?	*¿Cuándo?*	¿KWAHN-doh?
Have you also been sexually abused?	*¿También ha sido abusada(o) sexualmente?*	¿Tahm-BYEHN ah SEE-doh ah-boo-SAH-dah(doh) sehk-SWAHL-mehn-teh?
You can trust me with your answer.	*Me puede confiar con su respuesta.*	Meh PWEH-deh kohn-fee-AHR kohn soo rehs-PWEHS-tah.
PATIENT	***PACIENTE***	
I don't want to talk about it.	*No quiero hablar de eso.*	Noh KYEH-roh ah-BLAHR deh EH-soh.
I was…	*Me…*	Me…
• raped.	• *violó.*	• vyoh-LOH.
• sodomized.	• *la metió por atrás.*	• meh lah meh-TYOH pohr ah-TRAHS.
• forced to have oral sex.	• *la metió en la boca.*	• lah meh-TYOH pohr lah BOH-kah.
• whipped.	• *dio latigazos.*	• dyoh lah-tee-GAH-sohs.
• burned.	• *quemó.*	• keh-MOH.
• tied up.	• *amarró.*	• ah-mah-RROH.
• confined.	• *encerró.*	• ehn-seh-RROH.
DOCTOR	**DOCTOR**	
Have you ever been…	*¿Alguna vez la (lo) ha(n)…*	¿Ahl-GOON-ah vehs lah (loh) ah(n)…
• burned?	• *quemado?*	• keh-MAH-doh?
• slashed?	• *cortado?*	• kohr-TAH-doh?
• whipped?	• *dado latigazos?*	• DAH-doh lah-tee-GAH-sohs?
• confined?	• *encerrado?*	• ehn-seh-RRAH-doh?
When?	*¿Cuándo?*	¿KWAHN-doh?

I need to know so that I can help you.	*Necesito saberlo para poder ayudarla(lo).*	Neh-seh-SEE-toh sah-BEHR-loh PAH-rah poh-DEHR ah-yoo-DAHR-lah(loh).
DOCTOR	***DOCTOR***	
Has this person victimized anybody else?	*¿Esta persona ha abusado de alguien más?*	EHS-tah pehr-SOH-nah ah ah-boo-SAH doh deh AHL-gyehn mahs?
Nothing will happen to you if you tell me.	*No le pasará nada si me lo dice.*	Noh leh pah-sah-RAH NAH-dah see meh loh DEE-seh.
PATIENT	***PACIENTE***	
She/he has victimized…	*Ha abusado de…*	Ah ah-boo-SAH-doh deh…
• my father/mother.	• *mi papá/mamá.*	• mee pah-PAH/mah-MAH.
• my brother/sister.	• *mi hermano/hermana.*	• mee ehr-MAH-noh/ehr-MAH-nah.
• my son/daughter.	• *mi hijo/hija.*	• mee EE-hoh/EE-hah.
DOCTOR	***DOCTOR***	
Have you ever sought help?	*¿Alguna vez ha pedido ayuda?*	¿Ahl-GOO-nah vehs ah peh-DEE-doh ah-YOO-dah.
PATIENT	***PACIENTE***	
I told…	*Le dije a…*	Le DEE-heh ah…
• a counselor.	• *un(a) consejero(a).*	• oon (OO-nah) kohn-seh-HEH-roh(rah).
• a neighbor.	• *un(a) vecino(a).*	• oon (OO-nah) veh-SEE-noh(nah).
• a friend.	• *un(a) amigo(a).*	• oon (OO-nah) ah-MEE-goh(gah).
• a teacher.	• *un(a) maestro(a).*	• oon (OO-nah) mah-EHS-troh(trah).
• a shelter.	• *un refugio.*	• oon reh-FOO-hyoh.
• the police.	• *la policía.*	• lah poh-lee-SEE-ah.
• a judge.	• *un juez.*	• oon hwehs.

DOCTOR	*DOCTOR*	
Will you…with this person?	*¿Va a…con esta persona?*	¿Vah ah…kohn EHS-tah pehr-SOH-nah?
• go on living	• *seguir viviendo*	• seh-GHEER vee-VYEHN-doh.
• stay	• *quedarse*	• keh-DAHR-seh
What are your plans?	*¿Qué planes tiene?*	¿Keh PLAH-nehs TYEH-neh?
PATIENT	***PACIENTE***	
I will go back to…	*Voy a regresar…*	Voy ah reh-greh-SAHR…
• the counselor.	• *a ver el (la) consejero(a).*	• kohn ehl (lah) kohn-seh-HEH-roh(rah).
• the shelter.	• *al refugio.*	• ahl reh-FOO-hyoh.
• the police.	• *a la policía.*	• ah lah poh-lee-SEE-ah.
• the judge.	• *a ver al juez.*	• ah vehr ahl hwehs.
I will…	*Voy a…*	Voy ah…
• stay with him/her.	• *quedarme con él/ella.*	• keh-DAHR-meh kohn EHL/EH-yah.
• move.	• *mudarme.*	• moo-DAHR-meh.
• get advice.	• *buscar consejos.*	• boos-KAHR kohn-SEH-hohs.
• stay with a friend.	• *quedarme con un(a) amigo(a).*	• keh-DAHR-meh kohn oon(OO-nah) ah-MEE-goh(gah).
DOCTOR	***DOCTOR***	
You are at risk of suffering a serious injury.	*Usted corre el riesgo de sufrir una herida grave.*	Oos-TEHD KOH-rreh ehl RYEHS-goh deh SOO-freer OO-nah eh-REE-dah GRAH-veh.
You need help.	*Usted necesita ayuda.*	Oos-TEHD neh-seh-SEE-tah ah-YOO-dah.
I am going to refer you to…	*La (lo) voy a mandar a ver…*	La (loh) voy ah mahn-DAHR ah vehr…

• a counselor.	• *un(a) consejero(a).*	• oon (OO-nah) kohn-seh-HEH-roh(rah).
• a social worker.	• *un(a) trabajador(a) social.*	• oon (OO-nah) trah-bah-hah-DOHR (DOH-rah) soh-SYAHL.
• a psychologist.	• *un(a) psicólogo(a).*	• oon (OO-nah) see-KOH-loh-goh(gah).
• a psychiatrist.	• *un(a) psiquiatra.*	• oon (OO-nah) see-kee-AH-trah.

VOCABULARY ••••

PHYSICAL ABUSE

abuse, to	*abusar*	ah-boo-SAHR
beating	*golpiza*	gohl-PEE-sah
disagreement	*desacuerdo*	dehs-ah-KWEHR-doh
discussion	*discusión*	dees-koo-SYOHN
fight, to	*pelear*	peh-leh-AHR
get along, to	*llevarse*	yeh-VAHR-seh
hit, to	*pegar/golpear*	PEH-gahr/GOHL-peh-ahr
hurt, to	*herir/doler*	eh-REER/doh-LEHR
judge	*juez*	hwehs
rape, to	*violar*	vyoh-LAHR
shelter	*refugio*	reh-FOO-gyoh
social worker	*trabajador(a) social*	trah-bah-hah-DOHR (DOH-rah) soh-SYAHL
tie, to	*amarrar*	ah-mah-RRAHR
victims	*víctimas*	VEEK-tee-mahs
violate, to	*violar*	vyoh-LAHR
whip, to	*dar latigazos*	dahr lah-tee-GAH-sohs

B. THE PATIENT WHO MAY HAVE BEEN EXPOSED TO HIV

GRAMMAR NOTE ••••

THE VERBS *SABER* AND *CONOCER* (TO KNOW)

The verb "to know" has two equivalents in Spanish: *saber* and *conocer*.

SABER (TO KNOW FACTS, TO KNOW ABOUT, TO KNOW HOW TO)

SINGULAR	PLURAL
sé	*sabemos*
sabes	*sabéis*
sabe	*saben*

I don't know what direction they took.	*Yo no sé por dónde se fueron.*
We know the truth.	*Sabemos la verdad.*
He knows how to speak English.	*Él sabe hablar inglés.*

CONOCER (TO KNOW PEOPLE OR PLACES, TO BE ACQUAINTED WITH)

SINGULAR	PLURAL
conozco	*conocemos*
conoces	*conocéis*
conoce	*conocen*

I know the patient.	*Conozco al paciente.*
They don't know the hospital.	*Ellos no conocen la clínica.*

DOCTOR	***DOCTOR***	
Do you have…	*¿Tiene usted relaciones sexuales con…*	¿TYEH-neh oos-TEHD reh-lah-SYOH-nehs sehk-SWAH-lehs kohn…
• a single sex partner?	• *una sóla persona?*	• OO-nah SOH-lah pehr-SOH-nah?

• multiple sex partners?	• *varias personas?*	• VAH-ryahs pehr-SOH-nahs?
What is the gender of…	*¿A qué sexo pertenece(n)…*	¿Ah KEH SEHK-soh pehr-teh-NEH-seh(sehn)…
• your partner?	• *su compañero(a)?*	• soo kohm-pah-NYEH-roh(rah)?
• each of your partners?	• *cada uno(a) de sus compañeros?*	• KAH-dah OO-noh(nah) deh soos kohm-pah-NYEH-rohs?
What do you know about the health of…	*¿Qué sabe usted acerca de la salud de…*	¿Keh SAH-beh oos-TEHD ah-SEHR-kah deh lah sah-LOOD deh…
• your partner?	• *su compañero(a)?*	• soo kohm-pah-NYEH-roh(rah)?
• each of your partners?	• *cada uno(a) de sus compañeros(as)?*	• KAH-dah OO-noh(nah) deh soos kohm-pah-NYEH-rohs(rahs)?
PATIENT	***PACIENTE***	
I know nothing.	*No sé nada.*	Noh seh NAH-dah.
I think she/he/one of them is infected with HIV/a sexually transmited disease.	*Me parece que ella/él uno de ellos está infectado con SIDA/una enfermedad venérea.*	Meh pah-REH-seh keh EH-yah/EHL/OO-noh deh eh-YOHS ehs-TAH een-fehk-TAH-doh kohn SEE-dah/OO-nah ehn-fehr-meh-DAHD veh-NEH-reh-ah.
I know that she/he/one of them has AIDS.	*Sé que ella/él/uno de ellos tiene SIDA.*	Seh keh eh-YAH/EHL/OO-noh deh eh-YOHS TYEH-neh SEE-dah.

DOCTOR	*DOCTOR*	
How often do you have sex with your partner(s)?	*¿Con qué frecuencia tiene relaciones sexuales con sus compañeros(as)?*	¿Kohn keh freh-KWEHN-syah TYEH-neh reh-lah SYOHN-ehs sehk-SWAH-lehs kohn-soo(s) kohm-pah-NYEH-rohs(rahs)?
What types of sexual activities do you and your partner(s) engage in?	*¿Qué típos de actividades sexuales practican usted y su(s) compañeros(as)?*	¿Keh TEE-pohs deh ahk-tee-vee-DAHD sehk-SWAH-lehs prahk TEE-kahn oos-TEHD ee soo(s) kohm-pah-NYEH-rohs(rahs)?
PATIENT	*PACIENTE*	
We like to have…	*Nos gusta sexo…*	Nohs GOOS-tah SEHK-soh…
• vaginal sex.	• *por la vagina.*	• pohr lah vah-HEE-nah.
• anal sex.	• *por atrás.*	• pohr ah-TRAHS.
• oral sex.	• *con la boca.*	• kohn lah BOH-kah.
DOCTOR	*DOCTOR*	
What do you do to protect yourself from being infected?	*¿Qué es lo que usted hace para protegerse de una infección?*	¿Keh ehs loh keh oos-TEHD AH-seh PAH-rah proh-teh-HEHR-seh deh OO-nah een-fehk-SYOHN?
PATIENT	*PACIENTE*	
Nothing.	*Nada.*	NAH-dah.
I put on a condom.	*Me pongo condón.*	Meh POHN-goh kohn-DOHN.
I make my partner put on a condom.	*Hago que mi compañero se ponga un condón.*	AH-goh keh mee kohm-pah-NYEH-roh seh POHN-gah oon kohn-DOHN.
I wash afterwards.	*Me lavo después.*	Meh LAH-voh dehs-PWEHS.
I douche afterwards.	*Me ducho al final.*	Meh DOO-choh ahl-FEE-nahl.

We practice safe sex.	*Hacemos el sexo seguro.*	Ah-SEH-mohs ehl SEHK-soh seh-GOO-roh.
We don't have intercourse.	*No tenemos sexo.*	Noh teh-NEH-mohs SEHKS-oh.
DOCTOR	***DOCTOR***	
I will have to order a test.	*Le voy a tener que hacer un examen de laboratorio.*	Leh voy ah teh-NEHR keh ah-SEHR oon ehks-AH-mehn deh lah-boh-rah-TOH-ryoh.
Just to make sure you're okay.	*Sólo para asegurarnos que está usted bien.*	SOH-loh PAH-rah ah-seh-goo-RAHR-nohs keh ehs-TAH oos-TEHD byehn.
We'll know...	*Lo sabremos...*	Loh sah-BREH-mohs...
• tomorrow. • soon. • in ten days.	• *mañana.* • *pronto.* • *en diez días.*	• mah-NYAH-nah. • PROHN-toh. • ehn dyehs DEE-ahs.
Don't worry.	*No se preocupe.*	Noh seh preh-oh-KOO-peh.
You'll be okay.	*Se sentirá bien.*	Seh sehn-tee-RAH byehn.
Would you like to learn how to protect yourself?	*¿Le gustaría aprender a protegerse?*	¿Leh goos-tah-REE-ah ah-prehn-DEHR ah proh-teh-HEHR-seh?
DOCTOR	***DOCTOR***	
Please read this booklet from the Department of Health.	*Por favor, lea este librito del Departamento de Salud.*	Pohr fah-VOHR, LEH-ah EHS-teh lee-BREE-toh dehl deh-pahr-tah-MEHN-toh deh sah-LOOD.
If you have any questions, please ask me.	*Si tiene alguna pregunta, por favor hagámela.*	See TYEH-neh ahl-GOO-nah preh-GOON-tah pohr fah-VOHR, ah-GAH-meh-lah.

SECTION D

MEDICAL PROCEDURES

1. General Instructions

DOCTOR/NURSE	*DOCTOR/ENFERMERA*	
Please undress...	*Por favor, desvístase...*	Por fah-VOHR, dehs-VEES-tah-seh...
• from the waist up.	• *de la cintura arriba.*	• de lah seen-TOO-rah ah-RREE-bah.
• from the waist down.	• *de la cintura abajo.*	• de lah seen-TOO-rah ah-BAH-hoh.
Put on this gown.	*Póngase esta bata.*	PON-gah-seh EHS-tah BAH-tah.
During the examination, I'll have to touch you.	*Durante la examinación, tendré que tocarlo(la).*	Doo-RAHN-teh lah ehks-ah-mee-nah-SYOHN tehn-DREH keh toh-KAHR-loh (lah).
Will you allow me to do so?	*¿Me lo permite?*	¿Meh loh per-MEE-teh?
Please let me know if it hurts.	*Por favor, dígame si le duele.*	Por fah-VOHR, DEE-gah-meh see leh DWEH-leh.

Do you want… present while I examine you?	*¿Quiere a…presente mientras lo(la) examino?*	¿KYEH-reh ah…preh-SEHN-teh MYEHN-trahs loh(lah) ehks-ah-MEE-noh?
• a nurse	• *un(a) enfermero(a)*	• oon (OO-nah) ehn-fer-MEH-roh(rah)
• your spouse	• *su esposo(a)*	• soo ehs-POH-soh (sah)
• your son/daughter	• *su hijo/hija*	• soo EE-hoh/EE-hah
Don't worry.	*No se preocupe.*	Noh seh preh-oh-KOO-peh.
I will only take a short time.	*Tomaré poco tiempo.*	Toh-mah-REH POH-koh TYEHM-poh.

2. Vital Signs

DOCTOR	*DOCTOR*	
I am going to…	*Le voy a…*	Leh voy ah…
• take your pulse.	• *tomar el pulso.*	• toh-MAHR ehl POOL-soh.
• count your respiratory movements.	• *contar las respiraciones.*	• Kohn-TAHR lahs rehs-pee-rah-SYOH-nehs.
• measure your blood pressure.	• *medir la presión arterial.*	• meh-DEER lah preh-SYOHN ahr-teh-RYAHL.
• measure your height.	• *medir su estatura.*	• meh-DEER soo ehs-tah-TOO-rah.
• weigh you.	• *pesarla(lo).*	• peh-SAHR-lah(loh).
May I have your wrist.	*Me permite su muñeca.*	Meh pehr-MEE-teh soo moo-NYEH-kah.
I will put this cuff around your arm.	*Le voy a poner esta banda alrededor del brazo.*	Voy ah poh-NEHR EHS-tah BAHN-dah ahl-reh-deh-DOHR dehl BRAH-soh.

Please stand here.	*Por favor, párese aquí.*	Pohr fah-VOHR, PAH-reh-seh ah-KEE.
Please step on the scale.	*Por favor, súbase a la báscula.*	Pohr fah-VOHR, SOO-bah-seh ah lah BAHS-koo-lah.

3. The Physical Examination

CULTURE NOTE ••••

DEALING WITH PATIENTS OF THE OPPOSITE SEX Latino patients, especially women who were born and raised in Latin America, are not used to undressing in front of others. Make sure your female patient is wearing a gown before you enter the room, and try to uncover only those parts of the body you are examining. If the doctor is male, the presence of a female nurse may be very reassuring. Allow the patient to cover herself immediately after the examination. Male patients are not used to having their genitalia or anal orifices handled by other males. Please make sure your patient understands that this is part of the examination. This rule should be observed by male and female doctors.

A. THE SKIN

DOCTOR	*DOCTOR*	
I have to uncover some parts of your body to examine your skin.	*Tengo que destapar algunas partes de su cuerpo para examinar cómo está su piel.*	TEHN-goh keh dehs-tah-PAHR ahl-GOO-nahs PAHR-tehs deh soo KWEHR-poh PAH-rah ehks-ah-mee-NAHR KOH-moh ehs-TAH soo pyehl.

If you feel pain or discomfort, please let me know.	*Si siente algún dolor o molestia, por favor avíseme.*	See SYEHN-teh ahl-GOON doh-LOHR oh moh-LEHS-tyah, pohr fah-VOHR ah-VEE-seh-meh.

B. THE LYMPH NODES

DOCTOR	*DOCTOR*	
I will put my hand on your body to examine your lymph glands.	*Voy a poner la mano sobre su cuerpo para examinar sus ganglios linfáticos.*	Voy ah poh-NEHR lah MAH-noh SOH-breh soo KWEHR-poh, PAH-rah ehx-ah-mee-NAHR soos GLAHN-glyohs leen-FAH-tee-kohs.

C. THE HEAD

DOCTOR	*DOCTOR*	
I have to palpate your head and touch your hair.	*Tengo que palparle la cabeza y tocarle el pelo.*	TEHN-goh keh pahl-PAHR-leh lah kah-BEH-sah ee toh-KAHR-leh ehl PEH-loh.

D. THE EYES

DOCTOR	*DOCTOR*	
I am going to examine your eyes.	*Le voy a examinar los ojos.*	Leh voy ah ehks-ah-mee-NAHR lohs OH-hohs.
Please look far away.	*Por favor, mire lejos.*	Pohr fah-VOHR, MEE-reh LEH-hohs.
Now, look at my finger.	*Ahora, mire mi dedo.*	Ah-OH-rah, MEE-reh mee DEH-doh.
Look at my eyes and tell me when you see my hands.	*Míreme a los ojos y dígame cuando vea mis manos.*	MEE-reh-meh ah lohs OH-hohs ee DEE-gah-meh KWAHN-doh VEH-ah mees MAH-nohs.

Tell me which one of my hands is moving.	*Dígame cuál de mis manos se está moviendo.*	DEE-gah-meh kwahl deh mees MAH-nohs seh ehs-TAH moh-VYEHN-doh.
I am going to shine a light in your eyes with a lamp.	*Voy a iluminarle los ojos con una lámpara.*	Voy ah ee-loo-mee-NAHR-leh lohs OH-hohs kohn OO-nah LAHM-pah-rah.
It will not hurt.	*No le molestará.*	Noh leh moh-lehs-tah-RAH.
I am going to see inside of your eyes with this instrument.	*Voy a mirar dentro de sus ojos con este instrumento.*	Voy a mee-RAHR DEHN-troh deh soos OH-hohs kohn EHS-teh eens-troo-MEHN-toh.

E. THE EARS/THE NOSE

DOCTOR	***DOCTOR***	
I have to examine your ears/nose.	*Tengo que examinarle los oídos/la nariz.*	TEHN-goh keh ehks-ah-mee-NAHR-leh lohs oh-EE-dohs/lah nah-REES.
I am going to put this instrument into your ears/nose.	*Voy a ponerle este instrumento en los oídos/la nariz.*	Voy ah poh-NEHR EHS-teh eens-troo-MEHN-toh ehn lohs oh-EE-dohs/lah nah-REES.
It will not hurt you.	*No le molestará.*	No leh moh-lehs-tah-RAH.
If it bothers you, please let me know.	*Si le molesta, me avisa.*	See leh moh-LEHS-tah, meh ah-VEE-sah.

F. THE MOUTH AND THROAT

DOCTOR	***DOCTOR***	
I have to examine your mouth and throat.	*Tengo que examinarle la boca y la garganta.*	TEHN-goh keh ehks-ah-mee-NAHR-leh lah BOH-kah ee lah gahr-GAHN-tah.

Please…	*Por favor,…*	Pohr fah-VOHR,…
• open your mouth.	• *abra la boca.*	• AH-brah lah BOH-kah.
• stick your tongue out.	• *saque la lengua.*	• SAH-keh lah LEHN-gwah.
• say "aah."	• *diga "aah."*	• DEE-gah "aah."
I am going to put this instrument inside your mouth.	*Voy a ponerle este instrumento en la boca.*	Voy ah poh-NEHR-leh EHS-teh een-stroo-MEHN-toh ehn lah BOH-kah.
You will feel slight discomfort.	*Va a sentir una pequeña incomodidad.*	Vah ah sehn-TEER OO-nah peh-KEH-nyah een-koh-moh-dee-DAHD.

G. THE NECK

DOCTOR	*DOCTOR*	
I have to examine your neck.	*Tengo que examinarle el cuello.*	TEHN-goh keh ehks-ah-mee-NAHR-leh ehl KWEH-yoh.
Please swallow.	*Por favor, trague.*	Pohr fah-VOHR, TRAH-geh.
Thanks.	*Gracias.*	GRAH-syahs.

H. THE BREASTS

DOCTOR	*DOCTOR*	
I have to examine your breasts.	*Tengo que examinarle los senos.*	TEHN-goh keh ehks-ah-mee-NAHR-leh lohs SEH-nohs.
May I touch you?	*¿Me permite tocarla?*	¿Meh pehr-MEE-teh toh-KAHR-lah?
If something hurts or feels uncomfortable, please tell me.	*Si le duele o le molesta algo, por favor dígamelo.*	See leh WEH-leh oh leh moh-LEHS-tah ahl-GOH, pohr fah-VOHR DEE-gah-meh-loh.

I. THORAX AND LUNGS

DOCTOR	*DOCTOR*	
I have to examine your chest, your back, and your lungs.	*Tengo que examinarle el pecho, la espalda, y los pulmones.*	TEHN-goh keh ehks-ah-mee-NAHR-leh ehl PEH-choh lah ehs-PAHL-dah, ee lohs pool-MOH-nehs.
Please…	*Por favor,…*	Pohr fah-VOHR,…
• sit like this.	• *siéntese así.*	• SYEHN-teh-seh ah-SEE.
• unbutton your dress.	• *desabróchese el vestido.*	• dehs-ah-BROH-cheh-seh ehl vehs-TEE-doh.
I have to put my hands over your chest and back.	*Tengo que ponerle las manos sobre su pecho y espalda.*	TEHN-goh keh poh-NEHR-leh lahs MAH-nohs SOH-breh soo PEH-choh ee ehs-PAHL-dah.
When I ask you to, please…	*Cuando se lo pida, por favor…*	KWAHN-doh seh loh PEE-dah, pohr fah-VOHR…
• say thirty-three.	• *diga treinta y tres.*	• DEE-gah TREHN-tah ee trehs.
• breathe deeply.	• *respire profundo.*	• rehs-PEE-reh proh-FOON-doh.
I have to…	*Tengo que…*	TEHN-goh keh…
• strike one hand with the other to hear the sound it makes.	• *pegar una mano con la otra para oír el sonido que hace.*	• peh-GAHR OO-nah MAH-noh kohn lah OH-trah PAH-rah oh-EER ehl soh-NEE-doh keh AH-seh.
• listen to your chest and back with this instrument.	• *oírle el pecho y la espalda con este instrumento.*	• oh-EER-leh ehl PEH-choh ee lah ehs-PAHL-dah kohn EHS-teh een-stroo-MEHN-toh.
It may be a little cold.	*Podría estar un poco frío.*	Poh-DREE-ah ehs-TAHR oon POH-koh-FREE-oh.

J. THE HEART

DOCTOR	DOCTOR	
Now, I am going to examine your heart.	*Ahora, voy a examinarle el corazón.*	Ah-OH-rah, voy ah ehks-ah-mee-NAHR-leh ehl koh-rah-SOHN.
I have…	*Tengo que…*	TEHN-goh keh…
• to strike one hand with the other to hear the sound it makes.	• *pegar una mano con la otra para oír el sonido que hace.*	• peh-GAHR OO-nah MAH-noh kohn lah OH-trah PAH-rah oh-EER ehl soh-NEE-doh keh AH-seh.
• listen to your heart with this instrument.	• *oír su corazón con este instrumento.*	• oh-EER soo koh-rah-SOHN kohn EHS-teh een-stroo-MEHN-toh.
Please lie on your side.	*Por favor, acuéstese de lado.*	Pohr fah-VOHR, ah-KWEHS-teh-seh deh LAH-doh.

K. THE ABDOMEN

DOCTOR	DOCTOR	
I have to examine your abdomen.	*Tengo que examinarle el abdomen.*	TEHN-goh keh ehks-ah-mee-NAHR-leh ehl ahb-DOH-mehn.
May I uncover you?	*¿Me permite que la (lo) destape?*	¿Meh pehr-MEE-teh keh lah (loh) dehs-TAH-peh?
I have to…	*Tengo que…*	TEHN-goh keh…
• put my hand over your abdomen to examine it.	• *ponerle las manos sobre el abdomen para examinarlo.*	• poh-NEHR-leh lahs MAH-nohs SOH-breh ehl ahb-DOH-mehn PAH-rah ehks-ah-mee-NAHR-loh.
• to strike one hand with the other to hear the sound it makes.	• *pegar una mano con la otra para oír el sonido que hace.*	• peh-GAHR OO-nah MAH-noh kohn lah OH-trah PAH-rah oh-EER ehl soh-NEE-doh keh AH-seh.

• to hear the noises in your abdomen with this instrument.	• *oír los ruidos de su abdomen con este instrumento.*	• oh-EER lohs ROO-ee-dohs deh soo-ahb-DOH-mehn kohn EHS-teh een-stroo-MEHN-toh.
If something hurts, please let me know.	*Si algo le duele, por favor me lo dice.*	See AHL-goh leh DWEH-leh, pohr fah-VOHR meh loh DEE-seh.

L. THE GENITALIA

DOCTOR	DOCTOR	
I have to examine your intimate parts.	*Tengo que examinarle las partes íntimas.*	TEHN-goh keh ehks-ah-mee-NAHR-leh lahs PAHR-tehs EEN-tee-mahs.
May I?	*¿Me lo permite?*	¿Meh loh pehr-MEE-teh?
If something hurts or bothers you, please tell me.	*Si le duele o le molesta algo, por favor dígamelo.*	See leh DWEH-leh oh leh moh-LEHS-tah AHL-goh pohr fah-VOHR DEE-gah-meh-loh.

If the patient is male:

DOCTOR	DOCTOR	
Please cough when I ask you to.	*Por favor, tosa cuando se lo pida.*	Pohr fah-VOHR, TOH-sah KWAHN-doh seh loh PEE-dah.

If the patient is female:

DOCTOR	DOCTOR	
Please lay down on the examining table.	*Por favor, acuéstese en la mesa de exploración.*	Pohr fah-VOHR, ah-KWEHS-teh-seh ehn lah MEH-sah deh ehx-ploh-rah-SYOHN.
The nurse will help you.	*La enfermera va a ayudarla.*	Lah ehn-fehr-MEH-rah vah ah ah-yoo-DAHR-lah.

Please put your feet on the stirrups.	*Por favor, ponga los pies en los estribos.*	Pohr fah-VOHR, POHN-gah lohs pyehs ehn lohs ehs-TREE-bohs.
Will you allow me to/ may I uncover you?	*¿Me permite/puedo destaparla?*	¿Meh pehr-MEE-teh/ PWEH-doh dehs-tah-PAHR-lah?
I am going to examine you with my right hand.	*Voy a examinarla con mi mano derecha.*	Voy ah ehks-ah-mee-NAHR-lah kohn mee MAH-noh deh-REH-chah.
I will try not to hurt you.	*Trataré de que no le duela.*	Trah-tah-REH deh keh noh leh DWEH-lah.
I am going to push over your pubis with my left hand in order to feel your organs better.	*Voy a empujar sobre su pubis con mi mano izquierda para sentir mejor sus órganos.*	Voy ah ehm-poo-HAHR SOH-breh soo POO-bees kohn mee ees-KYEHR-dah MAH-noh PAH-rah sehn-TEER meh-HOHR soos OHR-gah-nohs.
If something hurts or bothers you, please let me know.	*Si le duele o le molesta algo, por favor avíseme.*	See leh DWEH-leh oh leh moh-LEHS-tah AHL-goh, pohr fah-VOHR ah-VEE-seh-meh.
I am going to use an instrument to see your vagina and take samples.	*Voy a colocar un instrumento para poder ver su vagina y tomar muestras.*	Voy ah koh-loh-KAHR oon een-stroo-MEHN-toh PAH-rah POH-dehr vehr soo vah-HEE-nah ee toh-MAHR MWEHS-trahs.
It may be a little uncomfortable.	*Podría sentir una pequeña molestia.*	Poh-DREE-ah sehn-TEER OO-nah peh-keh-NYAH moh-lehs-TEE-ah.
Tell me if it's too uncomfortable.	*Dígame si le resulta muy molesto.*	DEE-gah-meh see leh reh-SOOL-tah moo-ee moh-LEHS-toh.

M. THE RECTAL EXAMINATION

DOCTOR	*DOCTOR*	
I have to examine your rectum with my finger.	*Tengo que examinarle el recto con el dedo.*	TEHN-goh keh ehks-ah-mee-NAHR-leh ehl REHK-toh kohn ehl DEH-doh.
May I?	*¿Puedo?*	¿PWEH-doh?
Please lay on your side.	*Por favor, acuéstese de lado.*	Pohr fah-VOHR, ah-KWEHS-teh-seh deh LAH-doh.
It may be a little uncomfortable.	*Podría sentir una pequeña molestia.*	Poh-DREE-ah sehn-TEER OO-nah peh-keh-NYAH moh-lehs-TEE-ah.

N. THE EXTREMITIES

DOCTOR	*DOCTOR*	
I have to examine your arms, legs, and spine.	*Tengo que examinarle los brazos, las piernas, y la columna vertebral.*	TEHN-goh keh ehks-ah-mee-NAHR-leh lohs BRAH-sohs, lahs PYEHR-nahs ee lah koh-LOOM-nah vehr-teh-BRAHL.
When I ask you to move the part I indicate, please do.	*Cuando se lo pida mover la parte que le señale, por favor hágalo.*	KWAHN-doh seh loh PEE-dah moh-VEHR lah PAHR-teh keh leh seh-NYAH-leh, pohr fah-VOHR AH-gah-loh.
Please move your…	*Por favor, mueva el (la/los/las)…*	Pohr fah-VOHR, MWEH-vah ehl (lah/lohs/lahs)…
• head.	• *cabeza.*	• kah-BEH-sah.
• neck.	• *cuello.*	• KWEH-yoh.
• shoulder.	• *hombro.*	• OHM-broh.
• arm.	• *brazo.*	• BRAH-soh.
• hand.	• *mano.*	• MAH-noh.
• fingers.	• *dedos.*	• DEH-dohs.
• leg.	• *pierna.*	• PYEHR-nah.

• feet.	• *pies.*	• pyehs.
• toes.	• *dedo del pie.*	• DEH-doh dehl pyeh.
DOCTOR	***DOCTOR***	
Now I am going to move your ____.	*Ahora yo le voy a mover el (la/los/las) ____.*	Ah-OH-rah leh voy ah moh-VEHR ehl (lah/lohs/lahs) ____.
Please relax.	*Por favor, relájese.*	Pohr fah-VOHR, reh-LAH-heh-seh.
Now, I need to see how strong you are.	*Ahora, necesito ver que fuerza tiene.*	Ah-OH-rah, neh-seh-SEE-toh vehr keh FWEHR-sah TYEH-neh.
Please use all your strength against me when I try to move your ____.	*Por favor, use toda su fuerza contra mí cuando trate de moverle el (la/los/las) ____.*	Pohr fah-VOHR, OO-seh TOH-dah soo FWEHR-sah KOHN-trah mee KWAHN-doh TRAH-teh deh moh-VEHR-leh ehl (lah/lohs/lahs) ____.

O. THE NEUROLOGICAL EXAMINATION

DOCTOR	***DOCTOR***	
I am going to…	*Voy a…*	Voy ah…
• examine your reflexes.	• *examinarle los reflejos.*	• ehks-ah-mee-NAHR-leh lohs reh-FLEH-hohs.
• use a rubber hammer.	• *usar un martillo de goma.*	• oo-SAHR oon mahr-TEE-yoh deh goh-mah.
Please relax.	*Por favor, tranquilícese.*	Pohr fah-VOHR, trahn-kee-LEE-seh-seh.
Close your eyes.	*Cierre los ojos.*	SYEH-rreh lohs OH-hohs.
Tell me if…	*Dígame si…*	DEE-gah-meh see…
• I am moving your finger/toe up or down.	• *le estoy moviendo el dedo hacia arriba o abajo.*	• leh ehs-TOY moh-VYEHN-doh ehl DEH-doh AH-syah ah-REE-bah oh ah-BAH-hoh.

• you feel the vibrations.	• *siente las vibraciones.*	• see SYEHN-teh lahs vee-brah-SYOH-nehs.
Please get up and walk a few steps.	*Por favor, levántese y camine unos pasos.*	Pohr fah-VOHR, leh-VAHN-teh-seh ee kah-MEE-neh OO-nohs PAH-sohs.
Stand with your eyes closed.	*Párese con los ojos cerrados.*	PAH-reh-seh kohn lohs OH-hohs seh-RRAH-dohs.
Tell me what am I touching you with.	*Dígame con que lo (la) estoy tocando.*	DEE-gah-meh kohn keh loh (lah) ehs-TOY toh-KAHN-doh.
PATIENT	*PACIENTE*	
With...	*Con...*	Kohn...
• a pin.	• *una aguja.*	• OO-nah ah-GOO-hah.
• a brush.	• *un cepillo.*	• oon seh-PEE-yoh.
• something soft/hard.	• *algo blando/duro.*	• AHL-goh BLAHN-doh/DOO-roh.
DOCTOR	*DOCTOR*	
Tell me if it feels hot or cold.	*Dígame si se siente caliente o frío.*	DEE-gah-meh see SYEHN-teh kah-LYEHN-teh oh FREE-oh.

4. Specific Medical Procedures

A. DRAWING BLOOD

If the patient has to return at a later point in time:

DOCTOR	*DOCTOR*	
I need to take a blood sample.	*Necesito tomar una muestra de sangre.*	Neh-seh-SEE-toh-MAHR OO-nah MWEHS-trah deh SAHN-greh.

We have to draw your blood before breakfast.	*Tenemos que sacar la sangre antes del desayuno.*	Teh-NEH-mohs keh sah-KAHR lah SAHN-greh AHN-tehs dehl dehs-ah-YOO-noh.
Go to sleep as usual.	*Duerma como siempre.*	DWEHR-mah KOH-moh SYEHM-preh.
Do not eat or drink anything after you wake up.	*No coma ni beba nada después de despertar.*	Noh KOH-moh nee BEH-bah NAH-dah dehs-PWEHS deh dehs-pehr-TAHR.
Come to the office as early as possible.	*Venga al consultorio tan pronto como pueda.*	VEHN-gah ahl kohn-sool-TOH-ryoh tahn PROHN-toh KOH-moh PWEH-dah.

If the patient is already in the office, ready to give blood:

Please give me your arm.	*Por favor, déme el brazo.*	Pohr ah-VOHR, DEH-meh ehl BRAH-soh.
This will cause a a little discomfort.	*Le causará un poco de molestia.*	Leh kahw-sah-RAH oon POH-koh deh moh-LEHS-tyah.
I am going to put a tournique around your arm.	*Le voy a poner un torniquete en el brazo.*	Leh voy ah poh-NEHR oon tohr-nee-KEH-teh ehn ehl BRAH-soh.

B. GETTING A URINE SAMPLE

DOCTOR	*DOCTOR*	
We need a urine sample.	*Necesitamos una muestra de orina.*	Neh-seh-see-TAH-mos OO-nah MWEHS-trah deh oh-REE-nah.
The urine has to be from midstream.	*La orina tiene que ser de la mitad del chorro.*	Lah oh-REE-nah TYEH-neh keh sehr deh lah mee-TAHD dehl KHOH-rroh.
Put the urine in this cup.	*Ponga la orina en este vaso.*	POHN-gah lah oh-REE-nah ehn EHS-teh VAH-soh.

The restroom is...	*El baño está...*	Ehl bah-NYOH ehs-TAH...
• down the hall.	• *al final del pasillo.*	• ahl fee-NAHL dehl pah-SEE-yoh.
• next door.	• *en la próxima puerta.*	• ehn lah PROHKS-ee-mah PWEHR-tah.
• to your left/right.	• *a la izquierda/derecha.*	• ah lah ees-KYEHR-dah/deh-REH-chah.
• right here.	• *aquí.*	• ah-KEE.

C. TAKING AN ELECTROCARDIOGRAM (EKG)

DOCTOR	DOCTOR	
I have to check what your heart is doing.	*Tengo que revisar lo que está haciendo su corazón.*	TEHN-goh keh reh-vee-SAHR loh keh ehs-TAH ah-SYEHN-doh soo koh-rah-SOHN.
Please take off your shirt/blouse and bra.	*Por favor, quítese la camisa/blusa y sostén.*	Pohr fah-VOHR, KEE-teh-seh lah kah-MEE-sah/BLOO-sah ee sohs-TEHN.
Put on this gown.	*Póngase esta bata.*	POHN-gah-seh EHS-tah BAH-tah.
Please lay down here.	*Por favor, acuéstese aquí.*	Pohr fah-VOHR, ah-KWEHS-teh-seh ah-KEE.
I am going to put electrodes on your body.	*Le voy a poner unos electrodos en el cuerpo.*	Leh voy ah poh-NEHR OO-nohs eh-lehk-TROH-dohs ehn ehl KWEHR-poh.
May I?	*¿Puedo?*	¿PWEH-doh?
Relax.	*Relájese.*	Reh-LAH-heh-seh.
It will not cause any discomfort.	*No le causará ninguna molestia.*	Noh leh kahw-sah-RAH neen-GOO-nah moh-LEHS-tyah.

D. THE CHEST X-RAY

DOCTOR	*DOCTOR*	
I have to take a chest X-ray.	*Tengo que tomarle una radiografía del tórax.*	TEHN-goh keh toh-MAHR-leh OO-nah rah-dyoh-grah-FEE-ah.
Please take off your shirt/blouse and bra.	*Por favor, quítese la camisa/blusa y sostén.*	Pohr fah-VOHR, KEE-teh-seh lah kah-MEE-sah/BLOO-sah ee sohs-TEHN.
Put on this gown.	*Póngase esta bata.*	POHN-gah-seh EHS-tah BAH-tah.
Please follow me.	*Por favor, sígame.*	Pohr fah-VOHR, SEE-gah-meh.
Stand here.	*Párese aquí.*	PAH-reh-seh ah-KEE.
Put your chin here.	*Ponga aquí el barba.*	POHN-gah ah-KEE ehl BAHR-bah.
Place your shoulders like this.	*Ponga así los hombros.*	POHN-gah ah-SEE lohs OHM-brohs.
Take a deep breath and hold it when I tell you.	*Respire hondo y detenga el aire adentro cuando le diga.*	Rehs-PEE-reh OHN-doh ee deh-TEHN-gah ehl ah-EE-reh ah-DEHN-troh KWAHN-doh leh DEE-gah.
Now, take a deep breath.	*Ahora, respire hondo.*	Ah-OH-rah, rehs-PEE-reh OHN-doh.
Thank you.	*Gracias.*	GRAH-syahs.

E. THE STOOL SPECIMEN

DOCTOR	*DOCTOR*	
I need a sample of your stool.	*Necesito una muestra de su excremento.*	Neh-seh-SEE-toh OO-nah MWEHS-trah deh soo ehks-kreh-MEHN-toh.
Please…	*Por favor,…*	Pohr fah-VOHR,…
• put a small amount in this cup.	• *ponga un poco en este vaso.*	• POHN-gah oon POH-koh ehn EHS-teh VAH-soh.

• bring it in tomorrow.	• *tráigala mañana.*	• TRAH-ee-gah-lah mah-NYAH-nah.

F. THE SPUTUM SPECIMEN

DOCTOR	*DOCTOR*	
I need a sample of your spit.	*Necesito una muestra de su esputo.*	Neh-seh-SEE-toh OO-nah MWEHS-trah deh soo ehs-POO-toh.
Please spit in this cup.	*Por favor, escupa en este vaso.*	Pohr fah-VOHR, ehs-KOO-pah ehn EHS-teh VAH-soh.
If you cannot spit now, please bring it in tomorrow.	*Si no puede escupir ahora, por favor me lo trae mañana.*	See noh PWEH-deh ehs-koo-PEER ah-OH-rah, pohr-fah-VOHR meh loh TRAH-eh mah-NYAH-nah.

G. DRAWING BLOOD FROM A FINGER OR HEEL

DOCTOR	*DOCTOR*	
I need to take a few drops of blood…	*Necesito sacarle unas gotas de sangre…*	Neh-seh-SEE-toh sah-KAHR-leh OO-nahs GOH-tahs deh SAHN-greh…
• from your fingers.	• *de uno de sus dedos.*	• deh OO-noh deh soos DEH-dohs.
• from the heel of your child.	• *de uno de los talones de su niño(a).*	• deh OO-noh deh lohs tah-LOH-nehs deh soo NEEN-yoh(ah).
I am going to puncture your finger/your heel.	*Voy a picarle el dedo/el talón.*	Voy ah pee-KAHR-leh ehl DEH-doh/ehl tah-LOHN.
You will feel a slight discomfort.	*Sentirá una pequeña molestia.*	Sehn-tee-RAH OO-nah peh-KEH-nyah moh-LEHS-tyah.

H. GETTING A THROAT CULTURE

DOCTOR	DOCTOR	
I need to take a sample from the back of your throat.	*Voy a tomarle una muestra de la garganta.*	Voy ah toh-MAHR-leh OO-nah MWEHS-trah deh lah gahr-GAHN-tah.
I am going to take the sample with this cotton swab.	*Voy a tomar la muestra con un hisopo.*	Voy a toh-NAHR lah MWEHS-trah kohn oon ee-SOH-poh.
It will just be a little uncomfortable.	*Sólo será un poco desagradable.*	SOH-loh seh-RAH oon POH-koh dehs-ah-grah-DAH-bleh.
Please stick your tongue out and say "aah."	*Por favor, saque la lengua y diga "aah."*	Pohr fah-VOHR, SAH-keh lah LEHN-gwah ee DEE-gah "aah."

I. GENERAL CLOSURE

DOCTOR	DOCTOR	
Thank you.	*Gracias.*	GRAH-syahs.
That's it.	*Eso es todo.*	EH-soh ehs TOH-doh.
You're all done.	*Ya hemos terminado.*	Yah HEH-mohs tehr-mee-NAH-doh.
You can get dressed now.	*Ya puede vestirse.*	Yah PWEH-deh vehs-TEER-seh.
I'll be back to discuss the results.	*Volveré para hablar sobre los resultados.*	Vohl-veh-REH PAH-rah ah-BLAHR-SOH-breh lohs reh-soohl-TAH-dohs.

THE PROGNOSIS

CULTURE NOTE ••••

MEDICAL TREATMENT AND THE FAMILY In Latino culture, medical problems are viewed not as an individual, but as a family matter. Not only the patient, but his or her entire family may need to be informed about the prognosis and the treatment plan. It therefore may be necessary that the patient has sufficient time to discuss matters with his or her family, or that you, as the medical provider, discuss matters with the entire family. In some cases, it may be better to call in an interpreter when discussing the prognosis and treatment plan, to make sure that your patient and his or her family do not misunderstand valuable and sensitive information. Particularly, if your patient is seriously ill, an interpreter may find more sensitive words to convey the bad news and to explain the complicated treatment plan.

1. Delivering and Discussing the Prognosis

DOCTOR	*DOCTOR*	
Fortunately, I have good news.	*Afortunadamente, tengo buenas noticias.*	Ah-fohr-too-NAH-dah-mehn-teh TEHN-goh BYEH-nahs noh-TEE-syahs.
There is nothing to worry about.	*No hay nada de que preocuparnos.*	Noh ay NAH-dah deh keh pre-oh-koo-PAHR-nohs.
Unfortunately, I do not have good news.	*Desafortunadamente, no tengo buenas noticias.*	Dehs-ah-fohr-too NAH-dah-mehn-teh, noh TEHN-goh BYEH-nahs noh-TEE-syahs.
Your/your father's/your mother's/your child's... suggest(s) that you are/your father/mother/child is healthy/sick.	*La/el... de usted/de su papá/mamá/de su hijo(a) sugiere(en) que usted/su papá/mamá/su hijo(a) está sano(a)/enfermo(a).*	Lah/ehl... deh oo-STEHD/deh soo pah-PAH/mah-MAH/deh soo EE-hoh(hah) soo-HYEH-rehn keh oos-TEHD/soo pah-PAH/mah-MAH/soo EE-hoh(hah) ehs-TAH SAH-noh(nah)/ehn-FEHR-moh(mah).
• history	• *historial*	• ees-TOH-ryahl
• examination	• *examen físico*	• ehx-AH-mehn FEE-see-koh
• lab results	• *resultados del laboratorio*	• reh-sool-TAH-dohs dehl lah-boh-rah-TOH-ryoh
I would like to...	*Me gustaría...*	Meh goos-tah-REE-ah...
• discuss your results.	• *discutir sus resultados.*	• dees-koo-TEER soos reh-sool-TAH-dohs.
• discuss your father's/mother's/child's results.	• *discutir los resultados de su papá/mamá/niño(a).*	• dees-koo-TEER lohs reh-sool-TAH-dohs deh soo pah-PAH/mah-MAH/NEEN-yoh(yah).

• offer you some options.	• *ofrecerle algunas opciones.*	• oh-freh-SEHR-leh ahl-GOO-nahs ohp-SYOH-nehs.
You will have to make some decisions about how we will proceed.	*Tendrá que hacer algunas decisiones sobre cómo procederemos.*	Tehn-DRAH keh ah-SEHR ahl-GOO-nahs deh-see-SYOHN-ehs SOH-breh KOH-moh proh-seh-deh-REH-mohs.
Would you like your spouse/son/daughter to be here?	*¿Le gustaría que su esposa(o)/hijo/hija estuviera aquí?*	¿Leh goos-tah-REE-ah keh soo ehs-POH-sah/EE-hoh/EE-hah ehs-too-VYEH-rah ah-KEE?
Would you feel more comfortable discussing this with an interpreter?	*¿Se sentiría más a gusto discutiendo esto con un intérprete?*	¿Seh sehn-tee-REE-ah MAHS ah GOOS-toh dees-koo-TYEHN-doh EHS-toh kohn oon een-TEHR-preh-teh?
An interpreter will be better able to convey what I want to say.	*Un intérprete podrá comunicar mejor lo que quiero decir.*	Oon een-TEHR-preh-teh poh-DRAH koh-moo-nee-KAHR meh-HOHR loh keh leh KYEH-roh DEH-seer.
I'll call someone who speaks Spanish who'll help us to discuss this.	*Llamaré a alguien que habla español para que nos ayude a hablar sobre esto.*	Yah-mah-REH ah ahl-GYEHN keh ah-BLAH ehs-pah-NYOHL PAH-rah keh nohs ah-YOO-deh ah ah-BLAHR SOH-breh EHS-toh.
PATIENT	***PACIENTE***	
What is wrong with me/him/her?	*¿De qué estoy/ está enfermo(a)?*	¿Deh keh ehs-TOY/ ehs-TAH ehn-FEHR-moh(mah)?
Is the disease serious?	*¿Es seria la enfermedad?*	¿Ehs SEH-ree-ah lah ehn-fehr-meh-DAHD?
Is it curable?	*¿Es curable la enfermedad?*	¿Ehs koo-RAH-bleh lah ehn-fehr-meh-DAHD?

Am I/is he/she going to be able to keep working?	*¿Voy/va a poder seguir trabajando?*	Voy/vah ah poh-DEHR seh-GHEER trah-bah-HAHN-doh?
Do I/does he/she have to go to the hospital?	*¿Tengo/tiene que ir al hospital?*	¿TEHN-goh/TYEH-neh keh eer ahl ohs-pee-TAHL?
Is an operation necessary?	*¿Va a ser necesaria una operación?*	¿Vah ah sehr neh-seh-SAH-ree-ah OO-nah oh-peh-rah-SYOHN?
DOCTOR	***DOCTOR***	
The disease that you have/he/she has is called...	*La enfermedad que usted/él/ella tiene se llama...*	Lah ehn-fehr-meh-DAHD keh oos-TEHD/EHL/EH-yah TYEH-neh seh YAH-mah _____.
• AIDS.	• *SIDA.*	• SEE-dah.
• Hepatitis.	• *Hepatitis.*	• eh-pah-TEE-tees.
• Syphilis.	• *Sífilis.*	• SEE-fee-lees.
• Gastritis.	• *Gastritis.*	• gahs-TREE-tees.
• Apendicitis.	• *Apendicitis.*	• Ah-pehn-dee-SEE-tees.
• Cancer.	• *Cáncer.*	• KAHN-sehr.
• Irritable Bowel Syndrome.	• *Colon Irritable.*	• KOH-lohn ee-ree-TAH-bleh.
It...	*La enfermedad...*	Lahn ehn-fehr-meh-DAHD...
• is (not) serious.	• *(no) es seria.*	• (noh) ehs SEH-ryah.
• is (not) acute.	• *(no) es aguda.*	• (noh) ehs ah-GOO-dah.
• is (not) curable.	• *(no) es curable.*	• (noh) ehs koo-RAH-bleh.
• is treated with an operation.	• *se trata con una operación.*	• seh trah-TAH kohn OO-nah oh-peh-rah-SYOHN.

You/he/she…	*Usted/él/ella…*	Oos-TEHD/ehl/EH-yah…
• will (not) be able to work.	• *(no) va a poder trabajar.*	• (noh) vah ah poh-DEHR trah-bah HAHR.
• will (not) have to go to the hospital.	• *(no) tendrá que hospitalizarse.*	• (noh) tehn-DRAH keh ohs-pee-tah-lee-SAHR-seh.
Fortunately, the disease that you have/he/she has is acute but curable.	*Afortunadamente, la enfermedad que usted/él/ella tiene aguda pero es curable.*	Ah-fohr-too-nah-DAH-mehn-teh, lah ehn-fehr-meh-DAH keh oos-TEHD/ehl/EH-yah TYEH-neh ah-GOO-dah peh-roh ehs koo-RAH-bleh.
PATIENT	***PACIENTE***	
How long am I/is he/she going to be sick?	*¿Cuánto tiempo voy/va a estar enfermo(a)?*	¿KWAHN-toh TYEHM-poh voy/vah ah ehs-TAHR ehn-FEHR-moh(mah)?
DOCTOR	***DOCTOR***	
You/he/she will be sick…	*Va a estar enfermo(a)…*	Vah ah ehs-TAHR ehn-FEHR-moh (mah)…
• a few days.	• *unos cuantos días.*	• OO-nohs KWAHN-tohs DEE-ahs.
• one week.	• *una semana.*	• OO-nah seh-MAH-nah.
• two or three weeks.	• *dos o tres semanas.*	• dohs oh trehs seh-MAH-nahs.
Unfortunately, the disease that you have/he/she has is chronic and incurable.	*Desafortunadamente, la enfermedad que usted/él/ella tiene es crónica e incurable.*	Dehs-ah-fohr-too-NAH-dah-mehn-teh, lah ehn-fehr-meh-DAHD keh oos-TEHD/ehl/EH-yah TYEH-neh ehs KROH-nee-kah ee een-koo-RAH-bleh.
PATIENT	***PACIENTE***	
I don't know what that means.	*No sé lo que significa eso.*	Noh seh loh keh seeg-nee-FEE-kah EH-soh.

DOCTOR	*DOCTOR*	
Your/his/her illness will always be there and cannot be cured.	*Su enfermedad va a durar para siempre y no tiene cura.*	Soo ehn-fehr-meh-DAHD vah ah DOO-rahr PAH-rah SYEHM-preh ee noh TYEH-neh KOO-rah.
To treat your/his/her disease...	*Para curar su enfermedad...*	PAH-rah KOO-rahr soo ehn-fehr-meh-DAHD...
• I will prescribe medications.	• *le recetaré unas medicinas.*	• leh reh-seh-tah-REH OO-nahs.
• you/he/she should change your/his/her lifestyle.	• *deberá cambiar su estilo de vida.*	• deh-beh-RAH kahm-BEE-AHR soo ehs-TEE-loh deh VEE-dah.
• you/he/she will need an operation.	• *tiene que operarse.*	• TYEH-neh keh oh-peh-RAHR-seh.
PATIENT	***PACIENTE***	
When can I go back to work?	*¿Cuándo puedo regresar al trabajo?*	¿KWAHN-doh PWEH-doh reh-greh-SAHR ahl trah-BAH-hoh?
Will it always hurt?	*¿Me va a doler siempre?*	¿Meh vah ah doh-LEHR SYEHM-preh?
Will I/he/she die?	*¿Me voy/se va a morir?*	¿Meh voy/seh vah ah moh-REER?
How long am I/is he/she going to live?	*¿Cuánto tiempo voy/va a vivir?*	¿KWAHN-toh TYEHM-poh voy/vah ah VEE-veer?
DOCTOR	***DOCTOR***	
You/he/she can expect to live _____ years with the treatment.	*Usted/él/ella puede esperar vivir _____ años con el tratamiento.*	Oos-TEHD/EHL/EH-yah PWEH-deh ehs-peh-RAHR vee-VEER _____ ah-NYOHS kohn ehl trah-tah-MYEHN-toh.
PATIENT	***PACIENTE***	
What happens if I don't/ he/she doesn't follow the treatment?	*¿Qué pasa si yo no sigo/ él/ella no sigue el tratamiento?*	¿Keh PAH-sah see yoh noh SEE-goh ehl/EH-yah noh SEE-geh ehl trah-tah-MYEHN-toh?

DOCTOR	***DOCTOR***	
Your/his/her illness will get worse.	*Su enfermedad empeorará.*	Soo ehn-fehr-meh-DAHD ehm-peh-oh-rah-RAH.
Patients that follow the treatment live well.	*Los pacientes que siguen el tratamiento viven bien.*	Lohs pah-SYEHN-tehs keh SEE-ghehn ehl trah-tah-MYEHN-toh VEE-vehn byehn.
PATIENT	***PACIENTE***	
Is the treatment very expensive?	*¿Es muy caro el tratamiento?*	¿Ehs MOO-ee KAH-roh ehl trah-tah-MYEHN-toh?
You will have to spend about _____ dollars a month.	*Va a tener que gastar como _____ dólares al mes.*	Vah ah teh-NEHR keh gahs-TAHR KOH-moh _____ DOH-lah-rehs ahl mehs.
Your insurance covers most of this.	*Su seguro cubre la mayor parte.*	Soo seh-GOO-roh KOO-breh lah mah-YOHR PAHR-teh.
PATIENT	***PACIENTE***	
Will I need special care at the end?	*¿Voy a necesitar cuidado especial al final?*	¿Voy ah neh-seh-see-TAHR KWEE-DAH-doh ehs-peh-SYAHL-ahl fee-NAHL?
DOCTOR	***DOCTOR***	
You may need…	*Puede necesitar…*	PWEH-deh neh-seh-see-TAHR…
• home care.	• *cuidado a domicilio.*	• kwee-DAH-doh ah doh-mee-SEE-lyoh.
• to go to a nursing home.	• *ir a un hospicio.*	• eer ah oon ohs-PEE-syoh.
• to receive hospice care.	• *cuidado de hospicio.*	• kwee-DAH-doh deh ohs-PEE-syoh.
• to have a nasogastric tube.	• *una sonda nasogástrica.*	• OO-nah SOHN-dah nah-soh-GAHS-tree-kah.
• to be on a ventilator.	• *estar en un ventilador.*	• ehs-TAHR ehn oon vehn-tee-lah-DOHR.

Do you have any questions?	*¿Tiene alguna pregunta?*	¿TYEH-neh ahl-GOO-nah preh-GOON-tah?

VOCABULARY ••••

COMFORTING PHRASES

Don't worry.	*No se preocupe.*	Noh seh preh-oh-KOO-peh.
We'll take care of you.	*Nosotros lo(la) vamos a cuidar.*	Noh-SOH-trohs loh (lah) VAH-mohs ah kwee-DAHR.
We'll help you.	*Nosotros lo(la) vamos a ayudar.*	Noh-SOH-trohs loh (lah) VAH-mohs ah ah-yoo-DAHR.
You will not be in pain.	*No sentirá dolor.*	Noh sehn-tee-RAH doh-LOHR.
There are many good treatment options.	*Hay muchas opciónes de tratamiento muy buenas.*	Ay MOO-chahs ohp-SYOH-nehs deh trah-tah-MYEHN-toh moo-ee BWEH-nohs.
We will make you as comfortable as possible.	*Lo (la) haremos sentirse lo más cómodo(a) posible.*	Loh (lah) ah-REH-mohs sehn-TEER-seh loh mahs KOH-moh-doh(dah) poh-SEE-bleh.
You will live a long and full life.	*Usted va a vivir una vida larga y saludable.*	Oos-TEHD vah ah VEE-veer OO-nah VEE-dah LAHR-gah ee sah-loo-DAH-bleh.
You have a very good chance of survival.	*Usted tiene probabilidades muy altas de sobrevivir.*	Oos-TEHD TYEH-neh proh-bah-bee-lee-DAH-dehs moo-ee AHL-tahs deh soh-breh-VEER.

(cont'd.)

Comforting Phrases *(cont'd.)*

Calm down.	*¡Cálmese!*	¡KAHL-meh-seh!
It's okay to be upset/to cry.	*Entiendo que esté enojado/quiera llorar.*	Ehn-tyehn-doh keh ehs-TEH eh-noh-HAH-doh/KYEH-rah yoh-RAHR.
Is there anything I can do to help you right now?	*¿Hay algo que puedo hacer para ayudarle ahorita?*	¿Ay AHL-goh keh PWEH-doh ah-SEHR PAH-rah ah-yoo-DAH-leh awoh-REE-tah?
Is there anyone you'd like me to call for you?	*¿Quiere que llame a alguien para que la acompañé?*	¿KYEH-reh keh yah-meh ah AHL-gyehn PAH-rah keh lah ah-kohm-pah-NYEH?

2. Referring the Patient

DOCTOR	*DOCTOR*	
I think you should see…	*Creo que debería ver…*	KREH-oh keh deh-beh-RYAH vehr…
• another doctor.	• *otro doctor.*	• OH-troh dohk-TOHR.
• a specialist.	• *un especialista.*	• oon ehs-peh-syah-LEES-tah.
I think you should get a second opinion.	*Creo que debería obtener una segunda opinión.*	KREH-oh keh deh-beh-REE-ah ohb-teh-NEHR OO-nah seh-GOON-dah oh-pee-NYOHN.
He/she will be able to tell us…	*Él/ella nos podrá decir…*	Ehl EH-yah nohs poh-DRAH deh-SEER…
• what is wrong.	• *lo que tiene.*	• loh keh TYEH-neh.
• what we should do for you.	• *lo que deberíamos hacer con usted.*	• loh keh deh-beh-REE-ah-mohs ah-SEHR kohn oos-TEHD.

• if there is something to worry about.	• *si tenemos algo de que preocuparnos.*	• see teh-NEH-mohs AHL-goh deh keh preh-oh-koo-PAHR-nohs.
Call me in my office... for the results.	*Llámeme al consultorio...para darle los resultados.*	YAH-meh-meh ahl kohn-sool-TOH-ryoh ...PAH-rah DAHR-leh lohs reh-sool-TAH-dohs.
• after you see Dr. ____.	• *después que vea al Doctor ____.*	• dehs-PWEHS keh VEH-ah ahl Dohk-TOHR ____.
• tomorrow.	• *mañana.*	• mah-NYAH-nah.
• in two days.	• *en dos días.*	• ehn dohs DEE-ahs.
• next week.	• *la semana que entra.*	• lah seh-MAH-nah keh EHN-trah.
We will call you...	*Nosotros lo (la) llamaremos...*	Nohs-OH-trohs loh (lah) yah-mah-REH-mohs...
• with the results.	• *con los resultados.*	• kohn lohs reh-soohl-TAH-dohs.
• to make an appointment to see me and discuss the results.	• *para hacer una cita conmigo y discutir los resultados.*	• PAH-rah ah-SEHR OO-nah SEE-tah kohn-MEE-goh ee dees-koo-TEER lohs reh-sool-TAH-dohs.

3. Discussing the Treatment

A. DISCUSSING THE MEDICAL INDICATIONS (WITH COMPETENT PATIENTS OR THEIR SURROGATES)

DOCTOR	*DOCTOR*	
Based on the diagnosis, we have to...	*En base al diagnóstico, tenemos que...*	Ehn BAH-seh ahl dee-ahg-NOHS-tee-koh, teh-NEH-mohs keh...
• give you some medications.	• *darle unas medicinas.*	• DAHR-leh OO-nahs meh-dee-SEE-nahs.
• give you radiation therapy.	• *darle radiación.*	• DAHR-leh rah-dee-ah-SYOHN.

• operate on you.	• *operarla(lo).*	• oh-peh-RAHR-lah(loh).
• ask you to...	• *perdirle que...*	• peh-DEER-leh keh...
• start/stop exercising.	• *empezar a/dejar de hacer ejercicio.*	• ehm-peh-SAHR ah/deh-HAHR deh ah-SEHR-eh-hehr-SEE-syoh.
• gain/lose weight.	• *ganar/perder peso.*	• gah-NAHR/pehr-DEHR PEH-soh.
• stop driving.	• *deje de manejar.*	• DEH-heh deh mah-neh-HAHR.
• practice safe sex.	• *practica sexo seguro.*	• prah-TEE-kah SEHK-soh seh-GOO-roh.
• learn to relax.	• *aprenda a descansar.*	• ah-PREHN-dah ah dehs-kahn-SAHR.
PATIENT	***PACIENTE***	
Why?	*¿Por qué?*	¿Pohr keh?
DOCTOR	***DOCTOR***	
Because we want to...	*Porque queremos...*	POHR-keh keh-REH-mohs...
• prevent you from getting worse.	• *prevenir que usted empeore.*	• preh-veh-NEER keh oos-TEHD ehm-peh-OH-reh.
• prevent a recurrence.	• *prevenir una recaída.*	• preh-veh-NEER OO-nah reh-kah-EE-dah.
• cure your disease.	• *curar su enfermedad.*	• koo-RAHR soo ehn-fehr-meh-DAHD.
• improve the quality of your life.	• *mejorar la calidad de su vida.*	• meh-hoh-RAHR lah kah-lee-DAHD deh soo VEE-dah.
• alleviate your pain.	• *aliviar su dolor.*	• ah-lee-VYAHR soo doh-LOHR.
• prevent you from dying prematurely.	• *prevenir que usted muera antes de tiempo.*	• preh-veh-NEER keh oos-TEHD MWEH-rah AHN-tehs deh TYEHM-poh.

B. DISCUSSING THE PATIENT'S PREFERENCES

What are the risks of the treatment?	*¿Cuáles con los riesgos del tratamiento?*	¿KWAH-lehs sohn lohs RYEHS-gohs dehl trah-tah-MYEHN-toh?
DOCTOR	*DOCTOR*	
The risk is that you…	*El riesgo es que…*	Ehl RYEHS-goh ehs keh…
• may not improve.	• *no mejore.*	• noh meh-HOH-reh.
• may suffer from side effects.	• *sufra un efecto secundario.*	• SOO-frah oon eh-FEHK-toh seh-koon-DAH-ryoh.
• may get worse.	• *empeore.*	• ehm-peh-OH-reh.
• may get very sick.	• *se ponga muy mal.*	• seh POHN-gah moo-ee mahl.
• may die.	• *se muera.*	• seh MWEH-rah.
The treatment has some unpleasant side effects.	*El tratamiento tiene algunos efectos secundarios que no son placenteros.*	Ehl trah-tah-MYEHN-toh TYEH-neh ahl-GOO-nohs eh-FEHK-tohs seh-koon-DAH-yohs keh noh sohn plah-sehn-TEH-rohs.
You may…	*Usted puede…*	Oos-TEHD PWEH-deh…
• feel nauseous.	• *sentirse con náusea.*	• sehn-TEER-seh kohn NWAH-seh-ah.
• gain/lose weight.	• *ganar/perder peso.*	• gah-NAHR/pehr-DEHR PEH-soh.
• loose your hair.	• *perder el pelo.*	• pehr-DEHR ehl PEH-loh.
• have diarrhea.	• *tener diarrea.*	• teh-NEHR dyah-REH-ah.
• feel weaker.	• *sentirse más débil.*	• sehn-TEER-seh MAHS DEH-beel.
• have some pain.	• *tener dolor.*	• teh-NEHR doh-LOHR.
• have an irregular heart beat.	• *tener latidos irregulares.*	• teh-NEHR lah-TEE-dohs ee-reh-goo-LAH-rehs.

• have a dry mouth.	• *tener la boca seca.*	• teh-NEHR lah BOH-kah SEH-kah.
• feel depressed.	• *sentirse deprimido(a).*	• sehn-TEER-seh deh-pree-MEE-doh(dah).
• feel anxious.	• *sentirse ansioso(a).*	• sehn-TEER-seh ahn-SYOH-soh(sah).
• lose interest in sex.	• *perder interés en el sexo.*	• pehr-DEHR een-teh-REHS ehn ehl SEHKS-oh.
But, it is unlikely that something like that will happen.	*Pero, es poco probable que algo así suceda.*	PEH-roh, ehs POH-koh proh-BAH-bleh keh AHL-goh ah-SEE soo-SEH-dah.
You are free to decide if you want this treatment or not.	*Usted tiene la libertad para decidir si quiere o no este tratamiento.*	Oos-TEHD TYEH-neh la lee-behr-TAHD PAH-rah deh-see-DEER see KYEH-reh oh noh EHS-teh trah-tah-MYEHN-toh.
You can take some time to make your decision.	*Puede tomarse un tiempo para decidir.*	PWEH-deh toh-MAHR-seh oon TYEHM-poh PAH-rah deh-see-DEER.
I need to know your decision by the _____ at _____ o'clock.	*Yo necesito saber cuál es su decisión para el día _____ a las _____.*	Yoh neh-seh-SEE-toh sah-BEHR KWAHL ehs soo deh-see-SYOHN PAH-rah ehl DEE-ah _____ ah lahs _____.
You may want to discuss this with your clergy/family/social worker.	*Tal vez usted quiere discutir esto con su pastor/familia/ trabajador(a) social.*	Tahl vehs OOS-tehd KYEH-reh dees-koo-TEER EHS-toh kohn soo PAHS-tohr/fah-MEE-lyah/trah-bah-HAH-dohr(DOH-rah) soh-SYAHL.
We do not have time to lose.	*No tenemos tiempo que perder.*	Noh teh-NEH-mohs TYEHM-poh keh pehr-DEHR.

PATIENT	***PACIENTE***	
When do you want to begin treatment?	*¿Cuándo quiere empezar el tratamiento?*	¿KWAHN-doh KYEH-reh ehm-peh-SAHR ehl trah-tah-MYEHN-toh?
DOCTOR	***DOCTOR***	
If you accept the treatment, we will start...	*Si usted acepta el tratamiento, empezaremos...*	See oos-TEHD ah SEHP-tah ehl trah-tah-MYEHN-toh, ehm-peh-sah-REH-mohs...
• immediately.	• *inmediatamente.*	• een-meh-DYAH-tah-mehn-teh.
• this afternoon.	• *esta tarde.*	• EHS-tah TAHR-deh.
• tomorrow.	• *mañana.*	• mah-NYAH-nah.
• next week.	• *la semana que entra.*	• lah seh-MAH-nah keh EHN-trah.
• as soon as the medications are ready.	• *tan pronto como preparen los medicamentos.*	• tahn PROHN-toh KOH-moh preh-PAH- rehn lohs meh-dee-kah-MEHN-tohs.
• as soon as they prepare the operating room.	• *tan pronto como preparen la sala de operaciones.*	• tahn PROHN-toh KOH-moh preh-PAH-rehn lah SAH-lah deh oh-peh-rah-SYOHN-ehs.
PATIENT	***PACIENTE***	
What will happen if I do not accept the treatment?	*¿Qué pasará si no acepto el tratamiento?*	¿Keh pah-sah-RAH see noh ah-SEHP-toh ehl trah-tah-MYEHN-toh?
DOCTOR	***DOCTOR***	
I will...	*Yo...*	Yoh...
• respect your decision.	• *respetaré su decisión.*	• rehs-peh-tah-REH soo deh-see-SYOHN.
• continue to be your physician.	• *seguiré siendo su médico.*	• seh-ghee-REH SYEHN-doh soo MEH-dee-koh.
• have to find another physician who will treat your	• *tendré que encontrar otro médico que trate*	• tehn-DREH keh ehn-kohn-TRAHR OH-troh MEH-dee-koh

illness the way you want.	*su enfermedad como usted quiere.*	keh TRAH-teh soo ehn-fehr-meh-DAH KOH-moh oos-TEHD KYEH-reh.
But I strongly advise you to accept the treatment.	*Perole le recomiendo que acepte el tratamiento.*	PEH-roh leh reh-koh-MYEHN-doh MOO-choh keh ah-SEHP-teh ehl trah-tah-MYEHN-toh.
Why will you not accept the treatment?	*¿Por qué no acepta el tratamiento?*	¿Pohr keh noh ah-SEPH-tah ehl trah-tah-MYEHN-toh?
What can I do convince you to accept the treatment?	*¿Qué puedo hacer para que acepte el tratamiento?*	¿Keh PWEH-doh ah-SEHR PAH-rah keh ah-SEPH-teh ehl trah-tah-MYEHN-toh?

VOCABULARY ••••

CONVINCING PEOPLE

I recommend ____.	*Yo recomiendo ____.*	Yoh reh-koh-MYEHN-doh ____.
I urge you to ____.	*Es urgente que ____.*	Ehs oor-HEHN-teh keh ____.
It is best if you ____.	*Seriá mejor que ____.*	Seh-REE-ah meh-HOHR keh ____.
It is in your best interest to ____.	*Es mejor para usted que ____.*	Ehs meh-HOHR pah-rah oos-TEHD ____.
According to medical research, this is your best option ____.	*Según las investigaciones médicas, ésta es su mejor opción ____.*	Seh-GOON lahs een-VEHS-tee-gah-SYOHN-ehs MEH-dee-kahs, EHS-tah ehs soo meh-HOHR ohp-SYOHN.

C. OBTAINING AN ADVANCED DIRECTIVE FROM A COMPETENT ADULT

CULTURE NOTE ••••

THE NEED FOR AN INTERPRETER Doctors are considered to be authority figures in Latino culture. Their word is taken at face value and very rarely questioned. Some Latino patients may not even ask questions if they don't understand your prognosis, the treatment option, the treatment plan, even if they didn't understand what you said due to a language problem. Therefore, it may be very important that you call in an interpreter whenever you and your patient have to make decisions pertaining to further treatment. Not only will an interpreter be able to rule out language problems, but he or she may also be able to elicit necessary questions from your patients that, due to the respect towards the doctor, would otherwise never be asked. Obviously, this is particularly important when you are discussing life and death situations, and may even be legally required in your state.

DOCTOR	*DOCTOR*	
We need to make some decisions about your treatment.	*Necesitamos tomar algunas decisiones sobre su tratamiento.*	Neh-seh-see-TAH-mohs toh-MAHR ahl-GOO-nahs deh-see-SYOH-nehs SOH-breh soo trah-tah-MYEHN-toh.

Sometimes the heart of a person stops beating suddenly.	*A veces el corazón de una persona deja de latir repentinamente.*	Ah VEH-sehs ehl koh-rah-SOHN deh OO-nah pehr-SOH-nah DEH-hah deh lah-TEER reh-pehn-TEE-nah-mehn-teh.
If this happens to you, would you like us to treat you as indicated?	*Si esto le pasa a usted, ¿quiere que le demos el tratamiento indicado?*	See EHS-toh leh PAH-sah ah oos-TEHD, ¿KYEH-reh keh leh DEH-mohs trah-tah-MYEHN-toh in-dee-KAH-doh?
If we don't treat you and try to make your heart beat again, you will die.	*Si no lo (la) tratamos e intentamos hacer que su corazón lata de nuevo, usted morirá.*	See noh loh (lah) trah-TAH-mohs eh een-tehn-TAH-mohs ah-SEHR keh soo koh-RAH-sohn LAH-tah deh noo-EH-voh, oos-TEHD moh-REE-rah.
On occasions, a person ceases or almost ceases breathing.	*En algunas ocasiones, una persona repentinamente deja o casi deja de respirar.*	Ehn ahl-GOO-nahs oh-kah-SYOH-nehs, OO-nah pehr-SOH-nah reh-pehn-TEE-nah-mehn-teh DEH-hah oh KAH-see DEH-hah deh rehs-pee-RAHR.
If you are not breathing as you should, can I give you the treatment indicated?	*Si usted no está respirando como debería, ¿le puedo dar el tratamiento indicado?*	See oos-TEHD noh ehs-TAH rehs-pee-RAHN-doh KOH-moh deh-beh-REE-ah, ¿leh PWEH-doh dahr ehl trah-tah-MYEHN-toh een-dee-KAH-doh?
If we don't give you this treatment and try to make you breathe again, you will die.	*Si no lo (la) tratamos e intentamos que usted respire de nuevo, usted morirá.*	See no loh (lah) trah-TAH-mohs eh een-tehn-TAH-mohs keh oos-TEHD rehs-pee-reh deh noo-EH-voh, oos-TEHD moh-REE-rah.

At the end of life, I can do only one of two things:	*Al final de la vida, sólo puedo hacer una de dos cosas:*	Ahl fee-NAHL deh lah VEE-dah, SOH-loh PWEH-doh ah-SEHR OO-nah deh dohs KOH-sahs:
Prolong your life as long as I can by putting you on/ giving you…	*Prolongar su vida todo lo que pueda poniéndolo (la)en/dándolo(la)…*	Proh-lohn-GAHR soo VEE-dah TOH-doh loh keh PWEH-dah poh-NYEHN-doh-loh(lah) ehn DAHN-doh-loh(lah)…
• a respirator.	• *un respirador.*	• oon rehs-pee-RAH-dohr.
• an artificial kidney.	• *una riñón artificial.*	• OO-nah ree-NYOHN ahr-tee-fee-SYAHL.
• a marcapaso.	• *un marcapaso.*	• Oon mahr-kah-PAH-soh.
• a heart-lung machine.	• *una máquina de corazón-pulmón.*	• OO-nah mah-kee-nah deh koh-rah-SOHN-pool-MOHN.
• a peg tube.	• *un tubo intragástrico transcutáneo.*	• Oon TOO-boh een-trah GAHS-tree-koh trahns-koo-tah-NEH-oh.
• a nasogastric tube.	• *una sonda nasogástrica.*	• OO-nah SOHN-dah nah-soh-gahs-tree-kah.
Make you as comfortable as you can be.	*Hacer que usted éste lo más cómodo(a) posible.*	Ah-SEHR keh oos-TEHD ehs-TEH loh MAHS KOH-moh-doh (dah) poh-SEE-bleh.
What do you prefer?	*¿Qué prefiere?*	¿Keh preh-FYEH-reh?
Very well, thank you.	*Muy bien, muchas gracias.*	Moo-ee byehn, MOO-chahs GRAH-syahs.
I am grateful for your answers.	*Le agradezco sus respuestas.*	Leh ah-grah-DEHS-koh soos rehs-PWEHS-tahs.
I also want you to know that you have the right to change	*También quiero que sepa que usted tiene el*	Tahm-BYEHN KYEH-roh keh SEH-pah keh oos-TEHD TYEH-neh

your answers whenever you wish.	*derecho de cambiar sus respuestas cuando quiera.*	ehl deh-REH-choh deh kahm-BEE-AHR soos rehs-PWEHS-tahs KWAHN-doh KYEH-rah.
All you have to do is tell me that your answers have changed.	*Todo lo que tiene que hacer es decirme que sus respuestas han cambiado.*	TOH-doh loh keh TYEH-neh keh ah-SEHR ehs deh-SEER-meh keh soos rehs-PWEHS-tahs ahn kahm-BYAH-doh.

D. DISCUSSING THE QUALITY OF LIFE OF THE TERMINALLY ILL PATIENT*

DOCTOR	*DOCTOR*	
The treatment will...	*El tratamiento...*	Ehl trah-tah-MYEHN-toh...
• keep you from suffering_____.	• *impedirá que usted sufra _____.*	• eem-peh-dee-RAH keh oos-TEHD SOO-frah _____.
• help you to continue living as you did before you got sick.	• *le ayudará a continuar viviendo como lo estaba haciendo antes de enfermarse.*	• leh ah-YOO-dah-RAH ah kohn-tee-NOO-AHR vee-VYEHN-doh KOH-moh loh ehs-TAH-bah ah-SYEHN-doh AHN-tehs de ehn-fehr-MAHR-seh.
• not be able to cure your disease completely.	• *no curar su enfermedad completamente.*	• no koo-RAHR soo ehn-fehr-meh-DAH kohm-PLEH tah-mehn-teh.
• improve your status, but you will not be able to continue	• *mejorará su estado pero no podrá seguir viviendo*	• meh-hoh-rah-RAH soo ehs-TAH-doh, PEH-roh noh poh-

*For more typical questions and answers, please refer to section C.9 on *The Most Common Questions for the Elderly.*

living as you did before you got sick.	*como lo hacía antes de enfermarse.*	DRAH seh-GHEER vee-VYEHN-doh KOH-moh loh ah-SEE-ah AHN-tchs deh ehn-fehr-MAHR-seh.
• not cure your disease, but alleviate your symptoms and your pain.	• *no curará su enfermedad, pero aliviará sus síntomas y el dolor.*	• noh koo-rah-RAH soo ehn-fehr-meh-DAHD, PEH-roh ah-lee-vyah-RAH soos SEEN-toh-mahs ee ehl doh-LOHR.
You will be able to continue living and doing everything that you are used to while you can.	*Usted podrá continuar viviendo y haciendo todo lo que acostumbra mientras pueda.*	Oos-TEHD poh-DRAH kohn-tee-NOO-AHR vee-VYEHN-doh TOH-doh loh keh ah-kohs-TOOM-brah MYEHN-trahs PWEH-dah.
During treatment you will have to…	*Durante el tratamiento usted tendrá que…*	Doo-RAHN-teh ehl trah-tah-MYEHN-toh oos-TEHD tehn-DRAH keh…
• make some changes in your lifestyle.	• *cambiar su estilo de vida.*	• kahm-BYAHR soo ehs-TEE-loh deh VEE-dah.
• stop working.	• *dejar de trabajar.*	• deh-HAHR deh trah-bah-HAHR.
• stop drinking.	• *dejar de tomar.*	• deh-HAHR deh toh-MAHR.
• stop smoking.	• *dejar de fumar.*	• deh-HAHR de foo-MAHR.
• go on a diet.	• *ponerse a dieta.*	• poh-NEHR-seh ah DYEH-tah.

E. DISCUSSING THE CONTEXTUAL FEATURES OF THE CASE

DOCTOR	*DOCTOR*	
Do you live alone?	*¿Vive usted sola(o)?*	¿VEE-veh oos-TEHD SOH-lah(loh)?

Do you have enough money…	*¿Tiene suficiente dinero…*	¿TYEH-neh soo-fee-SYEHN-teh dee NEH-roh …
• to pay for the lifestyle changes that you have to make?	• *para pagar los cambios que debe hacer en su estilo de vida?*	• PAH-rah pah-GAHR lohs kahm-BYOHS keh DEH-beh ah-SEHR ehn soo ehs-TEE-loh deh VEE-dah?
• to pay for the care that you need?	• *para pagar por el cuidado que necesita?*	• PAH-rah pah-GAHR pohr ehl kwee-DAH-doh keh neh-see-SEE-tah?
Do you live with someone who will help you make the necessary lifestyle changes?	*¿Vive usted con alguien que le ayudará a hacer los cambios necesarios en su estilo de vida?*	¿VEE-veh oos-TEHD kohn AHL-gyehn keh leh ah-YOO-dah-RAH ah ah-SEHR lohs KAHM-byohs neh-seh-SAH-ryohs ehn soo ehs-TEE-loh deh VEE-dah?
Do you want/need a nurse to visit you and help you?	*¿Desea/necesita que una enfermera la(lo) visite y le ayude?*	¿Deh-SEH-ah/neh-seh-SEE-tah keh OO-nah ehn-fehr-MEH-rah lah(loh) vee-SEE-teh ee leh ah-YOO-deh?
You may lose your capacity to make decisions.	*Puede perder su capacidad para tomar decisiones.*	PWEH-deh pehr-DEHR soo kah-pah-see-DAHD PAH-rah toh-MAHR deh-see SYOH-nehs.
Have you given your spouse/children/companion instructions about your future care?	*¿Le ha dado usted indicaciones a su esposo(a)/hijos/compañero(a) sobre su cuidado futuro?*	¿Leh ah DAH-doh oos-TEHD een-dee-kah-SYOH-nehs ah soo ehs-POH-soh(sah)/EE-hos/kohm-pah-NYEH-roh(rah) SOH-breh soo kweh-DAH-doh foo-TOO-roh?
I recommend that you discuss these issues with him/her/them.	*Le recomiendo que discuta estas cosas con él/ella/ellos(as).*	Leh reh-koh-MYEHN-doh keh dees-KOO-tah EHS-tahs KOH-sahs kohn Ehl/EH-yah/EH-yohs(yahs).

SECTION F

DISCUSSING THE FOLLOW-UP

1. The Follow-up Visit

DOCTOR	*DOCTOR*	
How have you been since the last time I saw you?	*¿Cómo ha estado desde la última vez que la (lo) vi?*	¿KOH-moh ah ehs-TAH-doh DEHS-deh lah OOL-tee-mah vehs keh lah (loh) vee?
Do you feel…	*¿Se siente…*	¿Seh SYEHN-teh…
• better?	• *mejor?*	• meh-HOHR?
• the same?	• *igual?*	• ee-GWAHL?
• worse?	• *peor?*	• peh-OHR?
Have you been taking your medications as I told you?	*¿Ha estado tomando las medicinas como le dije?*	¿Ah ehs-TAH-doh toh-MAHN-doh lahs meh-dee-SEE-nahs KOH-moh leh DEE-heh?
Why not?	*¿Por qué no?*	¿Pohr keh noh?
PATIENT	***PACIENTE***	
Because…	*Porque…*	POHR-keh…
• I have not bought them yet.	• *no las he comprado.*	• noh lahs eh kohm-PRAH-doh.

• I do not understand how to take them.	• *no entiendo como tomarlas.*	• noh ehn-TYEHN-doh KOH-moh toh-MAHR-lahs.
• I have no one to help me take them.	• *no tengo quien me ayude a tomármelas.*	• noh TEHN-goh kyehn meh ah-YOO-deh ah toh-MAHR-meh-lahs.
DOCTOR	***DOCTOR***	
How have you been taking them?	*¿Cómo se las ha estado tomando?*	¿KOH-moh seh lahs ah ehs-TAH-doh toh-MAHN-doh?
PATIENT	***PACIENTE***	
• Once.	• *Una vez.*	• OO-nah vehs.
• Twice.	• *Dos veces.*	• Dohs VEH-sehs.
• Three times.	• *Tres veces.*	• Trehs VEH-sehs.
• Four times.	• *Cuatro veces.*	• KWAH-troh VEH-sehs.
...a day.	*...al día.*	...ahl DEE-ah.
Before/after meals.	*Antes de/después de las comidas.*	AHN-tehs deh/dehs-PWEHS deh lahs koh-MEE-dahs...
Before going to bed.	*Antes de acostarme.*	AHN-tehs deh ah-kohs-TAHR-meh.
DOCTOR	***DOCTOR***	
Have you been following the diet as I told you?	*¿También ha seguido la dieta como le dije?*	¿Tahm-BYEHN ah seh-GHEE-doh lah DYEH-tah KOH-moh leh DEE-heh?
What have you been eating/doing?	*¿Qué ha estado comiendo/haciendo?*	¿KEH ah ehs-TAH-doh koh-MYEHN-doh/ah-SYEHN-doh?
PATIENT	***PACIENTE***	
I have/have not been eating like you told me.	*He/no he estado comiendo como me dijo.*	Eh/noh eh ehs-TAH-doh koh-MYEHN-doh KOH-moh meh-DEE-hoh.

English	Spanish	Pronunciation
I have stopped eating/drinking…	*He dejado de comer/beber…*	Eh deh-HAH-doh deh koh-MEHR/beh-BEHR…
• meat.	• *carne.*	• KAHR-neh.
• bread.	• *pan.*	• pahn.
• candy.	• *dulces.*	• DOOL-sehs.
• milk.	• *leche.*	• LEH-cheh.
• salt.	• *con sal.*	• kohn sahl.
• coffee.	• *café.*	• kah-FEH.
• soft drinks.	• *refrescos embotellados.*	• reh-FREHS-kohs ehm-boh-teh-YAH-dohs.
DOCTOR	*DOCTOR*	
Have you made the lifestyle changes I asked you to do?	*¿Cambió su estilo de vida como le pedí?*	¿Kahm-BYOH soo ehs-TEE-loh deh VEE-dah KOH-moh leh peh-DEE?
PATIENT	*PACIENTE*	
I stopped…	*Dejé de…*	Deh-HEH deh…
• drinking.	• *beber.*	• beh-BEHR.
• smoking.	• *fumar.*	• foo-MAHR.
• exercising.	• *hacer ejercicio.*	• ah-SEHR eh-hehr-SEE-syoh.
• working overtime.	• *trabajar extra.*	• trah-bah-HAHR EHKS-trah.
I started exercising.	*Empecé a hacer ejercicio.*	• Ehm-peh-SEH ah ah-SEHR eh-hehr-SEE-syoh.
DOCTOR	*DOCTOR*	
This visit we will…	*Lo que vamos a hacer en esta visita es…*	Loh keh VAH-mohs ah ah-SEHR ehn EHS-tah vee-SEE-tah ehs…
• draw a blood sample.	• *sacar una muestra de sangre.*	• sah-KAHR OO-nah MWEHS-trah deh SAHN-greh.

• take an X-ray.	• *tomarle una radiografía.*	• toh-MAHR-leh OO-nah rah-dyoh-grah-FEE-ah.
• check your blood/ urine sugar.	• *revisar el azúcar en la sangre/orina.*	• reh-vee-SAHR ehl ah-SOO-kahr ehn la SAHN-greh/ oh-REE-nah.
Do you have a problem that we need to talk about?	*¿Tiene algún problema del que necesitamos hablar?*	¿TYEH-neh ahl-GOON proh-BLEH-mah dehl keh neh-seh-see-TAH-mohs ah-BLAHR?
PATIENT	*PACIENTE*	
I want to know…	*Quiero saber…*	KYEH-roh sah-BEHR…
• when I am going to feel better.	• *cuándo voy a sentirme mejor.*	• KWAHN-doh voy ah sehn-TEER-meh meh-HOHR.
• why I am not improving.	• *por qué no estoy mejorando.*	• pohr keh noh ehs-TOY meh-hoh-RAHN-doh.
• when I am going to be able to eat everything.	• *cuándo voy a poder comer de todo.*	• KWAHN-doh voh-ee ah poh-DEHR koh-MEHR deh TOH-doh.
• when I can go back to work.	• *cuándo puedo volver a trabajar.*	• KWAHN-doh PWEH-doh vohl-VEHR ah trah-bah-HAHR?
• when you are going to operate on me.	• *cuándo me va a operar.*	• KWAHN-doh meh vah ah oh-peh-RAHR.
DOCTOR	*DOCTOR*	
We are going to run more tests to find out.	*Vamos a pedir otros estudios para saberlo.*	VAH-mohs ah peh-DEER OH-trohs ehs-TOO-dyohs PAH-rah sah-BEHR.
When…	*Cuando…*	KWAHN-doh…
• you feel stronger/ better.	• *se sienta más fuerte/mejor.*	• seh SYEHN-tah MAHS FWEHR-teh/ meh-HOHR.

• you have improved.	• *haya mejorado.*	• AH-yah meh-hoh-RAH-doh.
I am going to ask you to come back in…	*Le voy a pedir que regrese en…*	Leh voy ah peh-DEER keh reh-GREH-seh ehn…
• one week.	• *una semana.*	• OO-nah seh-MAH-nah.
• 15 days.	• *quince días.*	• KEEN-seh DEE-ahs.
• one month.	• *un mes.*	• oon mehs.
• after you have seen the specialist.	• *después que haya visto al especialista.*	• dehs-PWEHS keh AH-ee ah VEES-toh ahl ehs-peh-syah-LEES-ta.
• if you feel worse.	• *si se siente peor.*	• see seh SYEHN-teh peh-OHR.
What we will do when you come back is…	*Lo que vamos a hacer cuando regrese es…*	Loh keh VAH-mohs ah ah-SEHR KWAHN-doh reh-GREH-seh ehs…
• check your blood pressure.	• *revisar su presión.*	• reh-vee-SAHR soo preh-SYOHN.
• check your blood sugar.	• *revisar su azúcar.*	• reh-vee-SAHR soo ah-SOO-kahr.
• see how you have felt with the medications.	• *ver cómo se ha sentido con las medicinas.*	• vehr-KOH-moh seh ah sehn-TEE-doh kohn lahs meh-dee-SEE-nahs.
Call this office…	*Llame al consultorio.*	YAH-meh ahl kohn-sool-TOH-ree-oh.
• to set up an appointment.	• *para hacer una cita.*	• PAH-rah ah-SEHR OO-nah SEE-tah.
• to get the test results.	• *para saber los resultados de los exámenes.*	• PAH-rah sah-BEHR lohs reh-sool-TA-dohs deh los ehx-AH-meh-nehs.
• if you need any help with…	• *si necesita ayuda con…*	• see neh-seh-SEE-tah ah-YOO-dah kohn…
• the medication.	• *los medicamentos.*	• lohs meh-dee-kah-MEHN-tohs.

• the diet.	• *la dieta.*	• lah DYEH-tah.
Okay?	*¿Estamos de acuerdo?*	¿Ehs-TAH-mohs deh ah-KWEHR-doh?

2. The Discharge

Mr./Mrs. ____, I think that your problem has/has not…	*Señor/Señora ____, creo que su problema ha/no ha…*	Seh-NYOHR/Seh-NYOH-rah ____, KREH-oh keh soo proh-BLEH-mah ah/noh hah…
• been resolved.	• *sido resuelto.*	• SEE-doh reh-SWEHL-toh.
• improved.	• *mejorado.*	• meh-hohr-RAH-doh.
You are ready to…	*Está listo(a) para…*	Ehs-TAH LEES-toh (tah) PAH-rah…
• go home.	• *irse a casa.*	• EER-seh ah KAH-sah.
• go to the rehabilitation facility.	• *ir a rehabilitación.*	• eer ah reh-hah-bee-lee-tah-SYOHN.
• go to the nursing home.	• *ir a la casa de hospicio para ancianos.*	• eer ah lah KAH-sah deh ohs-pee-SYOH PAH-rah ahn-SYAH-nohs.
There you will be cared for by…	*Ahí lo (la) cuidarán…*	Ah-EE loh (lah) kwee-dah-RAHN…
• your family.	• *su familia.*	• soo fah-MEE-lyah.
• your friends.	• *sus amistades.*	• soos ah-mees-TAH-dehs.
• home care specialists.	• *enfermeras a domicilio.*	• ehn-fehr-MEH-rahs ah doh-mee-SEE-lyoh.
• specialists in physical/occuaptional/speech therapy.	• *especialistas en terapia física/ocupacional/del lenguaje.*	• ehs-peh-syah-LEES-tahs ehn teh-RAH-pyah FEE-see-kah/oh-koo-pah-syoh-NAHL/dehl lehn-GWAH-heh.

To meet your needs, you should also call…	*Para sus necesidades, llame a…*	PAH-rah soos neh-seh-see-DAH-dehs, YAH-meh ah…
• meals on wheels.	• *comidas en ruedas.*	• koh-MEE-dahs ehn RWEH-dahs.
• home healthcare.	• *cuidados de salud en casa.*	• kwee-DAH-dohs deh sah-LOOD ehn KAH-sah.
• your insurance.	• *su seguro.*	• soo seh-GOO-roh.
• my nurse.	• *mi enfermera.*	• mee ehn-fehr-MEH-rah.
• the community health center.	• *el centro de salud comunitario.*	• ehl SEHN-troh deh sah-LOOD koh-moo-nee-TAH-ryoh.
• the welfare agency.	• *la agencia del welfare.*	• lah ah-HEHN-syah dehl WEHL-fehr.
• your priest/rabbi/minister.	• *su sacerdote/rabino/ministro.*	• soo sah-sehr-DOH-teh/rah-BEE-noh/mee-NEES-troh.
Do only light chores for the next…	*Haga sólo tareas ligeras durante…*	AH-gah SOH-loh tah-REH-ahs lee-HEH-rahs doo-RAHN-teh…
• week.	• *una semana.*	• OO-nah seh-MAH-nah.
• two weeks.	• *dos semanas.*	• dohs seh-MAH-nahs.
• month.	• *un mes.*	• oon mehs.
Resume your usual level of activity in…	*Empiece su nivel normal de actividades en…*	Ehm-PYEH-seh soo NEE-vehl nohr-MAHL deh ahk-tee-vee-DAH-dehs ehn…
• one week.	• *una semana.*	• OO-nah seh MAH-nah.
• two weeks.	• *dos semanas.*	• dohs seh-MAH-nahs.
• one month.	• *un mes.*	• oon mehs.
You must take your medications…	*Debe tomar sus medicinas…*	DEH-beh toh-MAHR soos meh-dee-SEE-nahs…

• as directed.	• *como se le indicó.*	• KOH-moh seh leh een-dee-KOH.
• once a day.	• *una vez al día.*	• OO-nah vehs ahl DEE-ah.
• twice a day.	• *dos veces al día.*	• dohs VEH-sehs ahl DEE-ah.
• three times a day.	• *tres veces al día.*	• trehs VEH-sehs ahl DEE-ah.
• four times a day.	• *cuatro veces al día.*	• KWAH-troh VEH-VEH-sehs ahl DEE-ah.
• before your meals.	• *antes de comer.*	• AHN-tehs deh koh-MEHR.
• after your meals.	• *después de comer.*	• dehs-PWEHS deh koh-MEHR.
• when you go to bed.	• *al acostarse.*	• ahl ah-kohs-TAHR-seh.
You should continue the diet…	*Debe continuar la dieta…*	DEH-beh kohn-tee-NWAHR lah DEE-EH-tah…
• for one week.	• *durante una semana.*	• doo-RAHN-teh OO-nah seh-MAH-nah.
• for two weeks.	• *durante dos semanas.*	• doo-RAHN-teh dohs seh-MAH-nahs.
• for one month.	• *durante un mes.*	• doo-RAHN-teh oon mehs.
• until your next visit to my office.	• *hasta la siguiente visita a mi oficina.*	• AHS-tah lah see-GYEHN-teh vee-SEE-tah ah mee oh-fee-SEE-nah.
The physical/occupational/speech therapist will help you improve.	*El terapeuta físico/ocupacional/del lenguaje le ayudará a mejorar su habilidad/habla.*	Ehl teh-rah-PEH-OO-tah FEE-see-koh/oh-koo-pah-syoh-NAHL/dehl lehn-GWAH heh leh ah-yoo-dah-RAH ah meh-hoh-RAHR soo ah-bee-lee-DAHD/AH-blah.

The nurse will visit you…	*La enfermera lo(la) visitará…*	Lah ehn-fehr-MEH-rah loh(lah) vee-see-tah-RAH…
• every day.	• *a diario.*	• ah DYAH-ryoh.
• every other day.	• *cada otro día.*	• KAH-dah oh-TROH DEE-ah.
You also need support from a counselor/psychiatrist.	*También necesita apoyo de un consejero/psiquiatra.*	Tahm-BYEHN neh-seh-SEE-tah ah-POH-yoh deh oon kohn-seh-HEH-roh/see-kee-AH-trah.
I recommend that you call ____.	*Le recomiendo que llame a ____.*	Leh reh-koh-MYEHN-doh keh YAH-meh ____.
I have worked with him/her before.	*He trabajado con él/ella antes.*	Eh trah-bah-HAH-doh kohn ehl/EH-yah ahn-tehs.
I need to see you in my office (in)…	*Necesito verlo(la) en mi oficina (en)…*	Neh-seh-SEE-toh VEHR-loh(lah) ehn mee oh-fee-SEE-nah (ehn)…
• tomorrow.	• *mañana.*	• mah-NYAH-nah.
• one week.	• *una semana.*	• OO-nah seh-MAH-nah.
• two weeks.	• *dos semanas.*	• dohs seh-MAH-nahs.
• one month.	• *un mes.*	• oon mehs.
• six months.	• *seis meses.*	• sehs MEH-sehs.
If you need to see me before that, please call my office.	*Si necesita verme antes, por favor llámeme en mi oficina.*	See neh-seh-SEE-tah VEHR-meh AHN-tehs, pohr fah-VOHR YAH-meh-meh ehn mee oh-fee-SEE-nah.
My secretary will make an appointment.	*Mi secretaria le dará una cita.*	Mee seh-kreh-TAH-ryah leh dah-RAH OO-nah SEE-tah.
If you have an emergency call…	*Si tiene una emergencia, por favor llame a…*	See TYEH-neh OO-nah eh-mehr-HEHN-syah, pohr fah-VOHR YAH-meh ah…
• my office.	• *a mi oficina.*	• mee oh-fee-SEE-nah.

• Dr. _____ at _____.	• *al Dr.*_____ *al* _____.	• ahl dohk-TOHR _____ ahl _____.
• just come to my office.	• *venga a mi oficina.*	• VEHN-gah ah mee oh-fee-SEE-nah.
• go to the emergency room of _____ hospital.	• *vaya a emergencias del hospital* _____.	• VAH-yah a eh-meh-HEHN-syahs dehl ohs-pee-TAHL _____.
Before we discharge you...	*Antes de darlo(la) de alta...*	AHN-tehs deh DAHR-loh(lah) deh AHL-tah...
• the nurse will bring your belongings.	• *la enfermera le traerá sus cosas.*	• lah ehn-fehr-MEH-rah leh trah-eh-RAH soos KOH-sahs.
• you/your spouse/son/daughter/companion needs(s) to go to Patient Services.	• *usted/su esposo(a)/hijo/hija compañero(a) necesita ir a Servicios para Pacientes.*	• oos-TEHD/soo ehs-POH-sohs(sah)/EE-ho/EE-hah/kohm-pah-NYEH-roh(rah) neh-seh-SEE-tah eer ah sehr-VEE-sohs PAH-rah pah-SYEHN-tehs.
Before you go, please go to the front desk.	*Antes de irse, por favor pase por la recepción.*	AHN-tehs DEH EER-seh, pohr fah-VOHR PAH-seh pohr lah reh-sehp-SYOHN.
They need information about your insurance.	*Necesitan información sobre su seguro.*	Neh-seh-SEE-tahn een-fohr-mah-SYOHN SOH-breh soo seh-GOO-roh.
Please discuss payment with them.	*Por favor, hable con ellos sobre el pago.*	Pohr fah-VOHR, AH-bleh kohn EH-yohs SOH-breh ehl PAH-goh.
Thank you.	*Gracias.*	GRAH-syahs.
Good luck.	*Buena suerte.*	BWEH-nah SWEHR-teh.
I hope you'll feel better soon.	*Espero que se sienta mejor pronto.*	Ehs-PEH-roh keh seh SYEHN-tah meh-HOHR PROHN-toh.

SECTION G

EMERGENCY PROCEDURES

1. Diagnosis and Treatment in the Emergency Room

A. THE PATIENT IS CONSCIOUS AND COMPLAINS OF PAIN

DOCTOR	*DOCTOR*	
What is your name?	*¿Cómo se llama usted?*	¿KOH-moh seh YAH-mah oos-TEHD?
When did the pain begin?	*¿Cuándo le empezó el dolor?*	¿KWAHN-doh leh ehm-peh-SOH ehl doh-LOHR?
PATIENT	***PACIENTE***	
It began…	*Me empezó…*	Meh ehm-peh-SOH…
• just a while ago.	• *hace un rato.*	• AH-seh oon RAH-toh.
• this morning/afternoon.	• *en la mañana/tarde.*	• ehn lah mah NYAH nah/TAHR-deh.
• yesterday.	• *ayer.*	• ah-YEHR.
DOCTOR	***DOCTOR***	
What kind of pain is it?	*¿Cómo es el dolor?*	¿KOH-moh ehs ehl doh-LOHR?

PATIENT	*PACIENTE*	
It is like…	*Es como…*	Ehs KOH-moh…
• a punch.	• *una punzada.*	• OO-nah poon-SAH-dah.
• a knife.	• *un cuchillo.*	• oon koo-CHEE-yoh.
It's burning.	*Me arde.*	Meh AHR-deh.
DOCTOR	*DOCTOR*	
Is the pain a …sensation?	*¿El dolor es…*	¿Ehl doh-LOHR ehs…
• burning	• *como una quemadura?*	• KOH-moh OO-nah keh-mah-DOO-rah?
• pulsating	• *pulsante?*	• pool-SAHN-teh?
• stabbing	• *como una cuchillada?*	• KOH-moh OO-nah koo-CHEE-yah-dah?
Is the pain…	*¿El dolor está…*	¿Ehl doh-LOHR ehs-TAH…
• increasing/decreasing?	• *aumentado/disminuyendo?*	• awoo-mehn-TAHN-doh/dees-mee-noo-YEHN-doh?
• the same?	• *igual?*	• ee-GWAHL?
Is there anything that takes the pain away?	*¿Hay algo que le quite el dolor?*	¿Ay ahl-GOH keh leh KEE-the ehl doh-LOHR?
PATIENT	*PACIENTE*	
Nothing.	*Nada.*	NAH-dah.
Lying on one side.	*Acostarme de lado.*	Ah-kohs-TAHR-meh deh LAH-doh.
Tylenol/aspirin/Advil.	*Tylenol/aspirina/Advil.*	Tee-leh-NOHL/ahs-PEE-ree-nah ahd-VEEL.
DOCTOR	*DOCTOR*	
Where…	*¿Dónde…*	¿DOHN-deh…
• did the pain begin?	• *empezó el dolor?*	• ehm-peh-SOH ehl doh-LOHR?

• do you feel the pain now?	• *tiene dolor en este momento?*	• TYEH-neh doh-LOHR ehn EHS-teh moh-MEHN-toh?
PATIENT	**PACIENTE**	
It began here.	*Empezó aquí.*	Ehm-peh-SOH a-KEE.
This is where it began.	*Aquí está donde empezó.*	Ah-KEE ehs-TAH DOHN-deh ehm-peh-SOH.
In…	*En…*	Ehn…
• the head.	• *la cabeza.*	• lah kah-BEH-sah.
• the eye.	• *el ojo.*	• ehl OH-hoh.
• the jaw.	• *la quijada.*	• lah kee-HAH-dah.
• the chest.	• *el pecho.*	• ehl PEH-choh.
• the stomach.	• *la boca del estómago.*	• lah BOH-kah dehl ehs-TOH-mah-goh.
• the navel.	• *el ombligo.*	• ehl ohm-BLEE-goh.
• the groin.	• *la ingle.*	• lah EEN-gleh.
• the back.	• *la espalda.*	• lah ehs-PAHL-dah.
• the testicles.	• *los testículos.*	• lohs tehs-TEE-koo-lohs.
• the anus.	• *el ano.*	• ehl AH-noh.
DOCTOR	**DOCTOR**	
Is the pain stronger when you breathe?	*¿Es el dolor más fuerte cuando respira?*	¿Ehs ehl doh-LOHR mahs FWEHR-teh KWAHN-doh rehs-PEE-rah?
Is the pain constant?	*¿Es constante el dolor?*	¿Ehs kohn-STAN-teh ehl doh-LOHR?
PATIENT	**PACIENTE**	
No,…	*No,…*	Noh,…
• it comes and goes.	• *va y viene.*	• vah ee VYEH-neh.
• it gets better and worse.	• *sube y baja.*	• SOO-beh ee BAH-hah.

• it's like a colic.	• *es como un cólico.*	• ehs KOH-moh oon KOH-lee-koh.
DOCTOR	**DOCTOR**	
Has the pain moved to another part of your body?	*¿Se ha movido el dolor a alguna otra parte del cuerpo?*	¿Seh ah moh-VEE-doh ehl doh-LOHR ah ahl-GOO-nah PAHR-teh dehl KWEHR-poph?
Please show me where the pain moved to?	*Por favor, señáleme dónde se movió el dolor.*	Pohr fah-VOHR, seh-NYAH-leh-meh DOHN-deh seh moh-VYOH ehl doh-LOHR.
Has the pain made you…	*¿El dolor le ha hecho…*	¿Ehl doh-LOHR leh ah EH-choh…
• feel dizzy?	• *sentirse mareada(o)?*	• sehn-TEER-seh mah-reh-AH-dah(doh)?
• vomit?	• *vomitar?*	• voh-mee-TAHR?
• sweat?	• *sudar?*	• soo-DAHR?
• weak?	• *débil?*	• DEH-beel?
Have you had this pain before?	*¿Había tenido alguna vez antes este dolor?*	¿Ah-BEE-ah teh-NEE-doh ahl-GOO-nah vehs AHN-tehs EHS-teh doh-LOHR?
When?	*¿Cuándo?*	¿KWAHN-doh?
PATIENT	***PACIENTE***	
Yesterday.	*Ayer.*	Ah-YEHR.
About…ago.	*Hace…*	AH-seh…
• a week	• *una semana.*	• OO-nah seh-MAH-nah.
• a month	• *un mes.*	• oon mehs.
DOCTOR	**DOCTOR**	
Did you see a doctor?	*¿Fue a ver al doctor?*	¿FWEH ah vehr ahl dohk-TOHR?
What did the doctor say (you had)?	*¿Qué le dijo el doctor (que tenía)?*	¿Keh leh DEE-hoh ehl dohk-TOHR (keh teh-NEE-ah)?

PATIENT	*PACIENTE*	
That it was…	*Que tenía…*	Keh teh-NEE-ah…
• appendicitis.	• *apendicitis.*	• ah-peh-dee-SEE-tees.
• the gall bladder.	• *la vesícula inflamada.*	• lah veh-SEE-koo-lah een-flah-MAH-dah.
• heartburn.	• *acidez.*	• ah-see-dehs.
• a strained muscle.	• *un desgarro muscular.*	• oon dehs-GAH-rroh moos-koo-LAHR.
• an infarct.	• *un infarto.*	• oon een-FAHR-toh.
That I should not worry.	*Que no me preocupara.*	Keh noh me preh-oh-koo-PAH-rah.
DOCTOR	***DOCTOR***	
How was your pain treated?	*¿Con qué le trataron el dolor?*	¿Kohn keh leh trah-TAH-rohn ehl doh-LOHR?
PATIENT	***PACIENTE***	
I was…	*Me…*	Meh…
• put on leave from work.	• *pusieron en reposo.*	• poo-SYEH-rohn ehn reh-POH-soh.
• given some medications.	• *dieron unas medicinas.*	• DYEH-rohn OO-nahs meh-dee-SEE-nahs.
• operated on.	• *operaron.*	• oh-peh-RAH-rohn.
DOCTOR	***DOCTOR***	
Do you have…	*¿Ha estado enfermo…*	¿Ah ehs-TAH-doh ehn-FEHR-moh…
• heart disease?	• *del corazón?*	• dehl koh-rah-SOHN?
• diabetes?	• *de diabetes?*	• deh dyah-BEH-tehs?
• emphysema?	• *de enfisema?*	• deh ehn-fee-SEH-mah?
• bronchitis?	• *de bronquitis?*	• deh brohn-KEE-tees?
• asthma?	• *de asma?*	• deh AHS-mah?

Are you allergic to any medications?	*¿Es alérgico(a) a algunas medicinas?*	¿Ehs ahl-EHR-hee-koh(kah) ah ahl-GOO-nahs meh-dee-SEE-nahs?
PATIENT	*PACIENTE*	
I am allergic to…	*Soy alérgico(a)…*	Soh-ee ah-LEHR-hee-koh(kah)…
• penicillin.	• *a penicilina.*	• ah peh-nee-see-LEE-nah.
• aspirin.	• *a aspirina.*	• ah ahs-pee-REE-nah.
• Advil.	• *al Advil.*	• ahl AHD-veel.
• Tylenol.	• *al Tylenol.*	• ahl tee-leh-NOHL.
• corn-based products.	• *a los productos a base de maíz.*	• ah lohs proh-DOOK-tohs ah BAH-seh deh mah-EES.
I don't think so.	*Creo que no.*	KREH-oh keh noh.

2. Interviewing the Family or Friend of an Unconscious Patient or a Child

DOCTOR	*DOCTOR*	
What is your name?	*¿Cómo se llama usted?*	¿KOH-moh seh YAH-mah oos-TEHD?
What is your relationship to the patient?	*¿Cuál es su relación con el paciente?*	¿Kwahl ehs soo reh-lah-SYOHN kohn ehl pah-SYEHN-teh?
PERSON	*PERSONA*	
I am his/her…	*Soy su…*	Soy soo…
• spouse.	• *esposo(a).*	• ehs-POH-soh(sah).
• fiancee.	• *novio(a).*	• NOH-vyoh(vyah).
• father/mother.	• *papá/mamá.*	• pah-PAH/mah-MAH.
• relative.	• *familiar.*	• fah-mee-LYAHR.
• friend.	• *amigo(a).*	• ah-MEE-goh(gah).

DOCTOR	*DOCTOR*	
What happened to the patient?	*¿Qué le pasó al paciente?*	¿Keh leh pah-SOH ahl pah-SYEHN-teh?
PERSON	*PERSONA*	
I don't know.	*No sé.*	Noh seh.
I found her/him like that.	*Lo (la) encontré así.*	Loh (lah) ehn-kohn-TREH ah-SEE.
She/he…	*Ella/él…*	EH-yah/EHL…
• fainted.	• *se desmayó.*	• seh dehs-mah-YOH.
• fell.	• *se cayó.*	• seh kah-YOH.
• had an accident.	• *tuvo un accidente.*	• TOO-voh oon ahks-see-DEHN-teh.
DOCTOR	*DOCTOR*	
Do you know what kind of medication the patient is taking?	*¿Sabe que clase de medicina está tomando el paciente?*	¿SAH-beh keh KLAH-seh deh meh-dee-SEE-nahs ehs-TAH toh-MAHN-doh ehl pah-SYEHN-teh?
Do you know if…	*¿Sabe si…*	¿SAH-beh see…
• the patient has been outside of the country recently?	• *el paciente ha estado fuera del país recientemente?*	• ehl PAH-SYEHN-teh ah ehs-TAH-doh FWEHR-ah dehl pah-EES reh-syehn-teh-MEHN-teh?
• the patient has any relatives?	• *¿el paciente tiene parientes?*	• ¿ehl pah-SYEHN-teh TYEH-neh pah-ree-EHN-tehs?
Were you with the patient when she/he started to be sick?	*¿Estaba usted con el paciente cuando empezó a sentirse enferma(o)?*	¿Ehs-TAH-bah oos-TEHD kohn ehl pah-SYEHN-teh KWAHN-doh ehm-peh-SOH ah sehn-TEER-seh ehn-FEHR-mah(moh)?
What was the patient doing when she/he got sick?	*¿Qué estaba haciendo la/el paciente cuando se enfermó?*	¿Keh ehs-TAH-bah ah-SYEHN-doh lah/ehl pah-SYEHN-teh KWAHN-doh seh ehn-fehr-MOH?

PERSON	*PERSONA*	
We were…	*Estábamos…*	Ehs-TAH-bah-mohs…
• talking.	• *hablando.*	• hah-BLAHN-doh.
• playing.	• *jugando.*	• hoo-GAHN-doh.
• making love.	• *haciendo el amor.*	• ah-SYEHN-doh ehl ah-MOHR.
• drinking.	• *bebiendo.*	• beh-BYEHN-doh.
• smoking.	• *fumando.*	• foo-MAHN-doh.
• doing drugs.	• *drogándonos.*	• droh-GAHN-doh-nohs.
DOCTOR	***DOCTOR***	
What was she/he drinking?	*¿Qué es lo que estaba tomando?*	¿Keh ehs loh keh ehs-TAH-bah toh-MAHN-doh?
PERSON	***PERSONA***	
Wine.	*Vino.*	VEE-noh.
Beer.	*Cerveza.*	Sehr-VEH-sah.
Liquor.	*Licor.*	Lee-KOHR.
Something that we prepared ourselves.	*Algo que habíamos preparado.*	AHL-goh keh ah-BEE-ah-mohs preh-pah-RAH-doh.
DOCTOR	***DOCTOR***	
What was in the drink?	*¿Qué tenía la bebida?*	¿Keh teh-NEE-ah lah beh-BEE-dah?
PERSON	***PERSONA***	
Whiskey.	*Whiskey.*	WHEES-kee.
Rum.	*Ron.*	Rohn.
Tequila.	*Tequila.*	The-KEE-lah.
Vodka.	*Vodka.*	VOHD-kah.
Mescal.	*Mescal.*	Mehs-KAHL.
Pisco.	*Pisco.*	PEES-koh.
Pure alcohol.	*Alcohol puro.*	Ahl-koh-OHL POO-roh.

DOCTOR	***DOCTOR***	
What was she/he smoking?	*¿Qué estaba fumando?*	¿Keh ehs-TAH-bah foo-MAHN-doh?
PERSON	***PERSONA***	
Cigarettes.	*Cigarrillos.*	See-gah-REE-yohs.
Cigars.	*Puros.*	POO-rohs.
Marijuana.	*Marijuana.*	Mah-ree-HWAH-nah.
DOCTOR	***DOCTOR***	
What kind of drugs did you use?	*¿Qué tipo de drogas usaron?*	¿Keh TEE-poh-deh DROH-gahs oo-SAH-rohn?
PERSON	***PERSONA***	
Morphine.	*Morfina.*	Mohr-FEE-nah.
Heroin.	*Heroína.*	Eh-roh-EE-nah.
Cocaine.	*Cocaína.*	Koh-kah-EE-nah.
Amphetamines.	*Anfetaminas.*	Ahn-feh-tah-MEE-nahs.
LSD.	*LSD.*	Eh-leh-eh-seh-DEH.
Peyote.	*Peyote.*	Peh-YOH-teh.
Mushrooms.	*Hongos.*	OHN-gohs.
DOCTOR	***DOCTOR***	
How did you take/inject them?	*¿Cómo se las tomaron/inyectaron?*	¿KOH-moh seh lahs toh-MAH-rohn/een-yehk-TAH-rohn?
PERSON	***PERSONA***	
Through…	*Por…*	Pohr…
• the nose.	• *la nariz.*	• lah nah-REES.
• the mouth.	• *la boca.*	• lah BOH-kah.
• a vein.	• *una vena.*	• OO-nah VEH-nah.
• the jugular vein.	• *la vena yugular.*	• lah VEH-nah yoo-goo-LAHR.
• the anus.	• *el ano.*	• ehl AH-noh.

DOCTOR	*DOCTOR*	
Did she/he complain of anything before losing consciousness?	*¿Se quejó de algo antes de quedar inconsciente?*	¿Seh keh-HOH deh AHL-goh AHN-tehs deh keh-DAHR een-kohn-SYEHN-teh?
PERSON	***PERSONA***	
She/he said…	*Dijo…*	DEE-hoh…
• that she/he was feeling very bad.	• *que se estaba sintiendo muy mal.*	• keh seh ehs-TAH-bah seen-TYEHN-doh moo-ee mahl.
• that she/he was feeling dizzy.	• *que se estaba sintiendo mareado(a).*	• keh seh ehs-TAH-bah seen-TYEHN-doh mah-reh-AH-doh(dah).
• that she/he was dying.	• *que se estaba muriendo.*	• keh seh ehs-TAH-bah moo-RYEHN-doh.
DOCTOR	***DOCTOR***	
How much time went by from the moment she/he complained until she/he lost consciousness?	*¿Cuánto tiempo pasó desde que se quejó hasta que quedó inconsciente?*	¿KWAHN-toh TYEHM-poh pah-SOH DEHS-deh keh seh keh-HOH AHS-tah keh keh-DOH een-kohn-SYEHN-teh?
PERSON	***PERSONA***	
Almost none.	*Casi nada.*	KAH-see NAH-dah.
A brief moment.	*Un momentito.*	Oon moh-mehn-TEE-toh.
A moment.	*Un rato.*	Oon RAH-toh.
DOCTOR	***DOCTOR***	
Did she/he vomit before or after losing consciousness?	*¿Vomitó antes o después de quedarse inconsciente?*	¿Voh-mee-TOH AHN-tehs oh dehs-PWEHS-deh keh-DAHR-seh een-kohn-SYEHN-teh?
Has this ever happened to the patient?	*¿Le había pasado esto antes al paciente?*	¿Leh ah-BEE-ah pah-SAH-doh EHS-toh AHN-tehs ahl pah-SYEHN-teh?
When?	*¿Cuándo?*	¿KWAHN-doh?

PERSON	***PERSONA***	
Once when she/he...	*Una vez que...*	OO-nah vehs keh...
• got drunk.	• *se emborrachó.*	• seh ehm-boh-rrah-CHOH.
• smoked marijuana.	• *fumó marijuana.*	• foo-MOH mah-ree-HWAH-nah.
• injected a drug.	• *se inyectó una droga.*	• seh een-yehk-TOH OO-nah DROH-gah.
DOCTOR	***DOCTOR***	
How did they treat the patient that time?	*¿Cómo lo trataron al paciente esa vez?*	¿KOH-moh loh trah-TAH-rohn ahl pah-TAH-teh EH-sah vehs?
PERSON	***PERSONA***	
She/he woke up by herself/himself.	*Despertó sola(o).*	Dehs-pehr-TOH SOH-lah(loh).
We took her/him to the emergency room of a hospital.	*La (lo) llevamos a la sala de emergencia del hospital.*	Lah (loh) yeh-VAH-mohs ah lah sah-lah deh eh-mehr-HEHN-syah dehl ohs-pee-TAHL.
DOCTOR	***DOCTOR***	
Do you know anyone who may be able to give us more information about the patient?	*¿Conoce usted a alguien que nos pueda dar más información sobre el paciente?*	¿Koh-NOH-seh oos-TEHD ah AHL-gyehn keh nohs PWEH-dah dahr MAHS een-fohr-mah-SYOHN SOH-breh ehl pah-SYEHN-teh?
What is...	*¿Cuál es...*	¿Kwahl ehs...
• the name of that person?	• *el nombre de esa persona?*	• ehl NOHM-breh deh EH-sah pehr-SOH-nah?
• the phone number?	• *el teléfono?*	• ehl teh-LEH-foh-noh?
• the address?	• *la dirección?*	• lah dee-rehk-SYOHN?
What relationship does she/he have with the patient?	*¿Qué relación tiene con el paciente?*	¿Keh reh-lah-SYOHN TYEH-neh kohn ehl pah-SYEHN-teh?

Do you know if the patient has a personal doctor?	*¿Sabe usted si la/el paciente tiene un médico personal?*	¿SAH-beh oos-TEHD see lah/ehl pah-SYEHN-teh TYEH-neh oon meh-DEE-oh pehr-soh-NAHL?
What is...of the doctor?	*¿Cuál es...del médico?*	¿Kwahl ehs... dehl MEH-dee-koh?
• the name	• *el nombre*	• ehl NOHM-breh
• the phone number	• *el teléfono*	• ehl teh-LEH-foh-noh
• the address	• *la dirección*	• lah dee-rehk-SYOHN

DOCTOR **DOCTOR**

Do you know if the patient has...	*¿Sabe usted si la (el) paciente tiene...*	¿SAH-beh oos-TEHD see lah (ehl) pah-SYEHN-teh TYEH-neh...
• heart disease?	• *una enfermedad del corazón?*	• OO-nah ehn-fehr-meh-DAHD dehl koh-rah-SOHN?
• diabetes?	• *diabetes?*	• dyah-BEH-tehs?
• emphysema?	• *enfisema?*	• ehn-fee-SEH-mah?
• bronchitis?	• *bronquitis?*	• brohn-KEE-tees?
• asthma?	• *asma?*	• AHS-mah?

If the patient is a woman ask:

Do you know if she is pregnant?	*¿Sabe usted si está embarazada?*	¿SAH-beh oos-TEHD see ehs-TAH ehm-bah-rah-SAH-dah?

VOCABULARY ••••

DRUG-RELATED TERMINOLOGY

acid	*ácido*	AH-see-doh
amphetamine	*anfetas*	ahn-FEH-tahs
angel dust	*polvo de ángel*	POHL-voh deh AHN-hehl
booze	*pisto*	PEES-toh
cigarettes	*cigarrillos/frajos*	see-gah-REE-yohs/ FRAH-hohs
cocaine	*coca*	KOH-kah
crack	*crack*	krahk
downers	*diablos*	DYAH-blohs
drugs	*drogas*	DROH-gahs
heroine	*chiva, heroína*	CHEE-vah, eh-roh-EE-nah
marijuana	*marijuana, mota, yerba, grifa*	MOH-tah, YEHR-bah, GREE-fah
mushrooms	*sombrillas*	sohm-BREE-yahs
pills	*píldoras*	peel-DOH-rahs
speedball	*"chute"*	"CHOO-teh"
tranquilizer	*tranquilizante*	trahn-kee-lee-SAHN-teh
uppers	*camello*	kah-MEH-yoh
downers	*traficante*	trah-fee-KAHN-teh
ecstacy	*extacy*	EHKS-tah-see

3. Accidental Exposure to a Toxic Substance

DOCTOR	*DOCTOR*	
How did the exposure occur?	*¿Cómo ocurrió la exposición?*	¿KOH-moh oh-koo-RYOH lah ehks-poh-see-SYOHN?
PERSON	*PERSONA*	
During an accident...	*En un accidente en...*	Ehn oon ahk-see-DEHN-teh ehn...
• at the factory where I work/she/he works.	• *la fábrica donde trabajo/trabaja.*	• lah FAH-bree-kah DOHN-deh trah-BAH-hoh/trah-BAH-hah.
• on the highway.	• *la carretera.*	• lah kah-rreh-TEH-rah.
• at home.	• *la casa.*	• lah KAH-sah.
• in the fields.	• *los sembradios.*	• lohs sehm-BRAH-dyohs.
DOCTOR	*DOCTOR*	
Do you know...	*¿Sabe usted...*	¿SAH-beh oos-TEHD...
• what substance he/she was/you were exposed to?	• *a qué substancia estuvo expuesto(a)?*	• ah keh soob-STAHN-see-ah ehs-TOO-voh ehks PWEHS-toh(tah)?
• how long she/he was/you were exposed?	• *cuánto tiempo estuvo expuesto(a)?*	• KWAHN-toh TYEHM-poh ehs-TOO-voh ehks-PWEHS-toh(tah)?
• if she/he/you ate some of that substance?	• *si comió algo de esa substancia?*	• see koh-MYOH AHL-goh deh EH-sah soob-STAHN-syah?
• if she/he/you drank some of that substance?	• *bebió algo de esta substancia?*	• beh-BYOH AHL-goh deh EHS-ah soob-STAHN-syah?
• if she/he/you inhaled some of that substance?	• *si inhaló algo de esa substancia?*	• see een-ah-LOH AHL-goh deh EH-sah soob-STAHN-syah?

• if some of that substance fell in her/his/your eyes?	• *si le cayó algo de esa substancia en los ojos?*	• see leh kah-YOH AHL-goh deh EH-sah soob-STAHN-syah ehn lohs OH-hohs?
• if some of that substance fell on any part of her/his/your body?	• *si le cayó algo de esa substancia en alguna parte del cuerpo?*	• see leh kah-YOH AHL-goh deh EH-sah soob-STAHN-syah ehn ahl-GOO-nah PAHR-teh dehl KWEHR-poh?
What have you done since being exposed to protect him/her/yourself from that substance?	*¿Qué ha hecho usted desde la exposición para protegerlo(la)/protegerse de esa substancia?*	¿Keh ah EH-choh oos-TEHD DEHS-deh lah ehks-poh-see-SYOHN PAH-rah proh-teh-HEHR-loh(lah)/proh-teh-HEHR-seh deh EH-sah soob-STAHN-syah?
PATIENT	***PACIENTE***	
Nothing.	*Nada.*	NAH-dah.
I took a bath.	*Me bañé.*	Meh bah-NYEH.
I covered him/her/myself with a blanket.	*Lo/la/me cubrí con una colcha.*	Loh/lah/meh koo-BREE-kohn OO-nah KOHL-chah.

4. Emergency Medical Services

A. AUTOMOBILE ACCIDENTS

DOCTOR	***DOCTOR***	
How long ago did the accident happen?	*¿Cuánto tiempo hace que ocurrió el accidente?*	¿KWAHN-toh TYEHM-poh AH-seh keh oh-koo-RYOH ehl ahk-see-DEHN-teh?
PATIENT/PERSON	***PACIENTE/PERSONA***	
About... ago.	*Hace...*	AH-seh...
• a moment	• *un rato.*	• oon-RAH-toh.
• half an hour	• *media hora.*	• MEH-dyah OH-rah.

• one hour	• *una hora.*	• OO-nah OH-rah.
DOCTOR	*DOCTOR*	
How did the accident happen?	*¿Cómo ocurrió el accidente?*	¿KOH-moh oh-koo-RYOH ehl ahk-see-DEHN-teh?
PATIENT/PERSON	*PACIENTE/PERSONA*	
I/we…	*Yo/nosotros…*	Yoh/noh-SOH-trohs…
• hit another car.	• *choqué/chocamos con otro auto.*	• choh-KEH/choh-KAH-mohs kohn OH-troh WOO-toh.
• dove off the highway.	• *me/nos salí/salimos de la carretera.*	• meh/nohs sah-LEE/sah-LEE-mohs deh lah kah-rreh-TEH-rah.
• turned the car over.	• *me/nos volteé/volteamos.*	• meh/nohs vohl-tee-EH/vohl-TEH-ah-mohs.
• hit a wall.	• *choqué/chocamos contra una pared.*	• choh-KEH/choh-KAH-mohs KOHN-trah OO-nah pah-REHD.
DOCTOR	*DOCTOR*	
Who was driving?	*¿Quién estaba manejando?*	¿Kyehn ehs-TAH-bah mah-neh-HAHN-doh?
PATIENT	*PACIENTE*	
I was.	*Yo.*	Yoh.
She/he was.	*Él/ella.*	Ehl/EH-yah.
A friend.	*Un(a) amigo(a).*	Oon (OO-nah) ah-MEE-goh(gah).
DOCTOR	*DOCTOR*	
How many people were in the car?	*¿Cuántas personas iban en el automóvil?*	¿KWAHN-tahs pehr-SOH-nahs EE-bahn eh ehl woo-toh-MOH-veel?

DOCTOR	***DOCTOR***	
What kind of car is it?	*¿Qué tipo de automóvil es?*	¿Keh TEE-poh deh woo-toh-MOH-veel ehs?
Who were the people injured?	*¿Quiénes son las personas que están heridas?*	¿KYEH-nehs sohn lahs pehr-SOH-nahs keh ehs-TAHN eh-REE-dahs?
PATIENT	***PACIENTE***	
My father/mother/son/ daughter/spouse/friend.	*Mi papá/mamá/ hijo/hija/esposo(a)/ amigo(a).*	Mee pah-PAH/mah-MAH/EE-hoh/EE-hah/ehs-POH-soh(sah)/ ah-MEE-goh(gah).
A little child.	*Un(a) niñito(a).*	Oon(OO-nah) nee-NYEE-toh(tah).
I don't know.	*No sé.*	Noh seh.
DOCTOR	***DOCTOR***	
Have you done anything to the injured people?	*¿Les ha hecho algo a las personas heridas?*	¿Lehs ah EH-choh AHL-goh ah lahs pehr-SOH-nahs eh-REE-dahs?
PATIENT/PERSON	***PACIENTE/PERSONA***	
Nothing.	*Nada.*	NAH-dah.
Mouth-to-mouth resuscitation.	*Respiración boca-boca.*	Rehs-pee-rah-SYOHN BOH-kah-BOH-kah.
I covered him/her them with blankets	*Lo/la/las/los cubrimos con colchas.*	Loh/lah/lahs/lohs koo-BREE-mohs kohn KOHL-chahs.
We tried to stop the bleeding.	*Tratamos de parar la sangre.*	Trah-TAH-mohs deh pah-RAHR lah SAHN-greh.
DOCTOR	***DOCTOR***	
Did you call the ambulance?	*¿Llamaron a la ambulancia?*	¿Yah-MAH-rohn ah lah ahm-boo-LAHN-syah?
Who did?	*¿Quién?*	¿Kyehn?

B. DETERMINING THE LEVEL OF CONSCIOUSNESS

DOCTOR	*DOCTOR*	
Tell me your name.	*Dígame como se llama.*	DEE-gah-meh KOH-moh seh YAH-mah.
Do you know...	*¿Sabe...*	¿SAH-beh...
• where you are?	• *dónde está?*	• DOHN-deh ehs-TAH?
• what day it is?	• *qué día es?*	• keh DEE-ah ehs?
• what date it is?	• *qué fecha es?*	• keh FEH-chah ehs?
How many fingers am I showing you?	*¿Cuántos dedos le estoy mostrando?*	¿KWAHN-tohs DEH-dohs leh ehs-TOY mohs-TRAHN-doh?

GRAMMAR NOTE ••••

DATES AND BIRTH DATES In Spanish, the day is always mentioned first:

What is today's date?	*¿Qué día es hoy?*
Today is February 25, 1997.	*Hoy es el 25 de febrero de 1997.*
2/25/97	25/2/97
What's your date of birth?	*¿Cuál es su fecha de nacimiento?*
When were you born?	*¿Cuándo nació usted?*
My date of birth is February 15, 1968.	*Mi fecha de nacimiento es el quince de febrero de mil novecientos sesenta y ocho.*
I was born on February 15, 1968.	*Nací el 15 de febrero de 1968.*

C. EMERGENCY MEDICAL PROCEDURES

PARAMEDIC	***PARAMEDICO***	
My name is ____.	*Me llamo ____.*	Meh YAH-moh ____.
I am an officer from Emergency Services.	*Soy funcionario de los Servicios de Emergencia.*	SOH-ee foon-SYOH-nah-ryoh deh lohs sehr-VEE-syohs deh eh-mehr-HEHN-syah.
I am here to help you.	*Estoy aquí para ayudarlo(la).*	Ehs-TOY ah-KEE PAH-rah ah-yoo-DAHR-loh(lah).
What is the emergency?	*¿Cuál es la emergencia?*	¿Kwahl ehs lah eh-mehr-HEHN-syah?
PERSON	***PERSONA***	
I/my mother/father/ son/daughter/friend...	*Yo/mi papá/mamá/ hijo(a)/amigo(a)...*	Yoh/mee pah-PAH/ mah-MAH/EE-hoh(hah)/ah-MEE-goh(gah)...
• am/is bleeding.	• *estoy/está sangrando.*	• ehs-TOY/ehs-TAH sahn-GRAHN-doh.
• just burned myself/ herself/himself.	• *me/se acabo(a) de quemar.*	• meh/seh ah-KAH-boh(bah) deh keh-MAHR.
• am/is having a baby.	• *está dando luz.*	• ehs-TAH DAHN-doh loos.
• broke an arm/leg.	• *me/se quebré/ quebró un(a) brazo/pierna.*	• meh/seh keh-BREH/ keh-BROH oon (OO-nah) BRAH-soh/ PYEHR-nah.
• cannot get up.	• *no me puedo/se puede levantar.*	• noh meh PWEH-doh/seh PWEH-deh leh-vahn-TAHR.

• have/has intense chest pain.	• *tengo/tiene un dolor intenso en el pecho.*	• TEHN-goh/TYEH-neh oon doh-LOHR een-TEHN-soh ehn ehl PEH-choh.
• feel(s) very sick.	• *me siento/se siente muy mal.*	• meh-SYEHN-toh/ seh SYEHN-teh moo-ee mahl.
He/she is unconscious.	*Él/élla está inconsciente.*	Ehl/EH-yah ehs-TAH een-kohn-SYEHN-teh.
PARAMEDIC	***PARAMEDICO***	
Everything will be okay.	*Todo va a salir bien.*	TOH-doh vah ah sah-LEER byehn.
I am going to administer emergency treatment.	*Le voy a administrar el tratamiento de emergencia.*	Leh voy ah ahd-mee-nees-TRAHR ehl trah-tah-MYEHN-toh deh eh-mehr-HEHN-syah.
You are bleeding.	*Usted está sangrando.*	Oos-TEHD ehs-TAH sahn-GRAHN-doh.
I am going to apply pressure over the injury to stop the bleeding.	*Voy a aplicar presión sobre la herida para que deje de sangrar.*	Voy ah ah-plee-KAHR preh-SYOHN SOH-breh lah eh-REE-dah PAH-rah keh DEH-heh deh sahn-GRAHR.
I am going to put a splint on...to immobilize it.	*Voy a ponerle una férula en... para inmobilizarlo.*	Voy ah poh-NEHR-leh OO-nah FEH-roo-lah ehn ...PAH-rah een-moh-bee-lee-SAHR.
• your arm(s)/leg(s)	• *el (la/los/las) brazo(s)/pierna(s)*	• ehl/lah/lohs/lahs BRAH-soh(s)/ PYEHR-nah(s)
• your neck	• *el cuello*	• ehl KWEH-yoh
Several parts of your body are burned.	*Tiene varias partes del cuerpo quemadas.*	TYEH-neh VAH-ryahs PAHR-tehs dehl KWEHR-poh keh-MAH-dahs.

I am going to dress them for protection.	*Voy a cubrirlas para protegerlas.*	Voy ah koo-BREER-lahs PAH-rah proh-teh-HEHR-lahs.
Be calm.	*Mantenga la calma.*	Mahn-TEHN-gah lah KAHL-mah.
Don't worry.	*No se preocupe.*	Noh seh preh-oh-koo-peh.
I am going to call the emergency helicopter.	*Voy a llamar al helicóptero de emergencia.*	Voy a yah-MAHR ahl eh-lee-KOHP-teh-roh deh eh-mehr-HEHN-syah.
It will take…to the hospital.	*La/se llevará… al hospital.*	Lah/seh yeh-vah-RAH…ahl ohs-pee-TAHL.
• you	• *a usted*	• ah oos-TEHD
• the patient	• *al paciente*	• ahl pah-SYEHN-teh
I will deliver the baby now.	*Voy a atender el parto ahora.*	Voy ah ah-tehn-DEHR ehl PAHR-toh ah-OH-rah.
You will deliver your baby at the hospital.	*Va a tener su bebé en el hospital.*	Vah ah teh-NEHR soo beh-BEH ehn ehl ohs-pee-TAHL.
Bring a bag with the things you will need.	*Traiga una bolsa con lo que va a necesitar.*	TRAH-ee-gah OO-nah BOHL-sah kohn loh keh vah ah neh-seh-see-TAHR.
Everything will be okay.	*Todo va a salir bien.*	TOH-doh vah ah sah-LEER byehn.
We'll help you.	*Nosotros lo/la vamos a ayudar.*	Noh-SOH-trohs loh/lah VAH-mohs ah ah-yoo-DAHR.

SECTION H

PATIENTS WITH SPECIAL CONDITIONS

1. Pregnancy and Prenatal Care

CULTURE NOTE ••••

THE IMPORTANCE OF PRENATAL CARE Prenatal care is not very common in Latino countries. Pregnancy is not considered to be a medical "problem," and therefore, most pregnant women are not inclined to seek medical advice until they are in labor. Therefore, it is advisable to specifically stress the importance of prenatal care.

A. PRENATAL CARE

DOCTOR	*DOCTOR*	
When was your last regular period?	*¿Cuándo fue su última regla normal?*	¿KWAHN-doh fweh soo OOL-tee-mah REH-glah nohr-MAHL?
When did you first think that you were pregnant?	*¿Cuándo fue la primera vez que pensó que estaba embarazada?*	¿KWAHN-doh fweh lah pree-MEH-rah vehs keh pehn-SOH keh ehs-TAH-bah ehm-bah-rah-SAH-dah?
What made you think you were pregnant?	*¿Qué la hizo pensar que estaba embarazada?*	¿Keh lah EE-soh pehn-SAHR keh ehs-TAH-bah ehm-bah-rah-SAH-dah?
PATIENT	***PACIENTE***	
I did not bleed.	*No me bajó la regla.*	Noh meh bah-HOH lah REH-glah.
My period...	*Mi regla...*	Mee-REH-glah...
• was short.	• *fue corta.*	• fweh KOHR-tah.
• was light.	• *fue escasa.*	• fweh ehs-KAH-sah.
My breasts...	*Mis senos...*	Mees SEH-nohs...
• changed.	• *cambiaron.*	• kahm-BYAH-rohn.
• got bigger.	• *se hicieron más grandes.*	• seh ee-SYEH-rohn MAHS GRAHN-dehs.
DOCTOR	***DOCTOR***	
How much did you weigh before your pregnancy?	*¿Cuánto pesaba antes de empezar su embarazo?*	¿KWAHN-toh peh-SAH-bah AHN-tehs deh ehm-peh-SAHR soo ehm-bah-RAH-soh?
Have you taken any medications since you discovered that you were pregnant?	*¿Ha tomado alguna medicinas desde que descubrió que está embarazada?*	¿Ah toh-MAH-doh ahl-GOO-nahs meh-dee SEE-nah DEHS-deh keh dehs-koo-BRYOH keh ehs-TAH-ehm-bah-rah-SAH-dah?

What medications?	*¿Qué medicinas?*	¿Keh meh-dee-SEE-nahs?
PATIENT	***PACIENTE***	
Something for nausea.	*Algo para el mareo.*	AHL-goh PAH-rah ehl mah-REH-oh.
Aspirin.	*Aspirina.*	Ahs-pee-RHEE-nah.
Antibiotics.	*Antibióticos.*	Ahn-tee-BYOH-tee-kohs.
Hormones.	*Hormonas.*	Ohr-MOH-nahs.
Tranquilizers.	*Tranquilizantes.*	Trahn-kee-lee-SAHN-tehs.
Antidepressants.	*Antidepresivos.*	Ahn-tee-deh-preh-SEE-vohs.
Stimulants.	*Estimulantes.*	Ehs-tee-moo-LAHN-tehs.
I have used drugs.	*He usado drogas.*	Eh oo-SAH-doh DROH-gahs.
I smoke.	*Fumo.*	FOO-moh.
DOCTOR	***DOCTOR***	
Is this your first pregnancy?	*¿Es éste su primer embarazo?*	¿Ehs EHS-teh soo PREE-mehr ehm-bah-RAH-soh?
How many times have you been pregnant before?	*¿Cuántas veces ha estado embarazada antes?*	¿KWAHN-tahs VEH-sehs ah ehs-TAH-doh ehm-bah-rah-SAH-dah ahn-tehs?
How many…	*¿Cuántos…*	¿KWAHN-tohs…
• deliveries have you had?	• *partos ha tenido?*	• PAHR-tohs ah teh-NEE-doh?
• miscarriages/abortions have you had?	• *abortos ha tenido?*	• ah-BOHR-tohs ah teh-NEE-doh?
Were the miscarriages spontaneous/provoked?	*¿Los abortos fueron espontáneos/provocados?*	¿Lohs ah-BOHR-tohs FWEH-rohn ehs-pohn-TAH-neh-oh/proh-voh-KAH-dohs?

How were they provoked?	*¿Cómo fueron provocados?*	¿KOH-moh FWEH-rohn proh-voh-KAH-dohs?
PATIENT	***PACIENTE***	
I went to an abortion clinic.	*Fui a una clínica de abortos.*	Fwee ah OO-nah KLEE-nee-kah deh ah-BOHR-tohs.
I put something into my uterus.	*Me metí algo en la matriz.*	Meh meh-TEE-AHL-goh ehn lah mah-TREES.
DOCTOR	***DOCTOR***	
Have you…	*¿Ha…*	¿Ah…
• felt nausea and vomited?	• *tenido náuseas y vómitos?*	• teh-NEE-doh NAWH-seh-ahs ee VOH-mee-tohs?
• had headaches?	• *tenido dolores de cabeza?*	• teh-NEE-doh doh-LOHR-ehs deh kah-BEH-sah?
• had blurred vision?	• *tenido visión borrosa?*	• teh-NEE-doh vee-SYOHN boh-RROH-sah?
• had swollen hands/feet?	• *tenido las manos/los pies hinchadas(os)?*	• teh-NEE-doh lahs MAH-nohs/lohs pyehs een-CHAH-dahs(dohs)?
• had a change in your daily urine output?	• *tenido un cambio en la cantidad que orina al día?*	• teh-NEE-doh oon KAHM-byoh ehn lah kahn-tee-DAHD keh oh-REE-nah ahl DEE-ah?
• had spotting or hemorrhages?	• *sangra o tenido hemorragias?*	• ah SAHN-grah oh teh-NEE-doh eh-moh-RAH-hee-ahs?

B. LABOR AND DELIVERY

DOCTOR	***DOCTOR***	
Did your water break?	*¿Ya se le rompió la fuente?*	¿Yah seh leh rohm-PYOH lah FWEHN-teh?

When?	*¿Cuándo?*	¿KWAHN-doh?
PATIENT	***PACIENTE***	
It…	*Se me rompió…*	Seh meh rohm-PYOH…
• just broke.	• *hace un momentito.*	• AH-seh oon moh-mehn-TEE-toh.
• broke a while ago.	• *hace un rato.*	• AH-seh oon RAH-toh.
• broke this morning.	• *esta mañana.*	• EHS-tah mah-YNAH-nah.
• broke yesterday.	• *ayer.*	• ah-YEHR.
DOCTOR	***DOCTOR***	
At what time did your labor pains begin?	*¿A qué hora le empezaron los dolores de parto?*	¿Ah keh OH-rah leh ehm-peh-SAH-rohn lohs doh-LOH-rehs deh PAHR-toh?
How often are your contractions coming?	*¿Con qué frecuencia le viene los dolores?*	¿Kohn keh freh-KWEHN-syah leh VYEH-neh lohs doh-LOH-rehs?
PATIENT	***PACIENTE***	
Every once in a while.	*A cada rato.*	Ah KAH-dah RAH-toh.
Every ____ minutes.	*Cada ____ minutos.*	KAH-dah ____ mee-NOO-tohs.
DOCTOR	***DOCTOR***	
How long do the pains last?	*¿Cuánto tiempo le duran los dolores?*	¿KWAHN-toh TYEHM-poh leh DOO-rahn lohs doh-LOHR-ehs?
PATIENT	***PACIENTE***	
They are very short.	*Muy poquito.*	MOO-ee poh-KEE-toh.
Some ____ seconds.	*Unos ____ segundos.*	OO-nohs ____ seh-GOON-dohs.
One minute.	*Un minuto.*	Oon mee-NOO-toh.
DOCTOR	***DOCTOR***	
Do you have any other pains?	*¿Tiene algún otro dolor?*	¿TYEH-neh ahl-GOON OH-troh doh-LOHR?

I have to examine your genitalia.	*Tengo que examinarle las partes privadas.*	TEHN-goh keh ex-ah-mee-NAHR-leh PAHR-tehs pree-VAH-dahs.
Will you allow me?	*¿Me lo permite?*	¿Meh loh pehr-MEE-teh?
May I/Can I?	*¿Puedo?*	¿PWEH-doh?
Breathe through your mouth.	*Respire por la boca.*	Rehs-PEE-reh pohr lah BOH-kah.
Try to make yourself as comfortable as possible.	*Trate de estar tan a gusto como sea posible.*	TRAH-teh deh ehs-TAHR tahn ah-GOOS-toh KOH-moh SEH-ah poh-SEE-bleh.
It will be a few more ...before your baby is born.	*Pasarán algunas(os) ...antes de que nazca su bebé.*	Pah-sah-RAHN ahl-GOO-nahs(nohs)... AHN-tehs deh keh NAHS-kah soo beh-BEH.
• hours	• *horas*	• OH-rahs
• minutes	• *minutos*	• mee-NOO-tohs
Your baby is ready to be born.	*Su bebé está listo para nacer.*	Soo beh-BEH ehs-TAH LEES-toh PAH-rah nah-SEHR.
We are going to take you to the delivery room.	*La vamos a llevar a la sala de partos.*	Lah VAH-mohs ah yeh-VAHR ah lah SAH-lah deh PAHR-tohs.
Please help us move you to the delivery table.	*Por favor, ayúdenos a pasarla a la mesa de partos.*	Pohr fah-VOHR, ah-YOO-deh-nohs ah pah-SAHR-lah ah lah MEH-sah deh PAHR-tohs.
Please open your legs.	*Por favor, abra las piernas.*	Pohr fah-VOHR, AH-brah lahs PYEHR-nahs.
Put your feet in these stirrups.	*Ponga los pies en estos estribos.*	POHN-gah lohs pyehs ehn EHS-tohs ehs-TREE-bohs.
Push.	*Empuje.*	Ehm-POO-heh.
Do not push.	*No empuje.*	Noh ehm-POO-heh.

There are a few complications.	*Hay algunas complicaciones.*	Ay ahl-GOO-nahs kohm-plee-kah-SYOH-nehs.
Your baby...	*Su bebé...*	Soo beh-BEH...
• is too big.	*• es muy grande.*	• ehs moo-ee GRAHN-deh.
• is in a difficult position.	*• está en una posición dificil.*	• ehs-TAH ehn oo-nah poh-see-SYOHN dee-FEE-seel.
• is coming...	*• viene...*	• VYEH-neh...
• crossways.	*• atravesado.*	• ah-trah-veh-SAH-doh.
• butt first.	*• de nalgas.*	• deh NAHL-gahs.
I am going to listen to your baby's heart.	*Voy a escuchar el corazón de su bebé.*	Voy ah ehs-koo-CHAHR ehl koh-rah-SOHN deh soo beh-BEH.
His/her heart is very fast/slow.	*Su corazón va muy aprisa/despacio.*	Soo koh-rah-SOHN vah moo-ee ah-PREE-sah/dehs-PAH-syoh.
Your baby is at risk of suffering lasting damage.	*Su bebé está en riesgo de sufrir daño permanente.*	Soo beh-BEH ehs-TAH ehn RHYEHS-goh deh soo-FREER dah-NYOH pehr-mah-NEHN-teh.
We should do a cesarean section.	*Debemos hacer una operación cesárea.*	Deh-BEH-mohs ah-SEHR OO-nah oh-peh-rah-SYOHN seh-SAH-ree-ah.
We open your abdomen and your uterus and we bring the baby out through there.	*Le abrimos el vientre y la matriz y sacamos a su bebé por ahí.*	Leh ah-BREE-mohs ehl VYEHN-treh ee lah mah-TREES ee sah-KAH-mohs ah soo beh-BEH pohr ah-EE.
PATIENT	***PACIENTE***	
I need you to explain this to my husband.	*Necesito que le explique a mi esposo.*	Neh-seh-SEE-toh keh leh ehks-PLEE-keh ah mee ehs-POH-soh.

I need to discuss this with my husband.	*Necesito discutirlo con mi esposo.*	Neh-seh-SEE-toh dees-koo-TEER-loh kohn mee ehs-POH-soh.
DOCTOR	*DOCTOR*	
Do you authorize me to do a cesarean section?	*¿Me autoriza usted a que le hagamos la cesárea?*	¿Meh awoo-toh-REE-sah oos-TEHD ah keh leh ah-GAH-mohs lah seh-SAH-reh-ah?
We are going to anesthetize you for the operation.	*La vamos a anestesiar para poderle hacer la operación.*	Lah VAH-mohs ah ahn-ehs-teh-SYAHR PAH-rah poh-DEHR-leh ah-SEHR lah oh-peh-rah-SYOHN.
There are two types of anesthesia, epidural and general.	*Hay dos tipos de anestesia, epidural y general.*	Ay dohs TEE-pohs deh ah-nehs-TEH-syah, eh-pee-doo-RAHL ee heh-neh-RAHL.
With epidural anesthesia you will be awake, but you won't feel anything.	*Con la anestesia epidural usted estará despierta, pero no sentirá nada.*	Kohn lah ah-nehs-TEH-syah eh-pee-doo-RAHL oos-TEHD ehs-tah-RAH dehs-PYEHR-tah, PEH-roh noh sehn-tee-RAH NAH-dah.
You will see your baby immediately after he or she is born.	*Verá a su bebé inmediatamente después de nacer.*	Veh-RAH ah soo beh-BEH een-meh-DYAH-tah-mehn-teh dehs-PWEHS deh nah-SEHR.
With general anesthesia, you will be asleep and feel nothing.	*Con la anestesia general, usted estará dormida y no sentirá nada.*	Kohn lah ah-nehs-TEH-syah heh-neh-RAHL oos-TEHD ehs-tah-RAH, dohr-MEE-dah ee noh sehn-tee-RAH NAH-dah.
You will see your baby when you wake up.	*Verá a su bebé cuando despierte.*	Veh-RAH ah soo beh-BEH KWAHN-doh dehs-PYEHR-teh.
You and the anesthetist will choose the best anesthesia for you and your baby.	*Usted y el anestesista escogerán la mejor anestesia para usted y su bebé.*	OO-stehd ee ehl ah-nehs-teh-SEES-tah ehs-koh-heh-RAHN lah meh-HOHR ah-nehs-TEH-syah PAH-rah oos-TEHD ee soo beh-BEH.

Mrs. ____, you just had a healthy boy/girl.	*Señora ____, acaba de tener un varón/una niña fuerte.*	Seh-NYOH-rah ____, ah-KAH-bah deh teh-NEHR oon vah ROHN/OO-nah NEE-nyah FWEHR-teh.
Congratulations!	*¡Felicidades!*	¡Feh-lee-see-DAH-dehs!

C. POSTPARTUM

DOCTOR	***DOCTOR***	
Will you breast feed your baby?	*¿Le va a dar el pecho a su bebé?*	¿Leh vah ah dahr ehl PEH-choh ah soo beh-BEH?
It is very important that your breasts are ready to feed your baby.	*Es muy importante que sus senos estén listos para alimentar a su bebé.*	Ehs MOO-ee eem-pohr-TAHN-teh keh soos SEH-nohs ehs-TEHN LEES-tohs PAH-rah ah-lee-mehn-TAHR ah soo beh-BEH.
Do you know how to prepare your breasts to feed your baby?	*¿Sabe cómo preparar sus senos para alimentar a su bebé?*	¿SAH-beh KOH-moh preh-pah-RAHR soos MAH-mahs PAH-rah ah-lee-mehn-TAHR ah soo beh-BEH?
The nurse will teach you how.	*La (él) enfermera(o) la enseñará cómo.*	Lah/ehl ehn-fehr-MEH-rah(roh) leh ehn-seh-NYAH-RAH KOH-moh.
Do you have any questions about how to care for your baby?	*¿Tiene alguna pregunta acerca de cómo cuidar a su bebé?*	¿TYEH-neh ahl-GOO-nah preh-GOON-tah ah-SEHR-kah deh KOH-moh KWEE-dahr ah soo beh-BEH?
The nurse will help you.	*La enfermera le ayudará.*	Lah ehn-fehr-MEH-rah leh ah-yoo-dah-RAH.

Please remember that you should not have sex during the next six weeks.	*Por favor, recuerde que no debe tener relaciones sexuales durante las siguientes seis semanas.*	Pohr fah-VOHR, reh-KWEHR-deh keh noh DEH-beh TEH-nehr reh-lah-SYOH-nehs sehk-SWAH-lehs doo-RAHN-teh lahs see-GYEHN-tehs sehs seh-MAH-nahs.
You have to come to my office in ____ weeks.	*Tiene que ir a mi oficina en ____ semanas.*	TYEH-neh keh eer ah mee oh-fee-SEE-nah ehn ____ seh-MAH-nahs.

2. The Patient with a Mood Disorder

> ### CULTURE NOTE ••••
>
> **THE IMAGE OF MOOD DISORDERS** Mood disorders are not seen as a medical "problem." Your Latino patients may not expect a physician to be able to help them, and therefore, might not even mention mood swings in an interview, unless you specifically ask about them. Therefore, if you suspect a mood disorder to be at the root of the problem, make sure you ask specific questions to solicit the answers you need. If possible, call in an interpreter to discuss these sensitive emotional issues.

DOCTOR	*DOCTOR*	
Are you…	*¿Está…*	¿Ehs-TAH…
• having difficulty falling asleep?	• *teniendo dificultad para dormirse?*	• teh-NYEHN-doh dee-fee-kool-TAHD PAH-rah dohr-MEER-seh?

• sleeping too much?	• *durmiendo demasiado?*	• door-MYEHN-doh deh-mah-SEE-AH-doh?
• tired often?	• *cansada(o) con frecuencia?*	• kahn-SAH-dah(doh) kohn freh-KWEN-syah?
Do you…	*¿Siente…*	¿SYEHN-teh…
• feel you have no energy to do things?	• *que no tiene ánimos para hacer las cosas?*	• keh noh TYEH-neh AH-nee-mohs PAH-rah ah-SEHR lahs KOH-sahs?
• have poor appetite lately?	• *que tiene poco apetito últimamente?*	• keh TYEH-neh POH-koh ah-peh-TEE-toh OOL-tee-mah-mehn-teh?
Have you…	*¿Ha…*	¿Ah…
• been eating more than is usual for you?	• *estado comiendo más de lo que acostumbra?*	• ehs-TAH-doh koh-myehn-doh MAHS deh loh keh ah-kohs-TOOM-brah?
• lost interest in doing things?	• *perdido interés en hacer cosas?*	• pehr-DEE-doh een teh-REHS ehn ah-SEHR KOH-sahs?
Do you feel…	*¿(Se) siente…*	¿(Seh) SYEHN-teh…
• hopeless lately?	• *sin esperanzas últimamente?*	• seen ehs-peh-RAHN-sahs OOL-tee-mah mehn-teh?
• that your life is a failure?	• *que su vida es un fracaso?*	• keh soo VEE-dah ehs oon frah-KAH-soh?
• that you have trouble concentrating?	• *que tiene dificultad para concentrarse?*	• TYEH-neh dee-fee-kool-TAHD PAH-rah kohn-sehn-TRAHR-seh?
• restless lately?	• *muy inquieto(a) últimamente?*	• MOO-ee een-KEE-EH-toh(tah) OOL-tee-mah-mehn-teh?
• that it would be better to be dead?	• *que sería mejor estar muerta(o)?*	• keh seh-RHEE-ah meh-HOHR ehs-TAHR MWEHR-tah(toh)?

• that there has never been a time in which you felt even sadder than you do at this moment?	• *que nunca ha habido algún momento en que usted se sentía más triste de lo que se siente en este momento?*	• keh NOON-kah ah ah-BEE-doh ahl-GOON moh-MEHN-toh ehn keh oos-TEHD seh sehn-TEE-ah MAHS TRES-teh deh loh keh seh SYEHN-teh ehn EHS-teh moh-MEHN-toh?
Has a physician ever prescribed lithium for you?	*¿Alguna vez le recetó litio un médico?*	¿Ahl-GOO-nah vehs leh reh-seh-TOH LEE-tyoh oon meh-DEE koh?

3. The Anxious Patient

CULTURE NOTE ••••

SUSTO Anxiety may not be thought of as a problem to be treated by a physician. Latino patients of Mexican ancestry understand anxiety as *susto* which roughly translates as "being scared." Some of your patients may insist on treating *susto* the way their ancestors always have, with the presence of a folk healer. In such cases, it may be necessary to negotiate with the patient and the entire family to work out a compromise that will include the necessary medical treatment.

DOCTOR	*DOCTOR*	
Have you…	*¿Ha tenido…*	¿Ah teh-NEE-doh…
• had an attack of anxiety or fear?	• *un ataque de ansiedad/miedo?*	• oon ah-TAH-keh deh ahn-syeh-DAHD/ MYEH-doh?
• ever had more than four of these attacks in one month?	• *más de cuatro de estos ataques en un mes?*	• mahs deh KWAH-troh ah-TAH-kehs ehn oon mehs?

Does the attack come suddenly, without warning?	*¿El ataque le llega de repente, sin que lo esté esperando?*	¿Ehl ah-TAH-keh leh YEH-gah deh reh-PEHN-teh seen keh loh ehs-TEH ehs-peh-RAHN-doh?
When you had the last attack...	*¿Cuando tuvo el último ataque,...*	¿KWAHN-doh TOO-voh ehl OOL-tee-moh ah-TAH-keh,...
• were you short of breath?	• *¿le faltó la respiración?*	• ¿leh fahl-TOH lah rehs-pee-rah-SYOHN?
• was your heart pounding and racing?	• *¿se le quería salir el corazón del pecho?*	• ¿seh leh keh-RHEE-ah sah-LEER ehl koh-rah-SOHN dehl PEH-choh?
• did you feel pressure or pain over your heart?	• *¿sintió presión o dolor en el corazón?*	• ¿seen-TYOH preh-SYOHN oh doh-LOHR ehn ehl koh-rah-SOHN?
• did you begin to sweat?	• *¿empezó a sudar?*	• ¿ehm-peh-SOH ah soo-DAHR?
• did you feel as if you were choking?	• *¿se sintió como si se estuviera ahogando?*	• ¿seh seen-TYOH KOH-moh see seh ehs-too-VYEH-rah ah-oh-GAHN-doh?
• did you have hot flashes or chills?	• *¿tuvo bochornos o escalofríos?*	• ¿TOO-voh boh-CHOHR-nohs oh ehs-kah-loh-FREE-ohs?
• did you feel as if you were going to have diarrhea?	• *¿sintió como si le fuera a dar diarrea?*	• ¿seen-TYOH KOH-moh see leh FWEH-rah ah dahr dyah-RREH-ah?
• did you feel weak, as if you were going to faint?	• *¿se sintió débil, como si se fuera a desmayar?*	• ¿seh seen-TYOH DEH-beel KOH-moh see seh FWEH-rah ah dehs-mah-YAHR?
• did you begin to tremble?	• *¿empezó a temblar?*	• ¿ehm-peh-SOH ah tehm-BLAHR?

• did things appear to be unreal?	• *¿las cosas no parecían ser reales?*	• ¿lahs KOH-sahs noh pah-reh-SEE-ahn sehr reh-AHL-ehs?
• were you afraid of dying?	• *¿tenía miedo de morirse?*	• ¿teh-NEE-ah MYEH -doh deh moh-REER-seh?
• were you afraid of going crazy?	• *¿tenía miedo de volverse loca(o)?*	• ¿teh-NEE-ah MYEH-doh deh vohl-VEHR-seh LOH-kah(koh)?
Have you felt...	*¿(Se) ha sentido...*	(Seh) ah sehn-TEE-doh...
• nervous or anxious most of the last month?	• *nervioso(a) o ansioso(a) casi todo el mes pasado?*	• nehr-VYOH-soh (sah) oh ahn-SYOH-soh(sah) KAH-see TOH-doh ehl mehs pah-SAH-doh?
• that you could not sit still?	• *que no se puede sentar?*	• keh noh seh PWEH-deh sehn-TAHR?
• that you tire easily?	• *que se cansa fácilmente?*	• keh seh KAHN-sah FAH-seel-mehn-teh?
• that you get angry easily.	• *que se enoja fácilmente?*	• keh seh ehn-OH-hah FAH-seel-mehn-teh?
• that these problems do not allow you to...	• *que estos problemas le impiden...*	• keh EHS-tohs pro-BLEH-mahs leh eem-PEE-dehn...
• do things well?	• *hacer las cosas bien?*	• ah-SEHR lahs KOH-sahs byehn?
• get along with people?	• *llevarse bien con la gente?*	• yeh-VAHR-seh byehn kohn lah HEHN-teh?
• that these things preoccupy you?	• *que estas cosas lo preocupan?*	• keh EHS-tahs KOH-sahs loh preh-oh-KOO-pahn?

4. The Patient with an Eating Disorder

CULTURE NOTE ••••

EATING HABITS Problems like bulimia, anorexia or overeating, while common among Latinos as well, are not considered to be medical problems, but rather as an expression of personal eating habits. Your patients might be surprised about your interest in their eating habits, and may resist your diagnosis and treatment plan. Try to explain as clearly as possible that eating disorders are often just symptoms for an underlying medical or psychological problem.

DOCTOR	*DOCTOR*	
Do you...	*¿Usted...*	¿Oos-TEHD...
• eat in a two hour period what other persons would consider too much?	• *come en dos horas lo que otras personas considerarían demasiado?*	• KOH-meh ehn dohs OH-rahs loh keh OH-trahs pehr-SOH-nahs kohn-see-deh-rah-REE-ahn deh-mah-SYAH-doh?
• feel you cannot control the quantity that you eat?	• *siente que no puede controlar la cantidad que come?*	• SYEHN-teh keh noh PWEH-deh kohn-troh-LAHR lah kahn-tee-DAHD keh KOH-meh?
• do this at least twice a week?	• *hace esto por lo menos dos veces por semana?*	• AH-seh EHS-toh pohr loh MEH-nohs dohs VEH-sehs pohr seh-MAH-nah?

Have you…	*¿Usted…*	¿Oos-TEHD…
• done this for the last six months?	• *lo ha hecho durante los últimos seis meses?*	• loh ah EH-choh doo-RAHN-teh lohs OOL-tee-mohs sehs MEH-sehs?
• made yourself vomit in order not to gain weight?	• *se ha provocado vómitos para no engordarse?*	• seh ah proh-voh-KAH-doh VOH-mee-tohs PAH-rah noh ehn-gohr-DAHR-seh?
• taken laxatives so that you will not gain weight?	• *ha tomado purgantes para no engordarse?*	• ah toh-MAH-doh poor-GAHN-tehs PAH-rah noh ehn-gohr-DAHR-seh?
• done this about twice a week?	• *ha hecho esto como dos veces por semana?*	• ah EH-choh EHS-toh KOH-moh dohs VEH-sehs pohr seh-MAH-nah?
• done this for at least three months?	• *ha hecho esto por lo menos durante tres meses?*	• ah EH-choh EHS-toh pohr loh MEH-nohs doo-RAHN-teh trehs MEH-sehs?
I am asking these questions to find out if there is a hidden medical or psychological problem.	*Le hago estas preguntas para descrubrir si hay un problema médico o psicológico.*	Leh AH-goh EHS-tahs preh-GOON-tahs PAH-rah dehs-koo-BREER see ay oon proh-BLEH-mah MEH-dee-koh oh see-koh-LOH-hee-koh.

5. The Alcohol-Abusing Patient

CULTURE NOTE ••••

ALCOHOL IN LATINO CULTURE Drinking alcohol is considered part and parcel of a man's life. Men are expected to get drunk on holidays and during celebrations, and a hangover is considered "funny." Being drunk, or as it is colloquially called *estar pedo* (being with fart), is almost like a sign of one's manhood and easily forgiven. This is not at all true for women. While drinking may be seen as a rite of passage for a young man, a woman who drinks is always a shame to herself and her family. Latino women may, therefore, have a lot of trouble admitting to drinking alcohol, while Latino men may not consider their drinking a medical problem at all. Be sensitive to these cultural issues when you suspect alcohol abuse.

DOCTOR	DOCTOR	
Do you drink alcoholic beverages regularly?	*¿Toma usted bebidas alcohólicas regularmente?*	¿TOH-mah oos-TEHD beh-BEE-dahs ahl-koh-OH-lee-kahs reh-goo-LAHR-mehn-teh?
Do you think that you should cut down on your drinking?	*¿Piensa que debería tomar menos?*	¿PYEHN-sah keh deh-beh-REE-ah toh-MAHR MEH-nohs?
Has anyone complained about your drinking?	*¿Se ha quejado alguien de la manera en que usted bebe?*	¿Seh ah keh-HAH-doh AHL-gyehn deh lah mah-NEH-rah ehn keh oos-TEHD beh-BEH?

Do you feel guilty about your drinking?	*¿Se siente culpable por la manera en que toma?*	¿Seh SYEHN-teh kool-PAH-bleh pohr lah mah-NEH-rah ehn keh TOH-mah?
Do you need a drink when you wake up in order to begin your activities?	*¿Necesita tomarse alguna bebida cuando despierta para poder empezar sus actividades?*	¿Neh-seh-SEE-tah toh-MAHR-seh ahl-GOO-nah beh-BEE-dah KWAHN-doh deh-PYEHR-tah PAH-rah poh-DEHR ehm-peh-SAHR soos ahk-tee-vee-DAH-dehs?
Did a physician ever tell you that you should stop drinking because of a health problem?	*¿Alguna vez un médico le dijo que dejara de tomar por algún problema de salud?*	¿Ahl-GOO-nah vehs oon MEH-dee-koh leh DEE-hoh keh deh-HAH-rah deh toh-MAHR pohr ahl-GOON proh-BLEH-mah deh sah-LOOD?
Have you...because you were drinking, drunk, or hung over?	*¿Ha...porque estaba tomando, borracho, o crudo?*	¿Ah...POHR-keh ehs-TAH-bah toh-mahn-doh boh-RRAH-choh, oh KROO-doh?
• been late	• *llegado tarde*	• yeh-GAH-doh TAH-deh
• missed work	• *faltado a su trabajo*	• fahl-TAH-doh ah soo trah-BAH-hoh
• missed school	• *faltado a la escuela*	• fahl-TAH-doh ah lah ehs-KWEH-lah
• missed business meetings	• *faltado a sus negocios*	• fahl-TAH-doh ah soos neh-GOH-syohs
• had difficulty getting along	• *tenido dificultad para llevarse bien con otros*	• teh-NEE-doh dee-fee-kool-TAHD PAH-rah yeh-VAHR-se byehn kohn OH-trohs
• caused trouble at home	• *a causado problemas en su casa*	• ah kah-SAH-doh proh-BLEH-mahs ehn soo KAH-sah

6. The Patient Who Abuses Tobacco and Other Substances

CULTURE NOTE ••••

SMOKING is rather common among Latinos. Concern with medical problems resulting from smoking is not as strong, and your patients may not want to comply with your suggestion to cut down or quit smoking all together. A rather frequent phrase quips *de algo se tiene uno que morir* (you have to die of something), and thus you might as well die of something you enjoy.

DOCTOR	*DOCTOR*	
Do you use...	*¿Acostumbra usted...*	¿OOS-tehd ah-kohs-TOOM-brah...
• tobacco?	• *a fumar tabaco?*	• ah FOO-mahr tah-BAH-koh?
• a controlled or illegal substance?	• *a usar alguna substancia controlado o ilegal?*	• ah oo-SAHR ahl-GOO-nah soob-STAN-syah kohn-troh-LAH-dah oh ee-leh-GAHL?
What?	*¿Qué?*	¿Keh?
PATIENT	***PACIENTE***	
Only tobacco.	*Sólo tabaco.*	SOH-lo tah-BAH-koh.
Marijuana.	*Marijuana.*	Mah-rhee-HWAH-nah.
Morphine.	*Morfina.*	Mohr-FEE-nah.
Cocaine.	*Cocaína.*	Koh-kah-EE-nah.
Amphetamine.	*Anfetamina.*	Ahn-feh-tah-MEE-nah.

DOCTOR	*DOCTOR*	
Do you take more than one drug at the same time?	*¿Usa más de una droga al mismo tiempo?*	¿OO-sah MAHS deh OO-nah DROH-gah ahl MEES-moh TYEHM-poh?
Can you stop whenever you want?	*¿Puede dejarla(s) cuando usted quiere?*	¿PWEH-deh deh-HAHR-lah(s) KWAHN-doh KYEH-reh?
Do you have any complaints when you stop for sometime?	*¿Tiene alguna molestia cuando la(s) deja de usar por un tiempo?*	¿TYEH-neh ahl-GOO-nah moh-LEHS-tyah KWAHN-doh lah(s) DEH-hah deh hoo-SAHR pohr oon TYEHM-poh?
What complaints?	*¿Qué molestias?*	¿Keh moh-LEHS-tyahs?
PATIENT	*PACIENTE*	
None.	*Ninguna.*	NEEN-goo-nah.
I…	*Yo…*	Yoh…
• feel very nervous.	• *me siento muy nerviosa(o).*	• meh SYEHN-toh moo-ee nehr-VYOH-sah(soh).
• cannot focus.	• *no puedo concentrarme.*	• noh PWEH-doh kohn-sehn-TRAHR-meh.
• feel nauseous.	• *tengo náuseas.*	• TEHN-goh NWAH-seh-ahs.
• vomit.	• *vomito.*	• VOH-mee-toh.
• pass out.	• *me desmayo.*	• meh dehs-MAH-yoh.
DOCTOR	*DOCTOR*	
Do you have…	*¿Tiene…*	¿TYEH-neh…
• seizures?	• *ataques?*	• ah-TAH-kehs?
• infections?	• *infecciones?*	• een-fehk-SYOH-nehs?
• jaundice?	• *la piel amarilla?*	• lah pyehl ah-mah-REE-yah?
Are you HIV positive?	*¿VIH positivo?*	¿veh-ee-AH-cheh poh-see-TEE-voh?
Do you feel guilty because you take drugs?	*¿Se siente culpable porque usa drogas?*	¿Seh SYEHN-teh kool-PAH-bleh POHR-keh OO-sah DROH-gahs?

English	Spanish	Pronunciation
Has someone you know…	*¿Alguien que usted conoce ha…*	¿AHL-gyehn keh oos-TEHD koh-NOH-seh ah…
• expressed concern about your drug abuse?	• *dicho que está preocupado(a) por su abuso de drogas?*	• DEE-choh keh ehs-TAH preh-oh-koo-PAH-dah(doh) pohr soo ah-BOO-soh deh DROH-gahs?
• said that you should stop using drugs?	• *dicho que usted debería dejar de usar drogas?*	• DEE-choh keh oos-TEHD deh-beh-REE-ah deh-HAHR deh oo-SAHR DROH-gahs?
Did you ever…	*¿Alguna vez usted ha…*	¿Ahl-GOO-nah vehs oos-TEHD ah…
• miss work/school because you were on drugs?	• *tenido que faltar al trabajo/ a la escuela porque estaba drogado?*	• teh-NEE-doh keh fahl-TAHR ahl trah-BAH-hoh/hah lah ehs-KWEH-lah pohr-keh ehs-TAH-blah droh-GAH-doh?
• have problems with the law because of your abuse?	• *tenido problemas con la ley por su abuso?*	• teh-NEE-doh proh-BLEH-mahs kohn lah LEH-ee pohr soo ah-BOO-soh?
• participate in a treatment program?	• *participado en un programa de tratamiento?*	• pahr-tee-see-PAH-doh ehn oon proh-GRAH-mah deh trah-tah-MYEHN-toh?
How do you inject yourself?	*¿Cómo se inyecta?*	¿KOH-moh seh een-YEHK-tah?
Do you share needles?	*¿Comparte agujas?*	¿Kohm-PAHR-teh ah-GOO-hahs?
You must avoid doing so.	*Debe evitar hacerlo.*	DEH-beh eh-vee-TAHR ah-SEHR-loh.
Sharing needles puts you at risk for diseases.	*El compartir agujas le causa un alto riesgo de contraer enfermedades.*	Ehl kohm-pahr-TEER ah-HOO-yahs leh KAW-sah oon AHL-toh RYEHS-goh deh kohn-trah-EHR ehn-fehr-meh-DAH-dehs.

7. Home Healthcare for the Elderly and/or Physically Challenged

DOCTOR/NURSE	*DOCTOR/ENFERMERA*	
Mr./Mrs. _____,...	*Señor/Señora _____,...*	Seh-NYOHR/Seh-NYOH-rah _____,...
• did you take your medication(s)?	• *tomó sus(s) medicina(s)?*	• toh-MOH soo(s) meh-dee-SEE-nah(s)?
• you need to take your medication(s).	• *necesita tomar su(s) medicina(s).*	• neh-seh-SEE-tah toh-MAHR soo(s) meh-dee-SEE-nah(s).
Why are you not taking your medication?	*¿Por qué no se esta tomando sus medicinas?*	¿Pohr keh noh seh EHS-tah toh-MAHN-doh soos meh-dee-SEE-nahs?
PATIENT	*PACIENTE*	
Because...	*Porque...*	POHR-keh...
• I did not understand how to take it.	• *no entendí como tomármelas.*	• noh ehn-TEHN-dee KOH-moh toh-MAHR-meh-lahs.
• I have not bought it.	• *no las he comprado.*	• noh lahs eh kohm-PRAH-doh.
• I do not want to take it.	• *no quiero tomarlas.*	• noh KYEH-roh toh-MAHR-lahs.
• I do not have money to buy it.	• *no tengo dinero para comprarlas.*	• noh TEHN-goh dee-NEH-roh PAH-rah kohm-PRAHR-lahs.
• I do not want to get better.	• *no quiero mejorar.*	• noh KYEH-roh meh-hoh-RAHR.
DOCTOR/NURSE	*DOCTOR/ENFERMERA*	
Mr./Mrs. _____,...	*Señor/Señora _____,...*	Seh-NYOHR/Seh-NYOH-rah _____,...
• do you want me to help you take your medication(s)?	• *quiere que le ayude a tomar su(s) medicina(s)?*	• KYEH-reh keh leh ah-YOO-deh ah toh-MAHR soo(s) meh-dee-SEE-nahs?
• would you like to eat something?	• *¿le gustaría comer algo?*	• ¿leh goos-tah-REE-ah koh-MEHR AHL-goh?

• are you hungry?	• *¿tiene hambre?*	• ¿TYEH-neh AHM-breh?
• are you thirsty?	• *¿tiene sed?*	• ¿TYEH-neh sehd?
• do you want to eat breakfast/lunch/dinner?	• *¿quiere desayunar/comer/cenar?*	• ¿KYEH-reh dehs-ah-yoon-AHR/koh-MEHR/seh-NAHR?
PATIENT	***PACIENTE***	
What will you bring me?	*¿Qué me va a traer?*	¿Keh meh vah ah trah-EHR?
DOCTOR/NURSE	***DOCTOR/ENFERMERA***	
I am going to bring you...	*Le voy a traer...*	¿Leh voy ah trah-EHR...
• a really good meal.	• *una comida muy buena.*	• OO-nah koh-MEE-dah moo-ee BWEH-nah.
• whatever you like.	• *lo que usted guste.*	• loh keh oos-TEHD GOOS-teh.
• breakfast/lunch/dinner.	• *desayuno/comida/cena.*	• dehs-ah-YOO-noh/koh-MEE-dah/SEH-nah.
Mr./Mrs. ____,...	*Señor/Señora ____,...*	Seh-NYOHR/Seh-NYOH-rah ____,...
• do you have your dentures on?	• *¿tiene puesta su dentadura?*	• ¿TYEH-neh PWEHS-tah soo dehn-tah-DOO-rah?
• do you need help to put on your dentures?	• *¿necesita ayuda para ponerse la dentadura?*	• ¿neh-seh-SEE-tah ah-YOO-dah PAH-rah poh-NEHR-seh dehn-tah-DOO-rah?
• did you finish eating?	• *¿acabó de comer?*	• ¿ah-kah-BOH deh koh-MEHR?
• did you like the meal?	• *¿le gustó la comida?*	• ¿leh goos-TOH lah koh-MEE-dah?
• can I take this away?	• *¿puedo llevarme esto?*	• ¿PWEH-doh yeh-VAHR-meh EHS-toh?
Mr./Mrs. ____,...	*Señor/Señora ____,...*	Seh-NYOHR/Seh-NYOH-rah ____,...

• please call me when you need to use your wheelchair.	• *por favor, llámeme cuando necesite usar su silla de ruedas.*	• pohr fah-VOHR, YAH-meh-meh KWAHN-doh neh-seh-SEE-teh oo-SAHR soo SEE-ah deh RWEH-dahs.
• do you need help getting in your wheelchair?	• *¿necesita ayuda para sentarse en su silla de ruedas?*	• ¿neh-seh-SEE-tah ah-YOO-dah PAH-rah sehn-TAHR-seh ehn soo SEE-yah deh RWEH-dahs?
Mr./Mrs. _____,…	*Señor/Señora _____,…*	Seh-NYOHR/Seh-NYOH-rah _____,…
• please call me when you need to go to the bathroom.	• *por favor, llámeme cuando necesite ir al baño.*	• pohr fah-VOHR, YAH-meh-meh KWAHN-doh neh-seh-SEE-teh eer ahl bah NYOH.
• do you need to go to the bathroom now?	• *¿necesita ir al baño ahora?*	• ¿neh-seh-SEE-tah eer ahl bah-NYOH ah-OH-rah?
• leave the door unlocked when you are in there.	• *no ponga el cerrojo cuando esté en el baño.*	• noh POHN-gah ehl seh-RROH-hoh KWAHN-doh ehs-TEH ehn ehl bah-NYOH.
• are you finished?	• *¿ya terminó?*	• ¿yah tehr-mee-NOH?
• do you need the commode?	• *¿necesita la la bacinilla?*	• ¿neh-seh SEE-tah lah bah-see-NEE-yah?
• do you need the urinal?	• *¿necesita el orinal?*	• ¿neh-seh-SEE-tah ehl oo-rhee-NAHL?
• do you need help cleansing yourself?	• *¿necesita ayuda para limpiarse?*	• ¿neh-seh-SEE-tah ah-YOO-dah PAH-rah leem-PYAHR-seh?
Mr./Mrs. _____, please call me when you are ready for a walk.	*Señor/Señora _____, por favor, llámeme cuando esté lista(o) para una caminata.*	Seh-NYOHR/Seh-NYOH-rah _____, pohr fah-VOHR, YAH-meh-meh KWAHN-doh ehs-TEH LEES-tah(toh) PAH-rah OO-nah kah-mee-NAH-tah.

Are you ready for a walk now?	*¿Está lista(o) para una caminata en este momento?*	¿Ehs-TAH LEES-tah(oh) PAH-rah OO-nah kah-mee-NAH-tah ehn EHS-teh moh-MEHN-toh?
Where would you like to go?	*¿A dónde le gustaría ir?*	¿Ah DOHN-deh leh goos-tah-REE-ah eer?
PATIENT	**PACIENTE**	
I would like to go…	*Me gustaría ir…*	Meh goos-tah-REE-ah eer…
• to the same place as always.	• *al mismo lugar de siempre.*	• ahl MEES-moh loo-GAHR deh SYEHM-preh.
• somewhere we have never been before.	• *a un lugar donde nunca hemos ido.*	• ah oon loo-GAHR DOHN-deh NOON-kah EH-mohs EE-doh.
• somehwere near.	• *a un lugar cerca.*	• ah oon loo-GAHR SEHR-kah.
• wherever you want.	• *a donde usted quiera.*	• ah DOHN-deh oos-TEHD KYEH-rah.
• around the block.	• *alrededor de la manzana.*	• ahl-reh-deh-DOHR deh lah mahn-SAH-nah.
• to the pool.	• *a la alberca.*	• ah la ahl-BEHR-kah.
DOCTOR/NURSE	**DOCTOR/ENFERMERA**	
Mr./Mrs. ____, would you like…	*Señor/Señora ____, ¿le gustaría…*	Seh-NYOHR/Seh-NYOH-rah ____, ¿leh goo-tah-REE-ah…
• to play a game of…	• *jugar en juego de…*	• hoo-GAHR oon HWEH-goh deh…
• canasta?	• *canasta?*	• kah-NAHS-tah?
• bridge?	• *bridge?*	• BREED-ch?
• poker?	• *poker?*	• POH-kehr?
• bingo?	• *lotería?*	• loh-teh-REE-ah?
• solitaire?	• *solitario?*	• soh-lee-TAH-ryoh?
• to watch television?	• *ver la televisión?*	• vehr lah teh-leh-vee-SYOHN?

• to talk for a while?	• *platicar un rato?*	• plah-TEE-kahr oon RAH-toh?
• to be by yourself?	• *estar sola(o)?*	• ehs-TAHR SOH-lah(loh)?
• see your priest/rabbi/minister?	• *ver a su sacerdote/rabino/ministro?*	• vehr ah soo sah-sehr-DOH-teh/rah-BEE-noh/mee-NEES-troh?
Mr./Mrs. _____,…	*Señor/Señora _____,…*	Seh-NYOHR/Seh-NYOH-rah _____,…
• when was the last time that your wife/husband/son/daughter/friend visited you?	• *¿cuándo fue la última vez que lo (la) visitó su esposa/esposo/hijo/hija/amigo(a)?*	• ¿KWAHN-doh fweh lah OOL-tee-mah vehs keh lah (loh) vee-see-TOH soo ehs-POH-sah/ehs-POH-soh/EE-hoh/EE-hah/ah-MEE goh(gah)?
• would you like me to call your husband/wife/son/daughter/friend?	• *¿le gustaría que llamará a su esposo/esposa/hijo/hija/amigo(a)?*	• ¿leh goos-tah-REE-ah keh yah-mah-RAH ah soo ehs-POH-soh/ehs-POH-sah/EE-hoh/EE-hah/ah MEE-goh(gah)?
• what would you like me to tell him/her?	• *¿qué quiere que le dijera?*	• ¿Keh KYEH-reh keh leh DEE-HEH-rah?
PATIENT	***PACIENTE***	
Tell her/him…	*Dígale que…*	DEE-gah-leh keh…
• to call me.	• *me llame.*	• meh YAH-meh.
• to come visit me.	• *me venga a visitar.*	• meh VEHN-gah ah vee-see-TAHR.
• to bring me a good book.	• *me traiga un buen libro.*	• meh TRAH-ee-gah oon byehn LEE-broh.
• to write me a letter.	• *me escriba una carta.*	• meh ehs-KREE-bah OO-nah KAHR-tah.

DOCTOR/NURSE	*DOCTOR/ENFERMERA*	
Mr./Mrs. ____,...	*Señor/Señora ____,...*	Seh-NYOHR/Seh-NYOH-rah ____,...
• are you worried about money?	• *¿está usted preocupado(a) por cosas de dinero?*	• ¿ehs-TAH oos-TEHD preh-oh-koo-PAH-dah(doh) pohr KOH-sahs deh dee-NEH-roh?
• would you like to speak to a counselor?	• *¿le gustaría hablar con un(a) consejero(a)?*	• ¿leh goos-tah-RHEE-ah ah-BLAHR kohn OO-nah kohn-seh-HEH-roh(rah)?
• tell me when you are ready to speak to a counselor.	• *dígame cuando esté lista para hablar con un(a) consejero(a).*	• DEE-gah-meh KWAHN-doh ehs-TEH LEES-tah PAH-rah ah-BLAHR kohn OO-nah kohn-seh-HEH-roh(rah).
Mr./Mrs. ____,...	*Señor/Señora ____,...*	Seh-NYOHR/Seh-NYOH-rah ____,...
• call me when you are ready to go to bed.	• *llámeme cuando esté listo(a) para acostarse.*	• YAH-meh-meh KWAHN-doh ehs-TEH LEES-tah(toh) PAH-rah ah-kohs-TAHR-seh.
• are you ready to go to bed?	• *¿está listo(a) para acostarse?*	• ¿ehs-TAH LEES-tah(toh) PAH-rah ah-kohs-TAHR-seh?
• do you want me to help you get in bed?	• *¿necesita que lo(la) ayude a acostarse?*	• ¿neh-seh-SEE-tah keh lah(loh) ah-YOO-deh ah ah-kohs-TAHR-seh?
Good night.	*Buenas noches.*	BYEH-nahs NOH-chehs.
Sleep well.	*Que duerma bien.*	Keh-DWEHR-mah byehn.
I'll see you tomorrow.	*Hasta mañana.*	AHS-tah mah-NYAH-nah.

SECTION I

REFERENCE

1. Glossary of Grammatical Terms

active voice—*voz activa:* a verb form in which the actor (agent) is expressed as the grammatical subject. The girl ate the orange—*La chica comió la naranja.*

adjective—*adjetivo:* a word that describes a noun; e.g., pretty—*bonita.*

adverb—*adverbio:* a word that describes a verb, an adjective, or another adverb; e.g., quickly—*rápidamente.*

agreement—*concordancia:* the modification of words so that they match the words they describe or relate to.

auxiliary verb—*verbo auxiliar:* a helping verb used with another verb to express some facet of tense or mood.

compound—*compuesto:* verb forms composed of two parts, an auxiliary and a main verb.

conditional—*potencial simple:* the mood used for hypothetical (depending on a possible condition or circumstance) statements and questions. I would eat if…—*Comería si…*

conjugation—*conjugación:* the formation of verbs with their endings; i.e., the finite forms (vs. nonfinite forms such as the infinitive or participle).

conjunction—*conjunción:* a word that connects other words and phrases; e.g., and—*y*.

definite article—*artículo definido:* a word linked to a noun indicating it is specific; e.g., the—*el* (masculine singular).

demonstrative—*demonstrativo:* a word that indicates or highlights something referred to; e.g., in this book—*este libro,* this—*este* is a demonstrative adjective.

diphthong—*diptongo:* a sequence of two vowels that glide together and act as a single sound in English. In Spanish, they are two separate sounds; e.g., co-*mió; cuán-do.*

direct object—*objeto directo:* the person or thing that receives the action of a verb (accusative).

ending—*desinencia:* the suffix added to the stem that indicates subject, tense, etc.

gender—*género:* grammatical categories for nouns, loosely related to physical gender and/or word ending; Spanish has two; masculine and feminine; e.g., *el chico* (m.), *la chica* (f.).

imperative—*imperativo:* the command form.

imperfect—*imperfecto:* the past tense used for ongoing or habitual actions or states; useful for description.

impersonal verb—*verbo impersonal:* a verb in which the person, place, or thing affected is expressed as the indirect object rather than the subject. To like (to be pleasing to)—*gustar:* I like chicken—*Me gusta el pollo* (The chicken is pleasing to me).

indefinite article—*artículo indefinido:* a word linked to a noun indicating that it is nonspecific; e.g., a/an—*un* (masculine singular).

indicative—*indicativo:* the mood used for factual or objective statements and questions.

indirect object—*objeto indirecto:* the person or thing that receives the action of the direct object and/or is the object of a preposition (dative).

infinitive—*infinitivo:* the basic form of a verb found in the dictionary which does not specify the subject (person or number), tense, or mood; e.g., to speak—*hablar.*

intransitive verb—*verbo intransitivo:* a verb that does not take a direct object; e.g., to live—*vivir.*

mood—*modo:* the attitude toward what is expressed by the verb.

noun—*sustantivo:* a word referring to a person, place, or thing; e.g., house—*casa.*

number—*número:* the distinction between singular and plural.

participle—*participio:* an unconjugated, unchanging verb form often used with auxiliary verbs to form compound verb forms; e.g., present and past participles: eating/eaten—*comiendo/comido.*

passive voice—*voz pasiva:* a verb form in which the recipient of the action is expressed as the grammatical subject. The orange was eaten by the girl—*La naranja fue comida por la chica.*

perfect—*perfecto:* verb forms used for actions or states that are already completed. I have eaten—*He comido* (present perfect).

person—*persona:* the grammatical category that distinguishes between the speaker (first person), the person spoken to (second person), and the people and things spoken about (third person); often applies to pronouns and verbs.

pluperfect—*pluscuamperfecto:* the past perfect in Spanish that uses the imperfect of *haber*—to have (in either the indicative or the subjunctive) plus the past participle; e.g., *Había comido*—I had eaten.

possessive—*posesivo:* indicates ownership; e.g., my—*mi* is a possessive pronoun (genitive).

predicate—*predicado:* the part of the sentence containing the verb and expressing the action or state of the subject.

preposition—*preposición:* a word (often as part of a phrase) that expresses spatial, temporal, or other relationships; e.g., on—*en.*

preterite—*pretérito:* the past tense used for completed actions or states; useful for narration of events.

progressive—*progresivo:* verb form used for actions that are ongoing; continuous. I am eating—*Estoy comiendo* (present progressive).

pronoun—*pronombre:* a word taking the place of a noun; e.g., personal or demonstrative.

reflexive verb—*verbo reflexivo:* a verb whose action reflects back to the subject; e.g., to wash oneself—*lavarse.*

simple—*simple:* one-word verb forms conjugated by adding endings to a stem.

stem or *root*—*raíz:* the part of the infinitive that does not change during the conjugation of regular verbs, formed by dropping *-ar, er,* or *-ir;* e.g., *habl-* in *hablar.*

subject—*sujeto:* the person, place, or thing performing the action of the verb or being in the state described by it (nominative).

subjunctive—*subjuntivo:* the mood used for nonfactual or subjective statements or questions.

tense—*tiempo:* the time of an action or state, i.e., past, present, future.

transitive verb—*verbo transitivo:* a verb that takes a direct object; e.g., to send—*mandar.*

verb—*verbo:* a word expressing an action or state; e.g., (to) walk—*caminar.*

2. Grammar Summary

• THE DEFINITE ARTICLE—*EL ARTÍCULO DEFINIDO* •

	SINGULAR	PLURAL
MASCULINE	*el*	*los*
FEMININE	*la*	*las*

• THE INDEFINITE ARTICLE—*EL ARTÍCULO INDEFINIDO* •

	SINGULAR	PLURAL
MASCULINE	*un*	*unos*
FEMININE	*una*	*unas*

• GENDER—*GÉNERO* •

All Spanish nouns are either masculine or feminine. Some types of words can be grouped by gender, but there are exceptions, and it is best to learn the word with its appropriate article.

Masculine words: nouns that end in *-o, -r, -n,* and *-l;* names of items in nature (e.g., mountains); days of the week and months; words of Greek origin ending in *-ma, -pa,* or *-ta;* verbs, adjectives, etc. used as nouns.

Feminine words: nouns that end in *-a, -dad, -tad, -tud, -ción, -sión, -ez, -umbre,* and *-ie;* names of cities and towns.

• PLURAL FORMATION—*FORMACIÓN DEL PLURAL* •

To form the plural for words ending in a vowel, add *-s.*
For words ending in a consonant or a stressed *í* or *ú,* add *-es.*
Nouns ending in *z* change to *c* in the plural; e.g., *niños felices*—happy children.

• ADJECTIVES AND AGREEMENT—*ADJETIVOS Y CONCORDANCIA* •

All adjectives must agree in number and gender with the nouns they modify, or describe.

For use with plural nouns, add *-s* to the adjective, or *-es* if it ends in a consonant.

When an adjective ends in *-o* (in its masculine form), its ending changes into *-a* when it modifies a feminine noun, e.g., *la mujer rica*—the rich woman. For most adjectives ending in a consonant (or a vowel other than *-o*) in the masculine form, simply use the same form for both genders. However, for adjectives ending in *-dor, -ón,* or *-án,* and for adjectives of nationality that end in a consonant, add *-a* to make the feminine form. For example la mujer francesa—the French woman. Adjectives that end in *-e* do not change for masculine or feminine gender: For example: un hombre inteligente, una mujer inteligente.

• PRONOUNS—*PRONOMBRES* •

SUBJECT PRONOUNS

I	*yo*
you (familiar)	*tú*
he	*él*
she	*ella*
you (polite)	*usted (Ud.)**
we	*nosotros, nosotras*
you (familiar)	*vosotros, vosotras*
you (polite)	*ustedes (Uds.)*
they	*ellos, ellas*

Note: Subject pronouns are often omitted in Spanish since the verbal endings show who or what the subject is.

* *Usted* and *ustedes* are treated as if they were third person pronouns, though in meaning, they are second person (addressee) pronouns. In Latin America, *ustedes* is used as both familiar and polite and *vosotros,-as* is not used.

Other pronouns, listed according to their corresponding subject pronoun, are:

	yo	*tú*	*él/ella/ Ud.*	*nosotros, -as*	*vosotros, -as*	*ellos/ ellas/ Uds.*
DIRECT OBJECT:	*me*	*te*	*lo/la*	*nos*	*os*	*los/las*
INDIRECT OBJECT:	*me*	*te*	*le*	*nos*	*os*	*les*
REFLEXIVE:	*me*	*te*	*se*	*nos*	*os*	*se*
POSSESSIVE:	*mi*	*tu*	*su*	*nuestro/a*	*vuestro/a*	*su*

Use the subject pronouns as objects of prepositions, except instead of *yo* and *tú,* use *mí* and *ti.* In sentences with reflexive pronouns, an optional prepositional phrase (*a* + *mí/ti/sí/nosotros,-as/vosotros,-as/sí* + *mismo/a*[s]) may be used for emphasis (*mismo* = same). Note: *con* + *mí/ti/sí* becomes *conmigo/contigo/consigo.*

The possessive pronouns (adjectives) listed are used before the noun, as in *mi libro*—my book. The *nosotros/vosotros* forms agree in number and gender with the noun they pertain to, and the others only agree in number. Longer forms used after the noun for emphasis differ only in the *mi, tu,* and *su* forms: they are *mío, tuyo,* and *suyo.* They also show agreement in both gender and number, as in *Los libros míos están en la mesa*—My books are on the table. When these long forms are preceded by the appropriate definite article, they represent the noun and stand alone. For example, *Los libros míos están en la mesa, pero los tuyos están en tu cuarto*—My books are on the table, but yours are in your room.

• DEMONSTRATIVE ADJECTIVES AND PRONOUNS—*ADJETIVOS Y PRONOMBRES DEMOSTRATIVOS* •

DEMONSTRATIVE ADJECTIVES

this, these	*este, esta, estos, estas*
that, those	*ese, esa, esos, esas*
that, those (farther removed)	*aquel, aquella, aquellos, aquellas*

To form the pronouns, simply add an accent to the first *e* in the word, as in *No me gusta éste*—I don't like this one. There are also neuter pronouns used for general ideas or situations: *esto, eso, aquello.* When the demonstrative pronouns are followed by a noun, they do not have an accent. For example, yo quiero este coche.

• ADVERBS—*ADVERBIOS* •

Form adverbs simply by adding *-mente* (which corresponds to -ly in English) to the feminine form of an adjective, as in *obviamente*—obviously.

• NEGATION—*NEGACIÓN* •

Form negative sentences by adding *no* before the conjugated verb and any pronouns, as in *No lo tengo*—I don't have it.

Many other negative constructions require two negative words; e.g., *No tengo nada*—I don't have anything/I have nothing. (*Nada*—nothing; *algo*—something/anything.)

• COMPARISON—*COMPARACIÓN* •

Form comparative expressions using *más*—more and *menos*—less with adjectives and adverbs; e.g., *Juan es más grande que Pepe*—Juan is bigger than Pepe/*Juan corre más rápidamente que Pepe*—Juan runs faster than Pepe/*Juan es menos famoso*—

Juan is less famous. Use *de* instead of *que* to mean "than" before numbers.

To make equal comparisons, use the expressions *tan... como* (before adjectives and adverbs) and *tanto... como* (before nouns, with which *tanto* must agree). For example, *Juan es tan grande como Pepe*—Juan is as big as Pepe/*Juan tiene tanto dinero como Pepe*—Juan has as much money as Pepe.

Form superlatives by using an article (a definite article that shows agreement for adjectives, *lo* for adverbs) with the comparative expressions, e.g., *Juan es el más grande*—Juan is the biggest/*Ella es la menos grande del grupo*—She is the least big in the group/*Juan corre lo más rápidamente*—Juan runs the fastest.

The "absolute superlative" form is *-ísimo/a: hermosísimo*—very/most beautiful; *frecuentísimamente*—very/most frequently. Irregular comparative words:

ADJECTIVE	ADVERB	COMPARATIVE
bueno—good	*bien*—well	*mejor*—better
malo—bad	*mal*—badly	*peor*—worse
mucho—much	*mucho*—much	*más*—more
poco—little	*poco*—little	*menos*—less
grande—great, big		*más grande*—bigger BUT *mayor*—older
pequeño—small		*más pequeño*—smaller BUT *menor*—younger

• RELATIVE PRONOUNS—*PRONOMBRES RELATIVOS* •

that, who, which	*que*
who(m)	*quien, quienes*
who, which	*el/la cual, los/las cuales*
who, which, the one(s) that/who	*el/la/los/las que*
what, which (refers to an entire idea)	*lo que*
whose (relative adjective)	*cuyo, -a, -os, -as*

• CONTRACTIONS—*CONTRACCIONES* •

de + el = del
a + el = al

3. Tense Formation Guide

The endings will always be presented according to subject person and number in the following order: *yo, tú, él/ella/usted, nosotros/-as, vosotros/-as, ellos/ellas/ustedes.*

• THE SIMPLE VERB FORMS •

1. To form the **present indicative**—*presente de indicativo* of regular verbs, add the following endings to the stem of the infinitive*:

FOR -*AR* VERBS: *-o, -as, -a, -amos, -áis, -an*
FOR -*ER* VERBS: *-o, -es, -e, -emos, -éis, -en*
FOR -*IR* VERBS: *-o, -es, -e, -imos, -ís, -en*

2. To form the **preterite**—*pretérito* of regular verbs, add the following endings to the stem of the infinitive:

FOR -*AR* VERBS: *-é, -aste, -ó, -amos, -ásteis, -aron*
FOR -*ER* AND -*IR* VERBS: *-í, -iste, -ió, -imos, -ísteis, -ieron*

Several verbs that are irregular in the preterite follow a pattern. Conjugate them in the following manner:

tener—to have: *tuve, tuviste, tuvo, tuvimos, tuvisteis, tuvieron*
estar—to be: *estuve…*
andar—to walk: *anduve…*
haber—to have: *hube…*
poder—to be able: *pude…*
poner—to put: *puse…*
saber—to know: *supe…*
caber—to fit: *cupe…*
querer—to want: *quise…*

* The stem is formed by dropping the infinitive endings *-ar*, *-er*, and *-ir*.

venir—to come: *vine…*
hacer—to do, make: *hice, hiciste, hizo…*
decir—to say, tell: *dije…dijeron*
traer—to bring: *traje…trajeron*
producir—to produce: *produje…produjeron*

3. To form the **imperfect**—*imperfecto* of regular verbs, add the following endings to the stem of the infinitive:

FOR -*AR* VERBS: *-aba, -abas, -aba, -ábamos, -abais, -aban*
FOR -*ER* AND -*IR* VERBS: *-ía, -ías, -ía, -íamos, -íais, -ían*

There are only three irregular verbs in the imperfect:

ser—to be: *era, eras, era, éramos, erais, eran*
ir—to go: *iba, ibas, iba, íbamos, ibais, iban*
ver—to see: *veía, veías, veía, veíamos, veíais, veían*

4. To form the **future**—*futuro* of regular verbs, add the following endings to the entire infinitive:

FOR -*AR, ER,* AND -*IR* VERBS: *-é, -ás, -á, -emos, -éis, -án*

5. To form the **conditional**—*potencial simple* of regular verbs, add the following endings to the entire infinitive:

FOR -*AR, ER,* AND -*IR* VERBS: *-ía, -ías, -ía, -íamos, -íais, -ían*

The same set of verbs are irregular in the future and conditional. Add the regular endings to the following stems:

tener—to have: *tendr-*
venir—to come: *vendr-*
poner—to put, place: *pondr-*
salir—to leave: *saldr-*
valer—to be worth: *valdr-*

poder—to be able: *podr-*
saber—to know: *sabr-*
haber—to have: *habr-*
caber—to fit: *cabr-*
hacer—to do, make: *har-*
decir—to say, tell: *dir-*
querer—to want: *querr-*

6. To form the **present subjunctive**—*presente de subjuntivo* of regular verbs and many irregular ones, add the following endings to the *yo* form of the present indicative after dropping the *-o:*

FOR -*AR* VERBS: *-e, -es, -e, -emos, -éis, -en*
FOR -*ER* and -*IR* VERBS: *-a, -as, -a, -amos, -áis, -an*

7. To form the **past** (imperfect) **subjunctive**—*imperfecto de subjuntivo* of both regular and irregular verbs, add the following endings to the *ellos/ellas/ustedes* (third person plural) form of the preterite after dropping the *-ron:*

FOR -*AR*, -*ER*, AND -*IR* VERBS: *-ra, -ras, -ra, -ramos, -rais, -ran*
OR: *-se, -ses, -se, -semos, -seis, -sen*

The *nosotros/-as* (first person plural) form has an accent on the vowel directly before the ending, e.g., *habláramos*.

• THE COMPOUND VERB FORMS •

1. To form **progressive**—*progresivo* verb forms, conjugate the verb *estar*—to be in the appropriate tense (either the present or the imperfect; see verb charts) and add the present participle. Form the present participle of most verbs by adding the following endings to the stem of the infinitive:

FOR -*AR* VERBS: -*ando*
FOR -*ER* and -*IR* VERBS: -*iendo*

2. To form **perfect**—*perfecto* verb forms, conjugate the auxiliary verb *haber*—to have in the appropriate tense (the present indicative, the imperfect, the preterite, the future, the conditional, the present subjunctive, and the past subjunctive; see verb charts) and add the past participle. Form the past participle of most verbs by adding the following endings to the stem of the infinitive:

FOR -*AR* VERBS: -*ado*
FOR -*ER* AND -*IR* VERBS: -*ido*

The irregular past participles are:

abrir—to open: *abierto*
cubrir—to cover: *cubierto*
morir—to die: *muerto*
volver—to return: *vuelto*
poner—to put, place: *puesto*
ver—to see: *visto*
escribir—to write: *escrito*
romper—to break: *roto*
decir—to say, tell: *dicho*
hacer—to do, make: *hecho*

• THE IMPERATIVE/COMMANDS •

A sample conjugation using *hablar*—to speak:

fam. sing. affirm. *habla*
fam. pl. affirm. *hablad*
fam. sing. neg. *no hables*
fam. pl. neg. *no habléis*

pol. sing. affirm. *hable*
pol. pl. affirm. *hablen*
pol. sing. neg. *no hable*
pol. pl. neg. *no hablen*

1. To form **familiar** (informal) **singular** (*tú*) **affirmative commands** for most verbs, use the *él/ella/usted* (third person singular) form of the present indicative.

2. To form **familiar plural** (*vosotros/-as*) **affirmative commands** for all verbs, change the *-r* of the infinitive to *-d.*

3. To form **polite** (formal) **singular** (*usted*) and **plural** (*ustedes*) **affirmative commands** and **all negative commands** (singular and plural, familiar and polite), use the appropriate form of the present subjunctive. Form the negative in the usual way.

4. To form **first person plural** (we) **commands** (let's...), use the subjunctive in the affirmative and the negative. In the affirmative, another option is to use *Vamos + a* + infinitive.

5. Attach reflexive, indirect, and direct object pronouns directly to the affirmative commands. For example *¡Háblame!*—Speak to me! For *nosotros/-as* and *vosotros/-as* affirmative commands in reflexive verbs, the last letter is dropped when the reflexive pronouns is attached. For example, *¡Lavémonos!*—Let's wash ourselves! and *¡Lavaos!*—Wash yourselves!

In negative commands, place them before the verb in the usual manner. For example *¡No me hables!*—Don't speak to me!

6. There are several irregular familiar singular affirmative commands:

tener—to have: *ten*
hacer—to do, make: *haz*
venir—to come: *ven*
decir—to say, tell: *di*
poner—to put, place: *pon*
ser—to be: *sé*

salir—to leave: *sal*
ir—to go: *ve*

• IMPERSONAL VERBS •

To conjugate impersonal verbs, i.e., verbs like *gustar*—to be pleasing to, to like, and *doler*—to hurt, use the third person form of the appropriate tense, mood, etc. of the verb and the indirect object pronoun that corresponds to the person, place, or thing affected. Whether to use the singular or plural of the third person form of the verb depends on the number of items doing the affecting. For example: *Me gusta el Señor González*——I like Mr. González (Mr. González is pleasing to me)/*Me gustan los González*—I like the Gonzálezes.

• REFLEXIVE VERBS •

To form reflexive constructions, conjugate the infinitive (without the *-se*) and use the reflexive pronoun that corresponds to the subject. For example:

lavarse—to wash oneself
me lavo—I wash myself

• THE PASSIVE VOICE •

There are four ways to form the passive voice—*la voz pasiva* in Spanish. Two use a form of the reflexive construction just discussed.

1. To form the reflexive passive, or passive *se*, use *se* + the third person singular or plural of the verb, depending on the number of the items being discussed. For example, *Se habla español aquí*—Spanish is spoken here, but *Se comieron las naranjas*—The oranges were eaten. This form only occurs with transitive verbs.

2. Another version, impersonal, *se,* involves the use of *se* + the third person singular only of the verb. Unlike passive *se,* this construction can be used with both intransitive and transitive verbs, but is used mainly with intransitive ones. Its usage also indicates that people (but not specific individuals) are involved in the action of the verb. For example, *Se duerme muy bien en el campo*—One sleeps very well in the country.

3. When the agent (the actor) is not expressed, another possibility is to use the "impersonal they" construction. To form it, simply use the third person plural of a verb, e.g., *Dicen que es un hombre peligroso*—They say (it is said) that he is a dangerous man.

4. The true passive is formed using the appropriate conjugation of *ser* + the past participle. (also called the passive participle). It is used when the agent is expressed or strongly implied. The past participle agrees with the grammatical subject. In Spanish, only direct objects (not indirect objects) may serve as the grammatical subject in the passive voice.

subject + *ser* + past participle + *por* + agent

For example, *La cuenta fue pagada por la Señora Sánchez*—The bill was paid by Mrs. Sánchez.

• STEM-CHANGING VERBS •

There are three kinds of stem-changing verbs.

1. For verbs such as *querer*—to want and *encontrar*—to find, change *e* to *ie* and *o* to *ue* in the stems of all forms except *nosotros, -as* and *vosotros, -as* in the present indicative and present subjunctive. There are no *-ir* verbs in this category.

2. For verbs such as *sentir(se)*—to feel and *dormir*—to sleep, change e to ie and o to ue in the exact same places as in the first

kind, and change *e* to *i* and *o* to *u* in the *nosotros, -as* and *vosotros, -as* forms of the present subjunctive, in the *él/ella/usted* and *ellos/ellas/ustedes* forms of the preterite, in all forms of the past subjunctive, and in the present participle. Only *-ir* verbs are in this category.

3. For verbs such as *pedir*—to request, change *e* to *i* in all places where any change occurs in the second kind. Only *-ir* verbs are in this category.

• SPELLING CHANGES •

To keep pronunciation consistent and to preserve customary spelling in Spanish, some verbs in certain tenses change their spelling. The rules are:

In verbs ending in *-car, c* changes to *qu* before *e* to keep the sound hard; e.g., *busqué*—I looked (from *buscar*).

In verbs ending in *-quir, qu* changes to *c* before *o* and *a;* e.g., *delinco*—I commit a transgression (from *delinquir*).

In verbs ending in *-zar, z* changes to *c* before *e; comencé*—I began (from *comenzar*).

In verbs ending in *-gar, g* changes to *gu* before *e* to keep the *g* hard; e.g., *pagué*—I paid (from *pagar*).

In verbs ending in a consonant + *-cer/-cir, c* changes to *z* before *o* and *a* to keep the sound soft; e.g., *venzo*—I conquer (from *vencer*).

In verbs ending in *-ger/-gir, g* changes to *j* before *o* and *a* to keep the sound soft; e.g., *cojo*—I catch (from *coger*).

In verbs ending in *-guir, gu* changes to *g* before *o* and *a* to preserve the sound; e.g., *distingo*—I distinguish (from *distinguir*).

In verbs ending in *-guar, gu* changes to *gü* before *e* to keep the "gw" sound; e.g., *averigüé*—I ascertained (from *averiguar*).

In verbs ending in *-eer,* the unstressed *i* between vowels becomes a *y;* e.g., *leyó*—he read (from *leer*).

In stem-changing verbs ending in *-eír,* two consecutive *i*'s become one; e.g., *rio*—he laughed (from *reír*).

In stem-changing verbs beginning with a vowel, an *h* must precede the word-initial diphthong or the initial *i* of the diphthong becomes a *y;* e.g., *huelo*—I smell [sense] from *oler*); *yerro*—I err (from *errar*).

In verbs with stems ending in *ll* or *ñ*, the *i* of the diphthongs *ie* and *ió* disappears; e.g., *bullió*—it boiled (from *bullir*).

4. English-Spanish Glossary

A

Abdomen *Vientre*
Abortion *Aborto*
Abuse, to *Abusar*
Accept, to *Aceptar*
Accident *Accidente*
Accountant *Contador*
Active *Activo*
Addiction *Adicción*
Address *Dirección*
Administer *Administrar*
Administrator *Administrador*
Afternoon *Tarde*
Against *Contra*
Age *Edad*
Agnostic *Agnóstico*
Agricultural *Agrícola*
AIDS *SIDA*
Alcoholism *Alcoholismo*
Allergic *Alérgico(a)*
Allergy *Alergia*
Alleviate *Aliviar*
Alone *Solo(a)*
Amphetamines *Anfetaminas*
Anaesthetist *Anestesista*
Anaesthetize, to *Anestesiar*
Anemia *Anemia*
Angina *Angina*
Angry *Enojado(a)*
Angry, to get *Enojar*
Ankle *Tobillo*
Answer *Respuesta*
Antidepressant *Antidepresivo*
Anus *Ano*
Anxiety *Ansiedad*
Anxious *Ansioso(a)*
Apartment *Apartamento*
Appetite *Apetito*
Apply *Aplicar*
Appointment *Cita*
Architect *Arquitecto*
Arm *Brazo*
Army *Ejército*
Around *Alrededor*
Arrive, to *Llegar*
Arterial pressure *Presión arterial*
Arthritis *Artritis*
Ask for, to *Pedir*
Asthma *Asma*
Atheist *Ateo(a)*
Authorize *Autorizar*
Avoid, to *Evitar*

B

Baby *Bebé*
Back *Espalda*
Bad *Mal*
Bag *Bolsa*
Bag of water *Fuente de agua*
Baseball *Beisból*
Basketball *Baloncesto*
Bath, to take a *Bañarse*
Bathroom *Baño*
Be present, to *Estar presente*
Beans *Frijoles*
Beat *Latído*
Beat, to *Palpitar*
Beating *Golpiza*
Bed *Cama*
Bed, go to *Acostar*
Beef *Carne de res*
Beer *Cerveza*
Begin, to *Empezar*
Beginning *Principio*
Behave, to *Portarse*
Behind *Detrás*
Believe, to *Creer*
Bells, little *Campanitas*
Bend over *Agachar*
Benefit *Beneficio*
Better *Mejor*
Between *Entre*
Billiards *Billar*
Bingo *Lotería*
Birth *Nacimiento*
Birth pains *Dolores*
Bit, a little *Poquito*
Bite, to *Morder*
Black *Negro*
Blanket *Colcha*
Bleed, to *Sangrar*
Block *Manzana*
Blood *Sangre*
Blouse *Blusa*
Blow, to *Sonar*
Blurry *Borroso*
Body *Cuerpo*
Body hair *Vello*
Bone *Hueso*
Book *Libro*
Born, to be *Nacer*
Borough *Barrio*
Bother, to *Molestar*
Brain *Cerebro*
Break, to *Romper*
Breakfast, to have *Desayunar*

Breast *Pecho*
Breast-feed *Dar de mamar*
Breathe, to *Respirar*
Bridge *Puente*
Bring, to *Traer*
Bronchitis *Bronquitis*
Bruise *Descalabro*
Bullet *Bala*
Burn *Quemadura*
Burn, to *Quemar, Arder*
Burning *Ardiente*
Burp, to *Eructar*
Bus *Autobus*
Business *Negocios*
Butt *Nalgas*
Buy, to *Comprar*
Buzz, to *Zumbar*
By itself *Sola/Solo*

C

Call, to *Llamar*
Calm, to *Calmar*
Can, to *Poder*
Cancer *Cáncer*
Cane *Bastón*
Capacity *Capacidad*
Capsule *Cápsula*
Car *Carro*
Care *Cuidados*
Carried *Picado*
Catholic *Católico*
Cause, to *Causar*
Center *Centro*
Cereal *Cereal*
Chair *Silla*
Change, to *Cambiar*
Chart *Expediente*
Chemical *Substancia química*
Chemotherapy *Quimioterapia*
Chest *Pecho*
Chew *Masticar*
Chicken pox *Varicela*
Chin *Barba*
Cholic *Cólico*
Choose, to *Escojer*
Church *Iglesia*
Cigarettes *Cigarrillos*
Cigars *Puros/Cigarros*
Cinema *Cine*
City *Ciudad*
Clear *Cristalino*
Clinic *Clínica*
Clinical history *Historia clínica*
Coast Guard *Guardacostas*
Cocaine *Cocaína*
Coffee grounds *Asientos de café*
Coitus *Acto sexual*
Color *Color*
Column *Columna*
Combat *Combate*
Come to *Venir*
Commode *Comodo*
Common Cold *Resfriado*
Companion *Compañero(a)*
Complain *Quejar*
Complete, to *Completar*
Concentrate, to *Concentrar*
Condom *Condón*
Condominium *Condominio*
Confine, to *Encerrar*
Consciousness *Conocimiento*
Consider, to *Considerar*
Constantly *Constantemente*
Constipated *Estreñido(a)*
Constipation *Constipación*
Continue, to *Seguir*
Contractions *Contracciones*
Control, to *Controlar*
Controlled *Controlado(a)*
Cotton swab *Hisopo*
Counseling *Consejería*
Country *País*
Cover, to *Cubrir*
Cramps *Calambres*
Crazy *Loco(a)*
Cry *Llánto*
Cry, to *Llorar*
C-section *Cesárea*
Cuff *Manguito*
Cup *Vaso*
Curable *Curable*

D

Damage, to *Dañar*
Dangerous *Peligroso(a)*
Dark *Obscura*
Date *Fecha*
Daughter(s) *Hija(s)*
Dead *Muerto(a)*
Deaf *Sordo*
Decisions *Decisiones*
Deep *Hondo*
Defecate, to *Evacuar*
Delivery room *Sala de expulsión*
Delivery table *Mesa de partos*
Dentist *Dentista*
Dentures *Dentaduras postizas*
Depressed *Deprimido(a)*
Desire *Ganas*
Development *Desarrollo*
Devil *Diablo*
Diabetes *Diabetes*
Diagnosis *Diagnóstico*
Diarrhea *Diarrea*
Difficult, to be *Costar trabajo*
Difficulty *Dificultad*

Digest, to *Digerir*
Dine, to *Cenar*
Diphtheria *Difteria*
Disagreements *Desacuerdos*
Discharge *Descarga/Desecho*
Discussion *Discusión*
Divorced *Divorciado(a)*
Dizziness *Mareo*
Doctorate *Doctorado*
Double *Doble*
Dress *Vestido*
Dress oneself, to *Vestirse*
Drink, to *Beber*
Drive, to *Manejar*
Drown, to *Ahogar*
Drug oneself, to *Drogar*
Drugstore *Farmacia*
Drunk *Borracho*
Drunk, to get *Emborrachar*
Dry *Seco*

E

Each *Cada*
Ear *Oído*
Eat, to *Comer*
Editor *Editor(a)*
Elbow *Codo*
Elderly (endearing) *Viejitos*
Electric cart *Carrito eléctrico*
Electrocardiogram *Eléctrocardiograma*
Electrodes *Electródos*
Electroshock *Electrochoque*
Emergency services *Servicios de emergencia*
Emphysema *Enfisema*
Employment *Empleo*
Enchiladas *Enchiladas*
End *Final*
Enema *Lavativa*
Enough for, to be *Alcanzar*
Entire *Todo(a)*
Epidural anesthesia *Anestesia epidural*
Epilepsy *Epilepsia*
Equal *Igual*
Equilibrium *Equilibrio*
Evangelical *Evangélico*
Exam table *Mesa de exploración*
Examine *Examinar*
Excrement *Excremento*
Exercise *Ejercicio*
Expect *Esperar*
Explain, to *Explicar*
Exposure *Exposición*

F

Factory *Fábrica*
Factory worker *Obrero(a)*
Faint, to *Desmayar*
Faith *Fé*
Fall, to *Caer*
Family *Familia*
Far *Lejos*
Far-sighted *Hipermetrope*
Fast *Rápido/Aprisa*
Fat *Gordura*
Fatten, to *Engordar*
Fear *Miedo*
Feces *Caca/Heces*
Feel guilty, to *Sentirse culpable*
Feel okay, to *Sentirse bien*
Fever *Fiebre*
Fiancée *Novia*
Field *Campo*
Fight, to *Pelear*
Fighter *Peleador(a)*
Find, to *Encontrar*
Finish, to *Acabar, Terminar*
Floor *Suelo*
Folk healer *Curandero(a)*
Force *Fuerza*
Forceps *Fórceps*
Forms *Formas*
Formula *Fórmula*
Fortunately *Afortunadamente*
Foul/Ugly *Feo*
Fracture *Fractura*
Free *Libre*
Friend(s) *Amigo(a)(os)(as)*
Fruit *Fruta*
Future *Futuro*
Future care *Cuidados futuros*

G

Gall bladder *Vesícula*
Game *Juego*
Gang *Pandilla*
Gastric *Gástrico(a)*
Gastric area *Boca del estómago*
Gastritis *Gastritis*
General anesthesia *Anestesia general*
German measles *Rubeola*
Get, to *Conseguir*
Get along well *Llevarse bien*
Get out, to *Sacar*
Get up, to *Levantarse*
Gland *Glándula*
Go around, to *Dar vueltas*
Go for a drive, to *Salir a pasear*
Go out, to *Salir*
Go up, to *Subir*
God *Dios*
Good *Bueno(a)*
Gown *Bata*
Grandchildren *Nietos(as)*
Grateful, to be *Agradecer*
Green *Verde*
Greenish *Verdoso*
Grow, to *Crecer*

Guilty *Culpable*
Gun shot *Balazo*

H

Hair *Pelo*
Hallway *Pasillo*
Halo *Aureola*
Handicapped *Inválido(a)*
Hang, to *Colgar*
Happen, to *Suceder*
Hard *Duro(a)*
Have a baby, to *Tener un niño*
Head *Cabeza*
Heal, to *Curar*
Healthy *Sano(s)*
Hear *Oir*
Heart *Corazón*
Heartburn *Agruras*
Helicopter *Helicóptero*
Help, to *Ayudar*
Hemorrhoids *Hemorroides*
Hepatitis *Hepatitis*
Hernia *Hernia*
Heroin *Heroína*
High blood pressure *Presión alta de la sangre*
High school graduate *Bachiller*
Highway *Carretera*
Hip *Cadera*
Hit, to *Golpear/Pegar*
Hoarse *Ronco(a)*
Hold up *Asalto*
Home *Casa*
Home care *Cuidados a domicilio*
Hope *Esperanza*
Hormones *Hormonas*
Hospice care *Cuidados de hospicio*
Hospitalize, to *Hospitalizar*
Hot *Caliente*
Hot flashes *Bochornos*
Hung over *Crudo(a)*
Hungry, to be *Tener hambre*
Hurt, to *Herir*

I

Ill-defined complaints *Achaques*
Illicit *Ilícita*
Illuminate, to *Iluminar*
Immediately *Inmediatamente*
Immobilize *Inmobilizar*
Impotent *Impotente*
Improvement *Mejoría*
Income *Ingreso*
Incurable *Incurable*
Indicated *Indicado*
Indications *Indicaciones*
Induct *Inducir*
Infarct *Infarto*
Infection *Infección*
Inflamed *Inflamada*
Information *Información*
Inguinal region *Ingle*
Inhale, to *Inhalar*
Inject *Inyectar*
Injury *Herida*
Irregular *Irregular*
Irregularly *Irregularmente*
Instrument *Instrumento*
Insecure *Inseguro(a)*
Inside *Interior*
Intense *Intenso*
Interest *Interés*
Intimate *Intimas*
Irritated *Irritado(a)*
Itch *Comezón*

J

Jaw *Quijada*
Jew *Judío(a)*
Joints *Coyonturas*
Journalist *Periodista*
Judge *Juez*
Jugular vein *Vena yugular*
Juice *Jugo*
Jump, to *Saltar*

K

Keep from happening, to *Impedir*
Kidnap *Secuestrar*
Kidney *Riñón*
Kindergarten *Parvulos*
Kill, to *Matar*
Knife *Cuchillo*

L

Labor *Trabajo de parto*
Lamp *Lámpara*
Last, to *Durar*
Last night *Anoche*
Lately *Últimamente*
Law *Ley*
Lawyer *Abogado(a)*
Lax *Flojo*
Laxatives *Purgantes*
Lay, to *Acostar*
Learn, to *Aprender*
Leave, to *Dejar*
Left *Izquierda*
Leg *Pierna*
Lend, to *Prestar*
Let know, to *Avisar*
Letter *Carta*
Life *Vida*
Lift, to *Cargar*
Light(s) *Luz(ces)*
Lightning *Relámpago*
Like, to *Gustar*
Liquid *Líquido*

Liquor *Licór*
Lithium *Litio*
Liver *Hígado*
Living *Vivo(s)*
Load up, to *Cargar*
Lock *Cerradura*
Lose, to *Perder*
LSD *LSD*
Lung *Pulmón*
Lymphatics *Linfáticos*

M

Magazine *Revista*
Making love *Haciendo el amor*
Man *Hombre*
Market *Mercado*
Married *Casado(a)*
Master's degree *Maestría*
Meals *Alimentos*
Measles *Sarampión*
Meeting *Reunión*
Memory *Memoria*
Menstruate, to *Reglar*
Menstruation *Regla*
Merchant *Comerciante*
Mezcal *Mezcal*
Milk *Leche*
Mind *Razón*
Minister *Ministro*
Miss, to *Faltar*
Molar *Muela*
Mood *Estado de ánimo*
Morphine *Morfina*
Most of *Mayoría*
Mouth *Boca*
Move, to *Mover*
Mucus *Moco*
Mumps *Paperas*
Muscle sprain *Desgarro muscular*
Mushrooms *Hongos*

N

Nails *Uñas*
Name *Nombre*
Nausea *Náusea*
Navel *Ombligo*
Navy *Marina*
Near *Cerca*
Near-sighted *Miope*
Neck *Cuello*
Needle(s) *Aguja(s)*
Neighbor *Vecino(a)*
Neighborhood *Vecindario*
Nervous *Nervioso(a)*
Nervous system *Sistema nervioso*
Never *Nunca*
News *Noticias*
Nipple *Pezón*
Nodule *Bola*
Nodule *Nódulo/Bolita*
Noise *Ruido*
Noise, to make *Hacer ruido*
No one *Nadie*
Nose *Naríz*
Not quiet *Inquieta*
Nothing *Nada*
Nurse *Enfermero(a)*

O

Observe, to *Notar*
Offer, to *Ofrecer*
Office *Oficina*
Officer *Oficial*
Old *Viejo(a)*
One time *Una vez*
Open, to *Abrir*
Operate *Operar*
Options *Opciones*
Optometrist *Optometrista*
Organs *Organos*
Orgasm, to have an *Venirse*
Overdose *Sobredosis*

P

Pain *Dolor*
Paralysis *Parálisis*
Park *Parque*
Pass, to *Pasar*
Paste-like *Pastoso*
Pay, to *Pagar*
Pay attention, to *Fijar, Hacer caso*
Payment *Pago*
Penis *Miembro viril*
People *Gente*
Permanent *Permanente*
Persecute *Perseguir*
Personal physician *Médico personal*
Pertussis *Tosferina*
Peyote *Peyote*
Photographer *Fotógrafo(a)*
Physical examination *Examen físico*
Physician *Médico(a)*
Pillow *Almohada*
Pilot *Piloto*
Pisco *Pisco*
Pistol *Pistola*
Place, to *Colocar*
Plans *Planes*
Play, to *Jugar*
Pleasant *Placentero*
Pneumonia *Pulmonía*
Poison *Veneno*
Police *Policía*
Poor *Pobre*
Position *Posición*
Possible *Posible*
Pound(s) *Libra(s)*
Powdered milk *Leche en polvo*

Prefer *Preferir*
Pregnant *Embarazada*
Prenatal *Prenatal*
Prepare, to *Preparar*
Pressure *Presión*
Prevent, to *Prevenir*
Prick with pins *Enterrar alfileres*
Proceed, to *Proceder*
Products *Productos*
Prolong *Prolongar*
Prostate *Próstata*
Protect, to *Proteger*
Protestant *Protestante*
Provoke, to *Provocar*
Psychotherapy *Psicoterapia*
Psychotic *Psicótico(a)*
Pubis *Pubis*
Pulsating *Punzada*
Pulse *Pulso*
Pure *Puro*
Purulent secretions *Langañas*
Pus *Pús*
Push, to *Empujar*
Put, to *Poner*

Q

Quality *Calidad*
Quantity *Cantidad*
Questionnaire *Cuestionario*
Quiet *Quieto*

R

Radiation therapy *Radiación*
Rank *Rango*
Read, to *Leer*
Ready *Listo*
Recommend, to *Recomendar*
Rectum *Recto*
Red *Rojo*
Redden, to *Enrojecer*
Reddish *Rojizo*
Reflexes *Reflejos*
Register *Registrar*
Rehabilitation *Rehabilitación*
Relapse *Recaída*
Relation *Relación*
Relax, to *Aflojar*
Remember *Recordar*
Respect, to *Respetar*
Responsibility *Responsabilidad*
Rest *Reposo*
Rest, to *Descansar*
Results *Resultados*
Return *Regresar*
Rheumatism *Reumatismo*
Ribs *Agujas*
Right *Derecho(a)*
Risk *Riesgo*
Rope *Cuerda*
Rubber hammer *Martillo de goma*
Rum *Ron*
Run, to *Correr*

S

Sad *Triste*
Sample *Muestra*
Sand *Arena*
Satisfied *Satisfecha(o)*
Sausage *Chorizo*
Scale *Báscula*
Scalp *Cuero cabelludo*
Scare, to *Asustar*
Scared *Asustado(a)*
Scarlet fever *Escarlatina*
Scary event *Susto*
School *Escuela*
Scrotum *Escroto*
Seizures *Ataques*
Serious *Grave*
Sew, to *Coser*
Sexual relations *Relaciones sexuales*
Shake, to *Temblar*
Share, to *Compartir*
Shelter *Refúgio*
Shine *Brillo*
Shiny *Brillante*
Shirt *Camisa*
Should *Deber*
Shoulder *Hombro*
Show, to *Enseñar, Mostrar*
Sick person *Enfermo(a)*
Side *Lado*
Side effect *Efecto secundario*
Sideways *Atravesado*
Signal *Señal*
Signal, to *Señalar*
Single *Soltero(a)*
Sit down, to *Sentar*
Situation *Situación*
Skin *Piel*
Skull *Cráneo*
Sleep, to *Dormir*
Smell, to *Oler*
Smile *Sonreir*
Smoke, to *Fumar*
Sneeze, to *Estornudar*
Soccer *Soccer*
Soft *Blando(a)*
Soft drinks *Refrescos embotellados*
Solve, to *Resolver*
Someone *Alguien*
Son(s) *Hijo(s)*
Sound *Sonido*
Soup *Sopa*
Speak, to *Hablar*
Special care *Cuidados especiales*
Spell, to *Deletrear*
Spend, to *Gastar*

Spine *Columna vertebral*
Spit, to *Escupir*
Splint *Ferula*
Spontaneous *Espontáneo(a)*
Sport *Deporte*
Spouse *Esposo(a)*
Sprout, to *Brotar*
Sputum *Esputo*
Stab *Cuchillada*
Stain, to *Manchar*
Stained *Manchada(o)/Rayado(a)*
Stairs *Escalera*
State *Estado*
Step(s) *Paso(s)*
Stick inside *Meter*
Stick out, to *Sacar*
Stiff *Tieso(a)*
Stimulants *Estimulantes*
Stirrups *Estribos*
Stones *Piedras*
Store *Tienda*
Stream *Chorro*
Strength *Fuerza*
Stroke *Embolia*
Study *Estudio*
Stuffed *Tapadao*
Subway *Metro*
Suckle *Mamar*
Suddenly *Repentinamente*
Suffer *Sufrir*
Suggest, to *Sugerir*
Suicide, to commit *Suicidarse/suicidio*
Sun oneself, to *Asolear*
Support, to *Sostener*
Suppository *Supositorio*
Suture, to *Suturar*
Swallow *Tragar*
Swallow, to *Tragar*
Sweat, to *Sudar*
Sweets *Dulces*
Swell, to *Hinchar*
Swimming pool *Alberca*
Symptoms *Síntomas*

T

Take away, to *Quitar*
Take it, to *Aguantar*
Take, to *Tomar*
Take samples, to *Tomar muestras*
Take the top off, to *Destapar*
Talk, to *Platicar*
Tar *Asfalto*
Taste *Sabor*
Tea *Té*
Telephone *Teléfono*
Television *Televisión*
Temperature *Temperatura*
Temple(s) *Sien(es)*
Tender *Adolorida*
Tetanus *Tétanos*
Thefts *Robos*
Thermometer *Termómetro*
Thick *Grueso(a)*
Thirsty, to be *Tener sed*
Tie, to *Amarrar*
Tight *Apreteda(o)*
Tight, to be *Apretar*
Time *Horas*
Thin *Delgado(a)*
Thoughts *Pensamientos*
Throat *Garganta*
Thyroid *Tiroides*
Tobacco *Tabaco*
Toilet *Excusado*
Tongue *Lengua*
Tonsils *Anginas*
Too much *Demasiado*
Tooth *Diente*
Top, on *Encima*
Tortillas *Tortillas*
Touch, to *Tocar*
Tourniquet *Torniquete*
Toxic fumes *Humos tóxicos*
Tranquilize, to *Tranquilizar*
Tranquilizer *Tranquilizante*
Travel, to *Viajar*
Treatment program *Programa de tratamiento*
Tree *Árbol*
Trust, to *Confiar*
Try, to *Tratar*
Tuberculosis *Tuberculosis*
Tummy *Pancita*
Turn around *Voltear*

U

Ulcers *Granos/Úlceras*
Unbutton *Desabróchese*
Unconscious *Inconsciente*
Uncover, to *Descubrir*
Understand, to *Entender*
Undigested *Indigesto*
Unemployed *Desempleado(a)*
Unfortunately *Desafortunadamente*
University *Universidad*
Urgent *Urgente*
Urgently *Urgentemente*
Urine *Orina*
Urinal *Urinal*
Used to, to be *Acostumbrar*
Useful, to be *Servir*
Uterus *Matríz*

V

Vaccinate, to *Vacunar*
Vaccine *Vacuna*
Vagina *Vagina*
Vein *Vena*

Ventilator *Ventilador*
Vibrations *Vibraciones*
Victims *Víctimas*
Violate, to *Violar*
Violent *Violento*
Vision *Visión*
Visit, to *Visitar*
Vital signs *Signos vitales*
Voice *Voz*
Volleyball *Voleiból*
Volume *Volumen*

W

Wake up, to *Despertar*
Walk *Caminata*
Walk, to *Caminar*
Walker *Andador(a)*
Want, to *Querer*
Wash, to *Lavar*
Water *Agua*
Wax, ear *Cerilla*
Way *Via*
Weak *Debil*
Weakness *Debilidad*
Weather *Tiempo*
Week *Semana*
Wheel chair *Silla de ruedas*
When *Cuando*
While, a *Rato*
Whip, to *Latiguear*
White *Blanco(a)*
Who *Quien*
Widower/widow *Viudo(a)*
Wind/Gas *Aire*
Wine *Vino*
Without *Sin*
Woman *Mujer*
Work, to *Trabajar*
Work overtime, to *Trabajar extra*
World *Mundo*
Worry, to *Preocupar*
Worse *Peor*
Worsen, to *Empeorar*
Wrist *Muñeca*
Write, to *Escribir*

X

X-Ray *Radiografía*

Y, Z

Yellow *Amarillo*
Yellowish *Amarillento*
Yesterday *Ayer*

5. Spanish-English Glossary

A

Abogado(a) *Lawyer*
Aborto *Abortion/Miscarriage*
Abrir *Open, to*
Abusar *Abuse, to*
Acabar *Finish, to*
Accidente *Accident*
Aceptar *Accept, to*
Achaques *Ill-defined complaints*
Acostar *Bed, to go to*
Acostumbrar *Used to, to be*
Activo(a) *Active*
Acto sexual *Coitus*
Adicción *Addiction*
Administrador *Administrator*
Administrar(a) *Administer*
Adolorida *Tender*
Aflojar *Loosen, to/ Relax, to*
Afortunademente *Fortunately*
Agachar *Bend over*
Agnóstico(a) *Agnostic*
Agradecer *Grateful, to be*
Agrícola *Agricultural*
Agruras *Heartburn*
Agua *Water*
Aguantar *Take, to/Endure, to*
Aguja(s) *Needle(s)*
A gusto *Feel okay, to*
Ahogar *Drown, to*
Aire *Wind/Gas*
Alberca *Swimming pool*
Alcanzar *Enough for, to be*
Alcoholismo *Alcoholism*
Alergia *Allergy*
Alguien *Someone*
Alimentos *Meals*
Aliviar *Alleviate*
Almohada *Pillow*
Almorranas *Hemorrhoids*
Alrededor *Around*
Amarillento *Yellowish*
Amarillo *Yellow*
Amarrar *Tie, to*
Andador(a) *Walker*
Anemia *Anemia*
Anestesia epidural *Epidural anesthesia*
Anestesia general *General anesthesia*
Anestesiar *Anesthetize, to*
Anestesista *Anaesthetist*
Anfetaminas *Amphetamines*
Angina *Angina*

Anginas *Tonsils*
Ano *Anus*
Anoche *Last night*
Ansiedad *Anxiety*
Ansioso(a) *Anxious*
Antidepresivo *Antidepressant*
Apartamento *Apartment*
Apetito *Apetite*
Aplicar *Apply*
Aprender *Learn, to*
Apretada *Tight*
Apretar *Tight, to be*
Aprisa *Fast*
Árbol *Tree*
Arder *Burn, to*
Ardiente *Burning*
Arena *Sand*
Arquitecto(a) *Architect*
Artritis *Arthritis*
Asalto *Hold up*
Asfalto *Tar*
Asientos de café *Coffee grounds*
Asma *Asthma*
Asolear *Sun oneself, to*
Asustado(a) *Scared*
Asustar *Scare, to*
Ataques *Seizures*
Ateo(a) *Atheist*
Atravesado *Sideways*
Aureola *Halo*
Autorizar *Authorize*
Autobus *Bus*
Avisar *Let know, to*
Ayer *Yesterday*
Ayudar *Help, to*

B

Bachiller *High school graduate*
Bala *Bullet*
Balacera *Shoot-out*
Balazo *Gunshot*
Baloncesto *Basketball*
Bañarse *Bath, to take a*
Barba *Chin*
Barrio *Borough*
Báscula *Scale*
Bastón *Cane*
Bata *Gown*
Bebé *Baby*
Beber *Drink, to*
Beisból *Baseball*
Beneficio *Benefit*
Billar *Billiards*
Blanco(a) *White*
Blando(a) *Soft*
Blusa *Blouse*
Boca *Mouth*
Boca del estomago *Gastric area*
Bochornos *Hot flashes*
Bola *Nodule*
Bolita *Nodule*
Bolsa *Bag*
Borracho *Drunk*
Borroso *Blurry*
Brazo *Arm*
Brillante *Shiny*
Brillo(a) *Shine*
Bronquitis *Bronchitis*
Brotar *Sprout*
Bueno(a) *Good*

C

Cabeza *Head*
Caca/Heces *Feces*
Cada *Each/Every*
Cadera *Hip*
Caer *Fall, to*
Calambres *Cramps*
Calidad *Quality*
Caliente *Hot*
Calmar *Calm, to*
Cama *Bed*
Cambiar *Change, to*
Caminar *Walk, to*
Caminata *Walk*
Camisa *Shirt*
Campanitas *Bells, little*
Campo *Field*
Cáncer *Cancer*
Cantidad *Quantity*
Capacidad *Capacity*
Cápsula *Capsule*
Cargar *Lift, to/Load up, to*
Carne de res *Beef*
Carretera *Highway*
Carrito eléctrico *Electric cart*
Carro *Car*
Carta *Letter*
Casa *Home*
Casado(a) *Married*
Católico *Catholic*
Causar *Cause, to*
Cedrilla *Wax, ear*
Cenar *Dine, to*
Centro *Center*
Cepillo *Brush*
Cerca *Near*
Cereal *Cereal*
Cerebro *Brain*
Cerradura *Lock*
Cerveza *Beer*
Césarea *C-Section*
Chancro *Chancre*
Chorizo *Sausage*
Chorro *Stream*
Cigarrillos *Cigarettes*

Cine *Cinema*
Cita *Appointment*
Ciudad *City*
Clínica *Clinic*
Cocaína *Cocaine*
Codo *Elbow*
Colcha *Blanket*
Colgar *Hang, to*
Cólicos *Cholic*
Colocar *Place, to*
Colon, irritable *Bowel, irritable*
Color *Color*
Columna *Column*
Columna vertebral *Spine*
Combate *Combat*
Comer *Eat, to*
Comerciante *Merchant*
Comezón *Itch*
Comodo *Commode*
Compañero(a) *Companion*
Compartir *Share, to*
Completar *Complete, to*
Comprar *Buy, to*
Concentrar *Concentrate, to*
Condominio *Condominium*
Condón *Condom*
Confiar *Trust, to*
Conocido(a) *Acquaintance*
Conocimiento *Knowledge*
Conseguir *Get, to*
Consejería *Counseling*
Considerar *Consider, to*
Constantemente *Constantly*
Constipación *Constipation*
Contador *Accountant*
Continuar *Continue, to*
Contra *Against*
Contracciones *Contractions*
Controlada(o) *Controlled*
Controlar *Control, to*
Corazón *Heart*
Correr *Run, to*
Coser *Sew, to*
Costar trabajo *Difficult, to be*
Coyunturas *Joints*
Cráneo *Skull*
Creer *Believe, to*
Cristalino(a) *Clear*
Crudo(a) *Hung over*
Cuando *When*
Cubrir *Cover, to*
Cuchillo *Knife*
Cuello *Neck*
Cuerda *Rope*
Cuero cabelludo *Scalp*
Cuerpo *Body*
Cuestionario *Questionnaire*
Cuidado *Care*
Cuidados a domicilio *Home care*
Cuidados de hospicio *Hospice care*
Cuidados especiales *Special care*
Cuidados futuros *Future care*
Culpable *Guilty*
Curable *Curable*
Curandero(a) *Folk healer*
Curar *Heal, to*

D

Dañar *Damage, to*
Dar *Give, to*
Dar de mamar *Breast-feed*
Dar vueltas *Go around, to*
Deber *Should*
Débil *Weak*
Debilidad *Weakness*
Decisiones *Decisions*
Dejar *Leave, to*
Deletrear *Spell, to*
Delgado(a) *Thin*
Demasiado(a) *Too much*
Dentaduras postizas *Dentures*
Dentista *Dentist*
Deporte *Sport*
Deprimido(a) *Depressed*
Derecho(a) *Right*
Desabróchese *Unbutton*
Desacuerdos *Disagreements*
Desafortunadamente *Unfortunately*
Desarrollo *Development*
Desayunar *Breakfast, to*
Descalabro *Bruise*
Descansar *To rest*
Descarga *Discharge*
Desconocidos(as) *Unknown individuals*
Desempleado(a) *Unemployed*
Desgarro muscular *Muscle sprain*
Desmayar *Faint, to*
Despertar *Wake up, to*
Destapar *Take the top off/Uncover*
Detras *Behind*
Diabetes *Diabetes*
Diablo *Devil*
Diagnóstico *Diagnosis*
Diarrea *Diarrhea*
Diente *Tooth*
Dificultad *Difficulty*
Difteria *Diphtheria*
Digerir *Digest, to*
Dios *God*
Dirección *Address*
Discusión *Discussion*
Divorciado(a) *Divorced*
Divorciar *Divorce, to*
Doble *Double*
Doctorado *Doctorate*
Dolor *Pain*

Dolores de parto *Labor pains*
Dormir *To sleep*
Drogarse *Drug oneself, to*
Dulces *Sweets*
Durar *Last, to*
Duro *Hard*

E

Edad *Age*
Editor(a) *Editor*
Efecto secundario *Side effect*
Ejercicio *Exercise*
Ejército *Army*
Eléctrocardiograma *Electrocardiogram*
Electrochoques *Electroshock therapy*
Electrodos *Electrodes*
Embarazada *Pregnant*
Embolia *Stroke*
Emborrachar *Drunk, to get*
Empeorar *Worsen, to*
Empezar *Begin, to*
Empleo *Employment*
Empujar *Push, to*
Encerrar *Confine, to*
Enchiladas *Enchiladas*
Encima *Top, on*
Encontrar *Find, to*
Enfermero(a) *Nurse*
Enfermo(a) *Sick person*
Enfisema *Emphysema*
Engordar *Fat, to get*
Enojado(a) *Angry*
Enojar *Angry, to get*
Enrojecer *Red, to become*
Enseñar *Show, to*
Entender *Understand, to*
Enterrar alfileres *Prick with pins*
Entre *Between*
Epilepsia *Epilepsy*
Equilibrio *Equilibrium*
Equipo *Team*
Eructar *Burp, to*
Escalera *Stairs*
Escarlatina *Scarlet fever*
Escojer *Choose, to*
Escribir *Write, to*
Escroto *Scrotum*
Escuela *School*
Escupir *Spit, to*
Espalda *Back*
Esperanza *Hope*
Esperar *Expect, to*
Espontaneos *Spontaneous*
Esposo(a) *Spouse*
Esputo *Sputum*
Estado *State*
Estado de Ánimo *Mood*
Estar presente *Be present, to*
Estatura *Height*
Estimulantes *Stimulants*
Estornudar *Sneeze, to*
Estreñido *Constipated*
Estribos *Stirrups*
Estudio *Study*
Evacuar *Defecate, to*
Evangélico *Evangelical*
Evitar *Avoid, to*
Examen físico *Physical examination*
Examinar *Examine, to*
Excremento *Excrement*
Excusado *Toilet*
Expediente *Chart/File*
Explicar *Explain*
Exposición *Exposure*

F

Fábrica *Factory*
Fajitas *Fajitas*
Faltar *Miss, to*
Familia *Family*
Farmacia *Drugstore*
Fé *Faith*
Fecha *Date*
Feo *Foul*
Férula *Splint*
Fiebre *Fever*
Fijar *Pay attention, to*
Final *End*
Flojo(a) *Lax*
Forceps *Forceps*
Formas *Forms*
Fórmula *Formula*
Fotógrafo(a) *Photographer*
Fracaso *Failure*
Fractura *Fracture*
Frijoles *Beans*
Fruta *Fruit*
Fuente *Bag of water*
Fuerza *Strength*
Fumar *Smoke*
Futuro *Future*

G

Garganta *Throat*
Ganas *Desire*
Gastar *Spend, to*
Gástrico(a) *Gastric*
Gastritis *Gastritis*
Gente *People*
Glándula *Gland*
Golpear *Hit, to*
Golpiza *Beating*
Gordura *Fat*
Granos *Ulcers*
Grave *Serious*
Grueso *Thick*
Guardacostas *Coast Guard*
Gustar *Like, to*

H

Hablar *Speak to*
Hacer caso *Pay attention, to*
Hacer ruido *Noise, make*
Haciendo el amor *Making love*
Helicóptero *Helicopter*
Hepatitis *Hepatitis*
Herida *Injury*
Herir *Hurt, to*
Hernia *Hernia*
Heroína *Heroin*
Hígado *Liver*
Hijos(as) *Sons/daughters*
Hinchar *Swell, to*
Hipermétrope *Far-sighted*
Hisopo *Cotton swab*
Historia clínica *Clinical history*
Hombre *Man*
Hombro(s) *Shoulder(s)*
Hondo *Deep*
Hongos *Mushrooms*
Hora *Time*
Hormonas *Hormones*
Hospitalizar *Hospitalize, to*
Hueso *Bone*
Humos tóxicos *Toxic fumes*

I

Iglesia *Church*
Igual *Equal*
Ilícita *Illicit*
Iluminar *Illuminate, to*
Impedir *Keep from happening, to*
Impotente *Impotent*
Inconsciente *Unconscious*
Incurable *Incurable*
Indicaciones *Indications*
Indicado *Indicated*
Indigesto *Undigested*
Inducir *Induct*
Infarto *Infarct*
Infección *Infection*
Información *Information*
Ingle *Inguinal region*
Ingreso *Income*
Inhalar *Inhale, to*
Inmediatamente *Immediately*
Inmobilizar *Immobilize*
Inquieta *Restless*
Inseguro(a) *Insecure*
Instrumento *Instrument*
Intenso(a) *Intense*
Interés *Interest*
Interior *Inside*
Intimas *Intimate*
Inválido *Handicapped*
Inyectar *Inject, to*
Irregular *Irregular*
Irregularmente *Irregularly*
Irritado(a) *Irritated*
Izquierdo(A) *Left*

J

Judío(a) *Jew*
Juego *Game*
Juez *Judge*
Jugar *Play, to*
Jugo *Juice*

L

Lado *Side*
Lagañas *Purulent secretions*
Lámpara *Lamp*
Latido(s) *Beat*
Latiguear *Whip, to*
Lavar *Wash, to*
Lavativa *Enema*
Leche *Milk*
Leche en polvo *Powdered milk*
Leer *Read, to*
Lejos *Far*
Lengua *Tongue*
Levantarse *Get up, to*
Ley *Law*
Libra(s) *Pound(s)*
Libre *Free*
Libro *Book*
Licor *Liquor*
Limpiarse *Toilet oneself, to*
Linfáticos *Lymphatics*
Líquido *Liquid*
Listo *Ready*
Litio *Lithium*
Llamar *Call, to*
Llanto *Cry*
Llegar *Arrive, to*
Llevar bien *Get along well*
Llevarse *Get along, to*
Llorar *Cry, to*
Loco(a) *Crazy*
Loteria *Bingo*
LSD *LSD*
Luz(ces) *Light(s)*

M

Maestría *Master's degree*
Mal *Bad*
Mamar *Suckle, to*
Manchada *Stained*
Manchar *Stain, to*
Mandar al diablo *Send to the devil, to*
Manejar *Drive, to*
Manguito *Cuff*
Manzana *Block*
Mareo *Dizziness*
Marina *Navy*
Martillo de húle *Rubber hammer*

Masticar *Chew, to*
Matar *Kill, to*
Matríz *Uterus*
Mayoria *Most of*
Médico(a) *Physician*
Médico(a) personal *Personal physician*
Mejor *Better*
Mejoría *Improvement*
Memoria *Memory*
Mercado *Market*
Mesa de exploración *Exam table*
Mesa de partos *Delivery table*
Meter *Stick inside*
Metro *Subway*
Mezcal *Mezcal*
Miedo *Fear*
Miembro viril *Penis*
Mientras *While*
Ministro *Minister*
Miope *Near-sighted*
Moco *Mucus*
Molestar *Bother, to*
Morder *Bite, to*
Moretones *Bruises*
Morfina *Morphine*
Mostrar *Show, to*
Mover *Move, to*
Muelas *Molars*
Muerto(a) *Dead*
Muestra *Sample*
Mujer *Woman*
Mundo *World*
Muñeca *Wrist*

N

Nacer *Born, to be*
Nacimiento *Birth*
Nada *Nothing*
Nadie *No one*
Nalgas *Butt*
Nariz *Nose*
Náusea *Nausea*
Negocios *Business*
Negro(a) *Black*
Nervioso(a) *Nervous*
Nietos(as) *Grandchildren*
Ninguno(a) *No ____*
Nódulo *Nodule*
Nombre *Name*
Notar *Observe*
Noticias *News*
Novio(a) *Fiancee*
Nuca *Neck, back of*
Nunca *Never*

O

Obrero *Factory worker*
Obscura *Dark*
Ocupación *Occupation*
Oficial *Officer*
Oficina *Office*
Ofrecer *Offer, to*
Oído *Ear*
Oír *Hear, to*
Oler *Smell, to*
Ombligo *Navel*
Opciones *Options*
Operar *Operate*
Optometrista *Optometrist*
Organos *Organs*
Orina *Urine*

P

País *Country*
Pagar *Pay, to*
Pagos *Payments*
Palpitar *Beat, to*
Pandilla(s) *Gang(s)*
Panzita *Tummy*
Paperas *Mumps*
Parálisis *Paralysis*
Parque *Park*
Parvulos *Kindergarten*
Pasar *Pass, to*
Pasillo *Hallway*
Paso(s) *Step(s)*
Pastoso *Paste-like*
Pecho *Chest*
Pedir *Ask for, to*
Pegar *Hit, to*
Pelear *Fight, to*
Peleonero *Fighter*
Peligroso *Dangerous*
Pelo *Hair*
Pensamientos *Thoughts*
Peor *Worse*
Perder *Lose, to*
Periodista *Journalist*
Permanente *Permanent*
Perseguir *Persecute, to*
Peyote *Peyote*
Pezón *Nipple*
Piedras *Stones*
Piel *Skin*
Pierna *Leg*
Piloto *Pilot*
Pisco *Pisco*
Pistola *Pistol*
Placentero *Pleasant*
Planes *Plans*
Platicar *Talk, to*
Pobre *Poor*
Pocas *Few*
Poder *Can, to*
Policia *Police*
Poner *Put, to*
Poquito *Bit, a little*
Portarse *Behave oneself, to*

Posible *Possible*
Posición *Position*
Preferir *Prefer*
Prenatal *Prenatal*
Preocupar *Worry, to*
Preparar *Prepare, to*
Presión *Pressure*
Presión alta de la sangre *High blood pressure*
Presión arterial *Arterial pressure*
Prestar *Lend, to*
Prevenir *Prevent, to*
Principio *Beginning*
Proceder *Proceed, to*
Productos *Products*
Programa de tratamiento *Treatment program*
Prolongar *Prolong*
Próstata *Prostate*
Proteger *Protect, to*
Protestante *Protestant*
Provocar *To provoke*
Psicoterapia *Psychotherapy*
Psicótico(a) *Psychotic*
Pubis *Pubis*
Puente *Bridge*
Pulmón *Lung*
Pulmonía *Pneumonia*
Pulso *Pulse*
Punzada *Pulsating*
Purgantes *Laxatives*
Puro *Pure*
Puros *Cigars*
Pús *Pus*

Q

Quebrar *Break, to*
Quedito *Very quiet*
Quejar *Complain, to*
Quemadura *Burn*
Quemar *Burn, to*
Querer *Want, to*
Quien *Who*
Quieto *Quiet*
Quijada *Jaw*
Quimioterapia *Chemotherapy*
Quitar *Take away, to*

R

Radiación *Radiation therapy*
Radiografía *X Ray*
Rango *Rank*
Rápido *Fast*
Rato *While, a*
Rayado(a) *Stained*
Razón *Mind*
Recaída *Relapse*
Recomendar *Recommend, to*
Recordar *Remember, to*
Recto *Rectum*
Refléjo(s) *Reflex(es)*
Refrescos embotellados *Soft drinks*
Refugio *Shelter*
Registrar *Register*
Regla *Menstruation*
Reglar *Menstruate, to*
Regresar *Return*
Rehabilitación *Rehabilitation*
Relación *Relation*
Relaciones sexuales *Sexual relations*
Relámpago *Lightning*
Repentinamente *Suddenly*
Reposo *Rest*
Resfriado *Common cold*
Resolver *Solve, to*
Respetar *Respect, to*
Respirar *Breathe, to*
Responsabilidad *Responsibility*
Respuesta *Answer*
Resultados *Results*
Reumatismo *Rheumatism*
Reunión *Meeting*
Revista *Magazine*
Riesgo *Risk*
Riñón(es) *Kidney(s)*
Robos *Thefts*
Rodilla *Knee*
Rojizo(a) *Reddish*
Rojo(a) *Red*
Romper *Break*
Ron *Rum*
Ronca(o) *Hoarse*
Rubeola *German measles*
Ruido *Noise*

S

Sabor *Taste*
Sacar *Get out, to*
Sala de partos *Delivery room*
Salir *Go out*
Saltar *Jump, to*
Sangrar *Bleed, to*
Sangre *Blood*
Sano(s) *Healthy*
Sarampión *Measles*
Satisfecha *Satisfied*
Seco(a) *Dry*
Secuestrar *Kidnap*
Seguir *Continue, to*
Semana *Week*
Señal *Signal*
Señalar *Signal, to/Indicate, to*
Sentar *Sit down, to*
Sentirse culpable *Feel guilty, to*
Servicios de emergencia *Emergency services*
Servir *Useful, to be*
SIDA *AIDS*

Sien(es) *Temple(s)*
Sífilis *Syphilis*
Signos vitales *Vital signs*
Silla *Chair*
Silla de ruedas *Wheelchair*
Sin *Without*
Síntomas *Symptoms*
Sistema nervioso *Nervous system*
Situación *Situation*
Sobredosis *Overdose*
Soccer *Soccer*
Sóla(o) *By itself*
Solo(a) *Alone*
Soltero(a) *Single*
Sonar *Blow, to*
Sonido *Sound*
Sonreir *Smile, to*
Sopa *Soup*
Sordo *Deaf*
Sostener *Support*
Subir *Go up, to*
Substancia química *Chemical substance*
Suceder *Happen, to*
Sudar *Sweat, to*
Suelo *Floor*
Sufrir *Suffer*
Sugerir *Suggest*
Suicidar/Suicidio *Suicide, to commit/Suicide*
Supositorio *Suppository*
Susto *Scary event*
Suturar *Suture, to*

T

Tabaco *Tobacco*
Tabaquismo *Tobacco addiction*
Tapada(o) *Stuffed*
Tarde *Afternoon*
Té *Tea*
Teléfono *Telephone*
Televisión *Television*
Temblar *Shake, to*
Temperatura *Temperature*
Tener hambre *Hungry, to be*
Tener un niño *Have a baby, to*
Tener sed *Thirsty, to be*
Terminar *Finish, to*
Termómetro *Thermometer*
Testigo de Johová *Jehovah's Witness*
Tétanos *Tetanus*
Tiempo *Weather*
Tienda *Store*
Tieso(a) *Stiff*
Tiroides *Thyroid*
Tobillo *Ankle*
Tocar *touch, to*
Toda *Entire*
Tomar *Take, to*
Tomar muestras *Take samples, to*
Torniquete *Tourniquet*
Tortillas *Tortillas*
Tosferina *Pertussis*
Totopos *Totopos*
Trabajar *Work, to*
Trabajar extra *Work overtime, to*
Trabajardor(a) social *Social worker*
Trabajo de parto *Labor*
Traer *Bring, to*
Tragar *Swallow*
Tranquilizante *Tranquilizer*
Tranquilizar *Tranquilize, to*
Tratar *Try, to*
Triste *Sad*
Tuberculosis *Tuberculosis*

U

Ulceras *Ulcers*
Ultimamente *Lately*
Uñas *Nails*
Universidad *University*
Urgente *Urgent*
Urgentemente *Urgently*
Urinal *Urinal*

V

Vacuna *Vaccine*
Vacunar *Vaccinate, to*
Vagina *Vagina*
Varicela *Chicken pox*
Vaso *Cup*
Vecindario *Neighborhood*
Vecino(a) *Neighbor*
Vello *Body hair*
Vena *Vein*
Vena yugular *Jugular vein*
Veneno *Poison*
Venir *Come, to*
Venirse *Have an orgasm, to*
Ventilador *Ventilator*
Verde *Green*
Verdoso(a) *Greenish*
Vesícula *Gall bladder*
Vestido *Dress*
Vestirse *Dress oneself, to*
Vez *One time*
Via *Way*
Viajar *Travel, to*
Vibraciones *Vibrations*
Víctimas *Victims*
Vida *Life*
Viejitos(as) *Elderly (endearing)*
Viejo(a) *Old*
Vientre *Abdomen*
Vino *Wine*
Violar *Violate, to*
Visión *Vision*

Visitar *Visit, to*
Viudo(a) *Widower/widow*
Vivo(s) *Living*
Voleiból *Volleyball*
Voltear *Turn around*
Volumen *Volume*
Voz *Voice*

W, X, Y, Z

Zumbar *Buzz, to*

6. Index

This index lists all culture notes, grammar notes, and vocabulary in alphabetical order.